ARKANSAS'S GILDED AGE

ARKANSAS'S GILDED AGE

THE RISE, DECLINE, & LEGACY OF POPULISM & WORKING-CLASS PROTEST

MATTHEW HILD

UNIVERSITY OF MISSOURI PRESS
Columbia

University of Missouri Press, Columbia, Missouri 65211
Printed and bound in the United States of America
 First printing, 2018.

Library of Congress Cataloging-in-Publication Data

Names: Hild, Matthew, author.
Title: Arkansas's Gilded Age : the rise, decline, and legacy of populism and working-class protest / Matthew Hild.
Description: Columbia : University of Missouri Press, [2018] | Includes bibliographical references. |
Identifiers: LCCN 2018021863 (print) | LCCN 2018025253 (ebook) | ISBN 9780826274182 (e-book) | ISBN 9780826221667 (hardcover : alk. paper)
Subjects: LCSH: Labor movement--Arkansas--History--19th century. | Populism--Arkansas--History--19th century. | Protest movements--Arkansas--History--19th century. | Working class--Arkansas--History--19th century. | Arkansas--Politics and government--To 1950. | Arkansas--History--1865-
Classification: LCC HD8083.A7 (ebook) | LCC HD8083.A7 H55 2018 (print) | DDC 320.56/620976709034--dc23
LC record available at https://lccn.loc.gov/2018021863

∞™ This paper meets the requirements of the American National Standard for Permanence of Paper for Printed Library Materials, Z39.48, 1984.

Typefaces: Herschel and Bembo

For Robert C. (Bob) McMath, consummate mentor, educator, and scholar.

CONTENTS

FOREWORD

THE PAST TWO DECADES HAVE witnessed a resurgence of scholarly interest in America's Gilded Age, the turbulent period encompassing the last three decades of the nineteenth century. Indeed, a number of recent books have altered our understanding of an era traditionally identified with robber barons, political corruption, and a culture of excess, refocusing our attention on a hardy tradition of political dissent led by agrarian radicals and organized labor. Perhaps most notable among these books are James Green's *Death in the Haymarket: A Story of Chicago, the First Labor Movement, and the Bombing That Divided Gilded Age America* (2006); Michael Kazin's *A Godly Hero: The Life of William Jennings Bryan* (2006); and Richard White's two magisterial works of synthesis, *Railroaded: The Transcontinentals and the Making of Modern America* (2011), and *The Republic for Which It Stands: The United States during Reconstruction and the Gilded Age, 1865–1896* (2017).

Now, with the publication of Matthew Hild's groundbreaking statewide study, *Arkansas's Gilded Age*, the intricate workings of this working-class protest tradition are revealed in all of their complexity and irony. Each state has a distinct political history that stands somewhat apart from national and regional norms, and Arkansas is no exception, having marched to its own drummer as much as any state in the nation. Yet, as Hild relates in a fascinating narrative of struggle, defeat, and perseverance, Arkansas's history of political dissent tells us a great deal about the limitations of political democracy in a nation rent with economic and racial inequality.

By narrowing his focus to a single state, Hild—the author of an imaginative 2007 survey of farmer-labor insurgency in the late-nineteenth-century South—is able to present a richly textured portrait of protest politics on the ground. Beginning with the immediate aftermath of Reconstruction, he takes us on a wild ride of agrarian and labor revolts against the Bourbon Democratic establishment. Along the way, he introduces us to a succession of related protest organizations: the Grange, the Greenback-Labor Party, the Knights of Labor, the Agricultural Wheel, the Brothers of Freedom, the Union Labor Party, the Farmers' Alliance, and the People's Party. All of these organizations eventually fell by the wayside, victims of the Arkansas Democratic Party's determination to crush third-party insurgency by any means necessary, including white supremacist demagoguery, assassination, disfranchisement, and mass violence.

The protest organizations' inability to overcome internal divisions, personal rivalries, discrimination related to race and gender, and persistent urban-rural tensions also contributed to their collective demise. But, as Hild points out, even with all of their problems and failures, the agrarian/labor radicals left a significant legacy that continued to influence Arkansas politics throughout the first half of the twentieth century. Their ideas lived on in the varied struggles waged by agrarian socialists, the United Mine Workers of America, Bryanist progressives, the Farmers' Union, the Working Class Union, the Progressive Farmers and Household Union of America (crushed in the infamous Elaine Race Massacre of 1919), and the Southern Tenant Farmers Union, formed in east Arkansas in 1934.

While working-class advocates never gained control of Arkansas politics, either during or after the Gilded Age, their persistent dissent against a thoroughly corrupt and antidemocratic political order merits our respect and admiration. The saga that Matthew Hild presents with authority and insight contains more heartache than redemption. But it is an American story worthy of close attention in the early twenty-first-century—an age buffeted by many of the same political and economic injustices that plagued the original Gilded Age of the nineteenth century.

Raymond Arsenault
John Hope Franklin Professor of Southern History
University of South Florida, St. Petersburg

ACKNOWLEDGMENTS

FIRST, I WOULD LIKE TO thank the helpful and efficient staff of the University of Missouri Press, especially Andrew J. Davidson and Mary Conley. I appreciate Ray Arsenault's willingness to write the foreword to this book; his biography of Jeff Davis remains essential reading for students of late nineteenth- and early twentieth-century Arkansas history. I am also grateful to Guy Lancaster and Carl H. Moneyhon, who read the manuscript for the press and offered thoughtful, helpful evaluations. Around the time that I started writing this book, Guy asked me to write an essay for his edited book *The Elaine Massacre and Arkansas: A Century of Atrocity and Resistance, 1819–1919*, which was published in 2018 by Butler Center Books of Little Rock. Writing my essay, "Labor Activism, Third-Party Politics, and African Americans in Arkansas, 1865–1892," for inclusion in that book proved to be a helpful exercise in refining my thoughts and ideas as I wrote this book. (I must also gratefully acknowledge the permission of Butler Center Books to reproduce that essay in *Arkansas's Gilded Age*, although only small portions of the essay appear here.)

I also must thank my friends and fellow historians of nineteenth-century America, Keri Leigh Merritt and Taylor Patterson, each of whom read portions of this study in its earlier forms and offered me valuable suggestions and encouragement. While I was writing this book, Keri Leigh and I were working together as the editors of a collection of original essays, *Reconsidering Southern Labor History: Race, Class, and Power* (University Press of Florida, 2018). While I would have completed *Arkansas's Gilded Age* sooner were it not for *Reconsidering Southern Labor History*, working with Keri Leigh and reading and editing the essays by the contributing authors greatly expanded and sharpened my knowledge and analysis of southern labor history; the delay was more than worthwhile in many respects.

Finally, I want to express my appreciation for the resources and helpful staff members at the Arkansas State Archives and the Special Collections

Divisions of the libraries of the University of Arkansas and the University of Arkansas at Little Rock. In Georgia, I am similarly beholden to the libraries and librarians of the Georgia Institute of Technology, Georgia State University, the University of Georgia, and the University of West Georgia. As is the case with university presses, these repositories of books, archival materials, and so many other educational resources are vital assets to our states and nation; they provide the foundations of knowledge that are essential to the democratic society that many of the men and women discussed in this book sacrificed and took real risks in order to build.

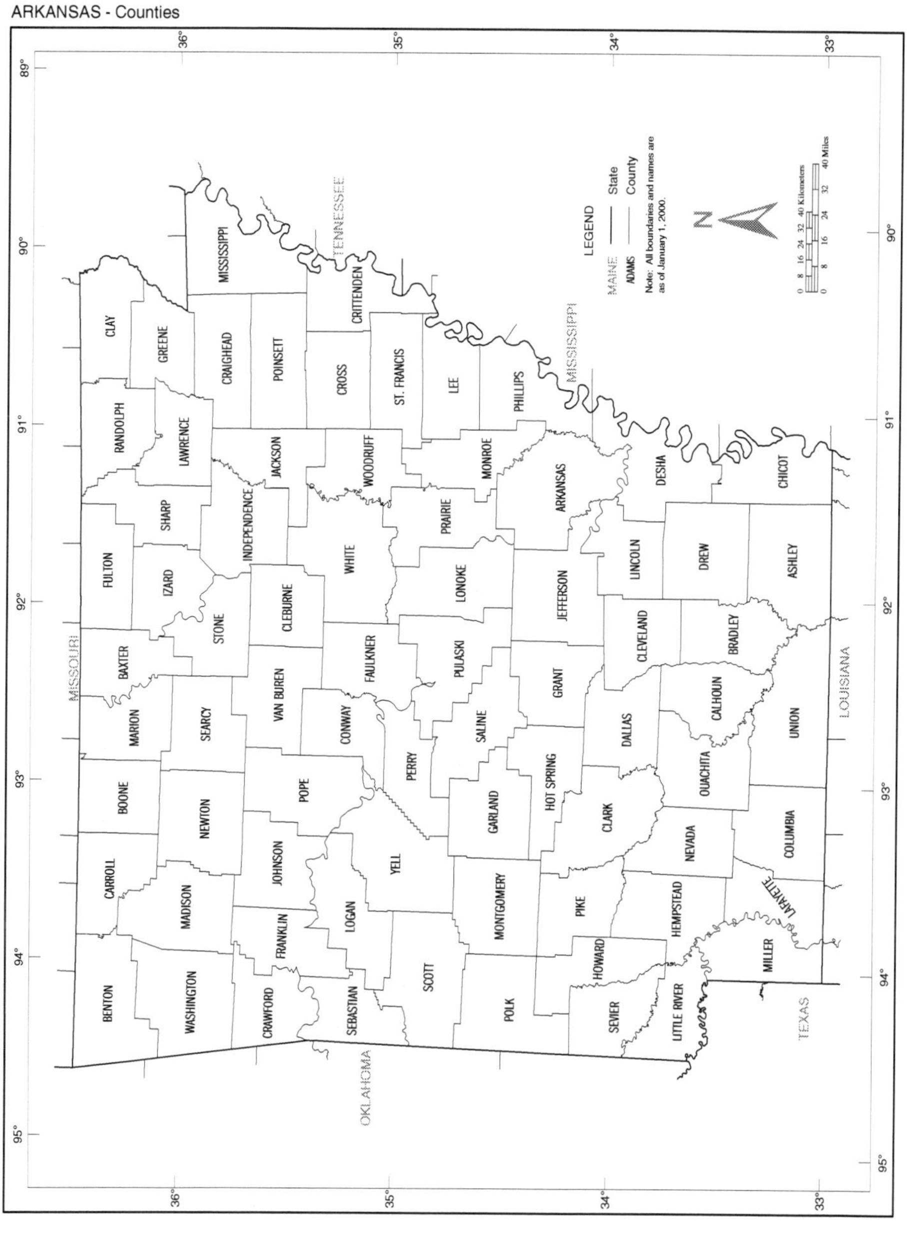

1. Arkansas county map. From the US Census Bureau, Census 2000. Retrieved from https://www2.census.gov/geo/maps/general_ref/stco_outline/cen2k_pgsz/stco_AR.pdf.

ARKANSAS'S GILDED AGE

INTRODUCTION

TODAY, IT IS UNLIKELY THAT many Americans think of Arkansas as a bastion of progressive reform movements. Most probably associate the Razorback State with Walmart, which is notorious for its unrelenting opposition to unions, and President Bill Clinton, who became decidedly less progressive after the Republican takeover of both houses of Congress in the elections of 1994.[1] During the late nineteenth century, however, working-class Arkansans, white and black alike—sometimes working together across the color line—waged a battle for economic, political, and (at times) social justice that made the state a figurative and occasionally even a literal battleground between reformers and defenders of the status quo. These efforts in behalf of reform, as well as the fierce opposition that they provoked, had consequences that reverberated well into the twentieth century.

The late nineteenth century became known in the United States as the Gilded Age after the publication in 1873 of a book by Mark Twain and Charles Dudley Warner titled *The Gilded Age: A Tale of To-day.*[2] This novel satirized the greed and shady business practices of the era's "robber barons" as well as the political corruption represented by kingpins such as William "Boss" Tweed of New York. While the term may have seemed more applicable to states like New York and Pennsylvania than southern states mired in post–Civil War poverty, even rural states with little industry exhibited some of the traits, or symptoms, of which Twain and Warner wrote. Economic inequality—the growing gap between the haves and the have-nots that was one of the hallmarks of the Gilded Age—was certainly as acute in the former Confederate states as any place else, especially considering that four million African Americans were released from slavery into, by and large, landless poverty at the end of the Civil War.[3] As for political corruption, the events that occurred in Arkansas during the Gilded Age, most notably during and after the campaigns of 1888, demonstrated that the South was rife with not only dirty politics but also that of a deadlier variety than elsewhere in the nation. Additionally, the race-related violence and injustice that plagued the South throughout the era meant that life in the region had a harsher edge than in the rest of the United States, a simmering tension that could explode at any time.

One of the ways that many working-class Americans tried to cope with the economic and political inequities of the Gilded Age was by joining organizations that seemed to hold the potential for alleviating some of these difficulties. Arkansas farmers formed organizations with odd names such as the Agricultural Wheel and the Brothers of Freedom, and laborers and farmers across the nation joined another group with a peculiar name—the Noble and Holy Order of the Knights of Labor. While each of these organizations was unique in certain ways, they shared, at least in a broad sense, a belief in the ideology of "producerism" and a conviction that the Jacksonian slogan of "Equal rights to all, special privilege to none" was being violated by "robber barons" and corrupt politicians.[4] Producerism essentially held that those who engaged in physical labor were the nation's real wealth producers and as such were entitled to their fair share of that wealth and a voice in how their communities, states, and nation were governed.[5] The prevailing mores of Gilded Age America regarding gender and race placed limits upon producerism, though. The People's (or Populist) Party, which revived the Jacksonian slogan as its own, refused to endorse women's suffrage during its maiden national campaign of 1892, although the Knights of Labor called for equal pay for equal work for both sexes.[6] The reform organizations of the Gilded Age practiced either total or at least partial segregation in the South. A landowning white farmer with black tenants or sharecroppers in Arkansas, or anywhere else in the South, was not likely to view them as being as entitled to either a share of the fruits of their labor or political representation as himself.

Nevertheless, by the late 1880s, enough adherents of the farmer and labor movements in Arkansas had found sufficient common ground to mount a significant third-party challenge to the state's dominant Democratic Party following the sharp post-Reconstruction decline of its Republican Party. In most southern and western states, this third-party movement emerged in the early 1890s under the guise of the Populist Party. In Arkansas, however, where the third party proved stronger than in most other southern states, it peaked from 1888 to 1890 in the form of the Union Labor Party, although it continued through the 1890s with the Populist Party. The emergence of a strong third party, supported by many white and black Arkansans, provoked Arkansas Democrats to stop at nothing to maintain their power. The story of farmer and labor protest in Arkansas during the Gilded Age, how it was conquered, and how it nevertheless laid the groundwork for some of the most significant political, economic, and social reforms of the twentieth century reveals a great deal about the democratic process in the United States (and how it can be subverted) and carries lessons that are still relevant today.

I. THE ROOTS OF DISCONTENT

DURING RECONSTRUCTION, ARKANSAS REPUBLICANS UNDER the leadership of Governor Powell Clayton (whose term was from 1868 to 1871) advocated a reformist agenda that included the establishment of a public school system and a state university, efforts to attract immigrants to the state, and the construction of levees and railroads. Unfortunately, though, as one historian has noted, this "bold and commendable" program was "barely under way . . . when it was beset by problems of inadequate finances, mismanagement, corruption, and intense political partisanship."[1] The Arkansas Republican Party then split in spectacular, and violent, fashion in the Brooks-Baxter War. This internecine clash followed a disputed gubernatorial election in 1872 in which the two claimants were rival Republicans; in 1874 the disagreement led to episodes of violence that resulted in more than two hundred deaths. Later that year, the Democratic Party won control of the governor's office and crushed any remaining hopes of the "activist government that . . . Clayton and the Republicans had pursued."[2] Arkansas Democrats proved less effective, however, at bringing financial stability or honest government to the state. Under the watch of Thomas J. Churchill, who served as the state treasurer from 1874 until winning the gubernatorial election of 1880, the state accumulated a shortfall of $294,876 in its accounts, which would be the equivalent of several million dollars today. Another shortage of $138,789 accrued during the tenure of Churchill's successor, Major William E. Woodruff, finally leading to condemnation from even the state's Democratic press in an era when most newspapers were clearly partisan.[3]

For working-class Arkansans, then, the "redemption" of the state by the Democratic Party meant a continuation of some of the worst problems of Reconstruction but a loss of the hopes for socioeconomic reform that Governor Clayton had put forth.[4] As noted by the historian Carl H. Moneyhon, "Individual Arkansans may have hoped for changes after 1874, but conditions in the state presented enormous barriers." In one of the most rural and poorest states in the nation—over 97 percent of Arkansans lived in rural communities in 1870, and the state's per capita income in 1880 (seventy-nine dollars) ranked fourth lowest in the nation—this did not bode well for most citizens.[5]

Even before 1874, some farmers began to express concerns about the new postbellum realities of Arkansas agriculture. During the late 1860s and early 1870s, the state's railroad network grew significantly. This development in turn opened new areas of the state to cotton cultivation and, subsequently, many farmers shifted from subsistence to commercial farming.[6] As Arkansas State (and National) Grange leader John Thompson Jones noted in 1877, however, many landowning Arkansas farmers had seen their "active capital . . . swept away by the war" to such an extent that many of them had sold "one-half or more of their well-improved farms."[7] For most Arkansas farmers, then, small landowners and tenants alike, commercial farming necessitated purchasing supplies on credit through a system known as the crop-lien, or as many farmers called it, the "anaconda" mortgage (named after the constricting snake), whereby the cotton crop served as the collateral for a loan that would have to be repaid at high interest. W. Scott Morgan, who during the 1880s became a leading figure in the state's agrarian revolt and ran for governor on the People's (or Populist) Party ticket in 1898, later described the anaconda mortgage as "wholesale robbery" characterized by the merchant (or, for tenant farmers, the landowner) "charging two and three prices for the goods furnished, thereby reducing his victims to extreme poverty, yes, to financial skeletons."[8] After 1875, a law passed by the "redeemed" Democratic state legislature ensured that these anaconda mortgages would have "the same force . . . as other mortgages."[9]

The Grange

The emergence of the National Grange of the Order of the Patrons of Husbandry (better known simply as the Grange) in Arkansas in 1872 represented, in part at least, a response to the economic difficulties confronting the state's farmers after the Civil War. The Grange began in 1867 as the brainchild of Oliver H. Kelley, who, while traveling through the South as an employee of the US Department of Agriculture, decided that "for the resuscitation of the country [meaning the South] and the recuperation of its farmers, whose wealth and resources had been swept away by the cruel hand of war, organization was a necessity." Before putting his plan into practice, Kelley further decided that the organization should not be confined to the South, since "there was vital need of organization among the farmers of the Union, North

2. The Honorable Powell Clayton of Arkansas. [Between 1860 and 1875] Photograph. Retrieved from the Library of Congress, accessed March 20, 2018, https://www.loc.gov/item/brh2003000845/PP/.

as well as South."[10] According to historian Gilbert C. Fite, "The objectives of the Grange were to enhance the comforts of farm homes and to improve rural social life, to oppose monopoly, to get better transportation facilities, to obtain improved education, to encourage crop diversification, and to establish business cooperatives as a means of eliminating middlemen and commission merchants." The Grange grew slowly at first, and primarily in the Midwest, but by the early 1870s it began to establish itself in the South.[11] The

Grange reached Arkansas in August 1872 after Kelley, who at that time was the organization's secretary, received a letter of inquiry from John Thompson Jones, a fifty-eight-year-old cotton planter living near Helena (Phillips County), Arkansas. Described by one historian as a man "of philosophic mien, with flowing beard and long unkempt locks," Jones was hardly the typical Arkansas farmer, having twice served as a district judge and been chosen as a Democratic US senator-elect in 1866 (although the Senate refused to seat him and Arkansas' other senator-elect, Augustus H. Garland, since the state was still "unreconstructed"). Nevertheless, this Virginia native certainly possessed knowledge of the conditions of agriculture, especially cotton agriculture, in Arkansas, having come to the state during the mid-1830s to become a cotton planter.[12]

The Grange grew rapidly in Arkansas. By May 1873, subordinate Granges (or local chapters) existed not only in Phillips County but also in Arkansas County and in the towns or cities of Trenton, Marvel, Planters, Richland, Clarendon, DeWitt, Mound Grove, Searcy, and Little Rock. In June, delegates from the subordinate Granges met in Helena and organized a State Grange. The first slate of officers elected included Jones as the Worthy Master. Fite noted that the Grange "admitted women on an equal basis with men," and indeed two of the seven officers were women (including Mrs. John Thompson Jones), although they held offices of lesser importance than did the male officers.[13] Grangers in Arkansas did not welcome African Americans (who constituted about one quarter of the state's population) into their organization though. In 1873, National Grange Master Dudley W. Adams declared that "the [Grange] Constitution is silent in regard to color. . . . If a Grange chooses to admit Negroes it may do so. . . . The matter is purely a local one." But in Arkansas the Grange was apparently an all-white organization.[14] Nevertheless, by October 1875 the Arkansas State Grange reported a membership of 20,471.[15]

Given that the population of Arkansas in 1875, interpolating from the census figures of 1870 and 1880, was about 650,000, the Grange possessed enough membership to potentially exercise some economic and political clout in the state. Historians have long debated, however, the role that the Grange played as an agent of reform in either of these realms. One of the first historians to examine the Arkansas Grange presented it as a do-nothing organization: "[Grangers] would meet, pledge themselves to prodigious tasks, and promptly forget most of them."[16] A more recent study, however, notes that during the 1870s, the Arkansas Grange "increasingly criticized banks, railroads, and middle men as the real culprits in the farmers' problems" and "sought legislation restricting the power of monopolies such as the railroads."[17] For example, at its annual meeting in January 1877, the Arkansas State Grange passed a resolution urging the Arkansas General Assembly "that some just and equitable law . . . be passed regulating the rates of passenger and freight tariffs on lines of railroads in this State, if it be within the power of the General Assembly to enact such a law."[18]

Yet as Edward L. Ayers noted in his study of the post-Reconstruction South, "The Grange sometimes fostered radicalism as well as conservatism," and a close look at the Arkansas Grange provides plenty of evidence of the latter.[19] While railroad freight rates were a problem that farmers of all classes could identify with, the proceedings of the State Grange session of January 1877 mention nary a word about the concerns of tenant farmers or even the crop-lien system. The prominent planter John Thompson Jones served as Worthy Master of the State Grange from its founding until 1877, also serving as the Master of the National Grange during his last two years at the helm of the Arkansas branch. His successor atop the State Grange, Simon P. Hughes, had once been an agricultural wage laborer, but by the early 1870s Hughes had become a successful lawyer, and subsequently he was able "to engage in extensive planting interests on the side."[20] The wealth of Jones and Hughes did not mean that they showed no interest in the problems facing farmers of lesser means, but on the other hand, they showed no inclination to make any radical proposals in their behalf, even while acknowledging that Grange programs were of limited use to small farmers and tenants. In 1877 Jones admitted that the cooperative purchasing efforts of the Arkansas Grange, while benefitting all farmers "in reducing the price, everywhere, of almost every article the farmer has to purchase," nevertheless "benefited . . . the small farmers not in just proportion to the larger ones."[21]

In politics, too, the Grange evinced elements of radicalism as well as conservatism. Ostensibly, the Grange was a nonpartisan organization. "No grange, if true to its obligations," stated the National Grange's Declaration of Purposes in 1874, "can discuss political or religious questions, nor call political conventions, nor nominate candidates, nor even discuss their merits in its meetings."[22] An Arkansas Grange newspaper in Van Buren County pointedly made note of this restriction in an editorial later that year.[23] Yet during the previous year, National Grange Master Dudley W. Adams had declared that Grangers felt it "a duty" to "scan very closely the acts of our public servants" and "to see to it that the candidates of all parties be men of integrity, whose interest is the welfare of the people, and not political ring-masters." Adams asserted the right of his rank and file to be actively involved in the political process, stating that "we, as producers, while we furnish food for millions, fight our nation's battles, defend its liberties in times of danger, should, of a right have an equal share as such in the making of these laws by which we are governed."[24] In Arkansas, as one historian noted, the Grange "never made a vigorous effort to participate in politics," yet "in one way or another, was involved in all the political campaigns conducted during its period of strength."[25]

The two men who stood at the helm of the Arkansas Grange during that period of strength—Jones and Hughes—certainly never tried to steer the organization away from the Democratic Party. Jones had nearly become a Democratic US senator in 1866; in 1878 he unsuccessfully tried again to become one of Arkansas's US senators as a Democrat. Hughes unsuccessfully sought the Democratic nomination for governor in 1876, and while he did not officially involve the Grange in his campaign, he nevertheless drew upon Grange support. Hughes made another failed bid for the Democratic Party's gubernatorial nomination in 1878, by which time he was the Worthy Master of the by-then-declining Arkansas Grange. Hughes eventually captured his prize in 1884, serving as the governor of Arkansas from 1885 to 1889.[26]

The Greenback and Greenback-Labor Parties

But as the Grange began to decline in 1876—in Arkansas, elsewhere in the South, and across the United States due to a host of problems including failing (and sometimes corrupt) cooperative enterprises, dissent over politics, and the inability of many members to pay dues—some prominent Grangers in Arkansas began to look away from the Democratic Party and toward more radical political alternatives.[27] Charles E. Tobey, an officer in the Arkansas State Grange, one of the state's first Grange organizers, and editor of the *Arkansas State Grange* newspaper, and Charles E. Cunningham, an active Granger who owned a saw and planing mill in Little Rock, both became active in the Greenback Party at this time. The Greenback movement began in the mid-1870s as a protest against the national system of money and banking that had developed since the Civil War, which coincided with a reduction in the amount of money in circulation in the United States from $30.35 per capita in 1865 to $19.36 by 1880.[28] As historian Charles Postel has noted, the Greenback movement espoused not only doctrines of currency reform but also of labor rights.[29] Tobey organized Greenback clubs in Arkansas in 1876; promoted the movement's "soft money" philosophy, which aimed to put more money into circulation; and tried to convince Grangers to support Greenback Party presidential candidate Peter Cooper.[30] Cunningham presided over what the *Arkansas Gazette* called a "very slimly attended" Greenback Party state convention in Little Rock on September 12, 1876, at which delegates appointed Tobey, a resident of Pope County, to the party's state central committee.[31] Only 289 Arkansas voters cast ballots for Cooper in November, but at the Arkansas State Grange's annual meeting of 1878, delegates passed a resolution sponsored by Cunningham that placed the organization's stamp of approval upon the doctrines of the Greenback platform.[32]

Yet while the Grange and the Greenback movement shared some ideas about currency reform and antimonopolism, the Arkansas Greenback movement differed sharply from the Arkansas State Grange where matters of race were involved.[33] Many African Americans in Arkansas already had demonstrated a willingness to engage in political activism and, in some instances, even labor activism in the years immediately following emancipation. The most striking instances of black labor activism in Arkansas occurred in John Thompson Jones's Phillips County, described by one historian as having been "the slave capital of the state" in 1860. Even before the Civil War ended, a group of newly freed black farm workers in Phillips County refused to work until their northern lessee agreed to their demands regarding wages and work rules. Then shortly after the war ended, a former slave named Bryant Singfield began organizing other former slaves in Phillips County who had stayed on the plantations of their former masters as contract laborers. Federal military commanders stationed in Helena "encouraged and assisted" Singfield in these efforts, according to the recollection of a former slave. Some of Singfield's followers then took the bold step of leaving their employers' plantations and moving onto an abandoned plot of land that they began farming as their own. A group of white planters, reportedly led by future county sheriff Bart Turner, retaliated by rounding up Singfield and several others who were involved in this budding labor protest and apparently killing them. Local legend later held that Singfield's ghost haunted a swamp where he was killed.[34]

While such labor protests were isolated events, many more African Americans in Arkansas asserted their rights by registering to vote. Assisted by the Union League, which was started by white northerners during the Civil War but drew many southern black followers after the war, some twenty-two thousand black men registered to vote in Arkansas between May and November of 1868. This required a great deal of resolve and courage, as the Ku Klux Klan emerged in Arkansas for the first time in late 1867 and began a campaign of violence and terror against Republicans of both races. As the presidential and congressional elections approached in 1868, the resultant death toll in the state reportedly exceeded two hundred citizens—mostly African Americans, as well as some white Unionists. In the southwestern Arkansas county of Lafayette, where opposition to the Democratic Party would be strong through the late nineteenth century, Klansmen killed about twenty men, most of them African Americans, that summer.[35]

African Americans would eventually play a significant role in the Greenback movement in Arkansas, but not in 1876. Little came of the Greenback Party's efforts in the state, where its one congressional candidate received 681 votes, or nationally that year. Few Americans viewed the octogenarian Peter Cooper as a serious presidential candidate. But by 1878, after the shockwaves generated by the Great Railroad Strike of 1877 and with the continuation of the depression that had begun with the Panic of 1873, the Greenback Party seemed more viable.[36] It would be revived in 1878 on February 22 (a favored date of reformers to hold conventions, being George Washington's birthday), when about 150 delegates came to Toledo, Ohio, for a "national convention of labor and currency reformers" and formed what they formally named the National Party, which soon became known as the Greenback-Labor Party.[37] Five months later, on July 13, the Arkansas Greenback-Labor Party held a state convention in Little Rock. The Pulaski County Greenback Club, which "drew its members," nearly three-quarters of whom were black, "from a curious assortment of Democrats, Grangers, and Republicans in the Little Rock area," dominated the state convention. The *Arkansas Gazette* reported that "about seven-eighths of the delegates present were colored," and "a row" nearly occurred at the convention when white delegates (including Charles E. Cunningham) took control of the newly appointed State Central Committee. The convention adjourned without appointing a slate of candidates for the upcoming state elections.[38]

The Arkansas Greenback-Labor Party supported the monetary demands of the national party, calling for the issue of paper currency to reverse the decline of the national per capita money supply, which Greenbackers argued would end deflation and lower the cost of credit, both vexing problems for farmers, especially in the South. In Arkansas, as well as most other southern states, the state debt coming out of the Civil War and Reconstruction loomed even larger in most citizens' minds than did national monetary reform. As early as 1874, some Arkansas Democrats began calling for the "repudiation" or disavowal of debts incurred by the state during Reconstruction under the rule of allegedly corrupt Republicans. As the repudiation movement spread across the South, the *New York Times* found a correlation between this "dishonesty" that was "the work of the southern Democrats" and the rise of the Greenback-Labor Party, which "now [in September 1878] springs up in the South to plague the politicians who have inculcated this monstrous doctrine." Arkansas Democrats, however, responded to the Greenback-Labor challenge in 1878 by co-opting much of the Greenbackers' inflationary, soft money platform (although they reversed that position shortly after the elections), and they held off on repudiating the state's "unjust" debt until 1884.[39]

In the state elections of 1878, the Arkansas Greenback-Labor Party proved to be a non-entity; it nominated a state ticket in July, only to have the ticket collapse in August as every candidate withdrew from the race. The Democrats' adoption of Greenback financial demands hurt the third-party cause, but probably even more damaging was Democrats' ability to associate the Greenback-Labor Party with African Americans and Republicans, given the composition of the state convention. In August, the *Arkansas Gazette* reported that "the *New York Evening Post* has just discovered that 'the Greenback party, in Alabama and Texas, is almost entirely made up of negroes,'" and then laconically commented, "We would respectfully invite the *Post* to extend its inquiries into all the other Southern States for similar discoveries.'"[40] Nevertheless, as Democrats swept all four of Arkansas's districts in the elections for the US House of Representatives in November, Greenback-Labor candidate Milton Rice received 48.8 percent of the vote in a two-man contest in the state's Third District, which included Pulaski County. Rice was the brother of Ben Rice, a Republican who had represented Arkansas in the US Senate during Reconstruction. In the Second District, located in southern Arkansas, Colonel John M. Bradley, who was referred to variously in the *Arkansas Gazette* as either a Greenbacker or an independent candidate, received 42.8 percent of the vote in a two-man contest. In the elections for the Arkansas state legislature, Greenback-Labor candidates won 7 of 124 seats. Victorious Greenbackers included the former slave and Union veteran Isaac T. Gillam, who at the time was serving as a Republican alderman in Little Rock. The Greenback-Labor Party did quite well in Little Rock that year, not only electing Gillam but also sweeping the municipal elections.[41] Carl H. Moneyhon found that farmers and "leaders and members of the labor unions forming in the state at that same time" were the party's strongest supporters, which would explain the party's success in the state's largest city, where some of these unions already existed.[42]

After the elections passed and Democrats dropped their support of the Greenbackers' soft money platform, some Arkansas Democrats joined the Greenback-Labor ranks. Most prominently, Rufus King Garland, brother of

Democratic US senator (and former governor) Augustus H. Garland, broke with the Democrats and became a Greenbacker in July 1879. Like his brother, Rufus Garland had been a "Redeemer"; he had participated in the Arkansas constitutional convention of 1874, and during the Civil War he served as both a captain and a member of the Confederate Congress. He declared that the Democrats' reversal of support for soft money was his reason for leaving the party, and he declared the struggle of the Greenback-Labor Party to be "the struggle of honest labor without scrip or purse against the grasp of the money power, which has been fostered by class legislation until it has grown insolent and tyrannical."[43] Under Garland's leadership, the state Greenback-Labor Party now supported repudiation of the state's debts, but in 1880 voters would reject a constitutional amendment to repudiate or readjust those debts. For many voters in Arkansas, as one scholar has noted, "Greenbackism became more an instrument of political opposition to the entrenched Democratic Party than a means of economic reform." In 1880, the Arkansas Republican and Greenback-Labor parties engaged in "fusion," an arrangement whereby the two parties shared nominations and agreed not to compete with each other for the same offices. Thus the Republicans endorsed Greenback-Labor gubernatorial candidate W. P. "Buck" Parks, an attorney from Lafayette County.[44] In August the party's presidential candidate, James B. Weaver of Iowa, campaigned for more than a week in Arkansas. At Little Rock, Charles E. Cunningham introduced him at a rally, and at Prescott, the former Union general was introduced by a one-legged Confederate veteran. Weaver's visit, however, failed to revive what had become a "moribund" state party. In the gubernatorial election, the official tally indicated 31,284 votes for Parks compared to 84,088 for Democrat Thomas J. Churchill. In November, Weaver received barely 4,000 votes in the state, and Rufus Garland, the only Greenbacker to run for Congress, received only 11.2 percent of the vote in a district (the third) where the Republicans did not honor the fusion agreement, leaving Garland in a distant third place. Statewide, too, fusion seemed to have its limits. In many heavily black counties, Parks received less support than Republicans had, although white voters in the state's hill counties (in the northern and western portions of the state) tended to support him.[45]

Thirty-two delegates attended the Arkansas Greenback-Labor convention of 1882 on June 20 in Little Rock. Familiar delegates at the convention included Isaac Gillam and the old Grangers Charles E. Cunningham and Charles E. Tobey. The party reaffirmed its support of the soft money national Greenback-Labor Party platform while, at the state level, indicating its continued support of repudiation of the state debt and expressing support for free public schools and immigration, "deprecat[ing] the fact that the Bourbon [Redeemer] element has so governed our state as to exclude the industrial classes." The party also called for state and county elections to be held at the same time as congressional elections "so that a fair vote and an honest count may be had, and the ballots of the people be kept from the hands of 'ticket clippers' and 'ballot-box stuffers.'" (This demand would seem quite prescient given what would happen in Arkansas elections six years later.) Finally, the party declared its desire for legislation regulating the freight and passenger tariffs on railroads, "and forcing these monopolies to recognize the fact that the people have some rights which should be respected." The party nominated a partial state ticket that included Rufus Garland for governor, Tobey for secretary of state, and one congressional candidate, Cunningham, for the state's seat as congressman-at-large.[46]

While fusion between the state Greenback-Labor and Republican parties had its limits in 1880, it collapsed altogether in 1882. On July 7, the Republican state convention nominated a complete state ticket with the exception of a candidate for congressman-at-large.[47] Garland finished third place in the gubernatorial election behind the Democratic victor James H. Berry and Republican William D. Slack, receiving only 10,142 votes, about one-third of the total received by Parks two years earlier.[48] In the election for congressman-at-large, Democrat Clifton R. Breckenridge received 66.6 percent of the votes cast compared to 32.7 percent for Cunningham.[49] Despite the Greenbackers' failure in the elections of 1882, the returns did reveal some areas of third-party strength in the state. These included some counties in predominantly white extreme northwestern Arkansas, such as Washington, which supported the party in this and earlier election years, and in the more diverse southwestern portion of the state. Historians have suggested that the Greenback-Labor Party's strength in the latter region reflected the personal popularity of gubernatorial candidates Parks and Garland, who both resided there, but one scholar has suggested that "voters in those counties, where considerable acreage of low yield soil was devoted to cotton, may also have been activated by the economic pinch." In Rufus Garland's Nevada County, the third party controlled the county offices from 1880 to 1884 and captured them again in 1886. The county later became a Populist Party stronghold in the 1890s.[50]

Nevada County was clearly exceptional, though, because the elections of 1882 proved to be the last time that the Greenback-Labor Party nominated any candidates for state or federal office in Arkansas.[51] The national party did not last much longer, falling apart after the presidential campaign of Massachusetts governor Ben Butler in 1884 attracted barely half the votes that James B. Weaver had four years earlier.[52] The Grange, while not actually disappearing, experienced a sharp decline of its own. "After the eclipse of the association in 1878," wrote historian Judith Barjenbruch, "former Grangers probably constituted much of the Greenback voting strength in the state [of Arkansas], but the absence of an official organization through which to channel their effort diminished their influence."[53] Technically, however, the Grange outlasted the Greenback-Labor Party in Arkansas, surviving into the early 1890s before merging into the Farmers' Alliance.[54]

Even as the Grange faded and the Greenback-Labor Party disintegrated, though, the problems confronting most of the state's farmers, which had sparked the rise of these organizations in the first place, persisted. Not surprisingly, then, both the Grange and the Greenback-Labor Party represented merely the beginning of farmers' organizations and farmer-labor oriented third parties in Arkansas. Moreover, the strength of the Greenback-Labor Party in Arkansas was hindered by the lack of a strong labor movement in the state during the party's brief period of existence, but as the party collapsed, the labor movement was starting to show clear signs of life.

Labor Strife

Those stirrings would begin even before the Greenback-Labor Party died. In particular, they began in two of the state's relatively new industries: railroads and coal mining. Railroad development did not begin in Arkansas until the 1850s, and in 1860 only one state (Oregon) had fewer miles of railroads.[55] The Civil War brought an end to railroad construction in Arkansas, but it began again in the late 1860s, and by the mid-1870s the state's basic rail network was in place and connected to the new national railroad system.[56] The development of the state's railroads facilitated the rise of coal mining in western Arkansas, which had been underway since the 1840s but which, according to an historical account written in 1906, "on a commercial scale . . . can hardly be considered to antedate the year 1883."[57] In 1880, western Arkansas mines produced 14,778 tons of coal; that production increased to nearly 400,000 tons ten years later.[58] In 1881 strikes would occur in both of these industries.

A series of railroad strikes shook the nation in the summer of 1877. As these strikes, the first of which began over wage cuts on July 16 in Martinsburg, West Virginia, spread to other towns and cities, they came to encompass many workers outside the railroad industry as well, becoming a general strike of sorts that earned the moniker "Great Railroad Strike of 1877." A strike leader in Baltimore explained that workers could no longer endure wages that were not sufficient for them to feed their children, and another striker who expressed the same grievance more bluntly stated that "we are strikin' for life." Over one hundred thousand workers joined these strikes, and they caused millions of dollars of property damage. Police forces, state militias, and finally federal troops dispatched by President Rutherford B. Hayes battled strikers in many locales. About two weeks after the strikes began, Hayes, who had been inaugurated in March following one of the most controversial, disputed elections in American history, was able to summarize the end of the strike succinctly: "The strikers have been put down by *force*." The death toll exceeded one hundred, and many more were injured.[59]

While the Great Railroad Strike of 1877 spread across much of the nation, it apparently did not extend into Arkansas. Four years later, though, on Sunday morning, June 12, 1881, about fifty freight brakemen employed by the Iron Mountain Railroad in Little Rock struck for higher wages. The job of a brakeman in this era, which entailed, among other tasks, coupling cars and setting hand brakes, often proved dangerous; thousands died on the job in the nineteenth century. The Iron Mountain brakemen demanded an increase from fifty to sixty dollars per month, claiming, according to the *Arkansas Gazette*, that their current salary was "not sufficient to repay them for the labor which they endure and the danger which they face." The brakemen "refused to take any trains out Sunday morning," and when their immediate negotiations with the general manager at Little Rock failed to produce a settlement, the railroad company sent assistant general superintendent Colonel Dudley from Texarkana on the noon train to meet with the strikers. Dudley and the strikers soon reached a settlement: three brakemen instead of two would be used on through freight trains, with the rear brakeman being paid fifty-five dollars per month, and on local freight trains, three brakemen would be used instead of four, with the head brakeman being paid sixty dollars per month and the other two fifty-five dollars. At ten o'clock on Monday morning, June 13, the freight trains started rolling again.[60]

Two months later, coal miners in the Johnson County hamlet of Spadra also struck for higher wages. The strike occurred at two mining companies, Steiwal & Co. and Bryan & Co., where miners demanded 87 ½ cents per ton instead of 75 cents. The *Arkansas Gazette* reported a standoff: "The miners seem to be determined to keep the mines idle until their demands are met, while on the other side the operators are quite willing to stop unless the men go in at the old prices." The *Gazette* also suggested some other possible developments, noting that "there has been no intimidation as yet; should there be the Quapaws [Indians] may again have a chance to rusticate."[61] Unfortunately, the outcome of this strike went unrecorded; the *Gazette* never reported on the strike again, and the rival *Arkansas Democrat* never reported on it at all. It seems safe to say, however, that it was not settled as quickly and amicably as the Iron Mountain Railroad strike had been. Spadra coal miners would strike again for higher wages in 1884 and 1885, and in 1886 they would join the Knights of Labor, the largest labor organization in the nation at that time.[62] In contrast to the farmers who had made up the bulk of the membership of the Grange in Arkansas, railroad workers and coal miners were far more likely to come from other parts of the United States or to have been born outside the United States. In Sebastian County, which by 1891 was producing over 80 percent of the entire state's coal output, the population increased from 19,560 in 1880 to 36,935 twenty years later. The foreign-born population in the county rose from 613 to 1,365 during those two decades. Immigrant miners came to Arkansas not only from northern states but also from Italy, Ireland, and Germany.[63] While the Great Railroad Strike of 1877 bypassed Arkansas, the equally calamitous "Great Southwest Railroad Strike" of 1886 and national coal miners' strike of 1894 would not.[64]

As the Greenback-Labor Party failed in its final campaigns in Arkansas in the autumn of 1882, it may have seemed that the state's Democratic Party (which had little to fear from the Arkansas GOP) could count on virtually uncontested control of the state in the years ahead. Furthermore, with the Arkansas State Grange reduced to a fraction of the 20,471 members that it had reported seven years earlier, the state's farmer movement may have appeared to be disintegrating as well. The state's labor movement had yet to ever appear threatening in the first place by this point. But the Greenback-Labor Party had suggested the possibility that disaffected white and black politicians and voters might make common cause in a third party, and even if the state's all-white Grange was led by loyal Redeemer Democratic planters, the party and the organization both gave voice to antimonopolist sentiment against railroads, corporations, and middlemen, as well as to grievances over the shortage of currency and credit that keenly affected so many Arkansans. Moreover, by the end of 1882, even as the Arkansas State Grange was decaying and the Greenback-Labor Party was dying, two farmers' organizations—both of which, unlike the Grange, began in Arkansas—were emerging to not only replace the Grange but also express the grievances of poor-to-middling farmers more sharply, and the Knights of Labor, which had begun to expand nationally shortly after the Great Railroad Strike of 1877, entered Arkansas to begin organizing farmers and industrial workers alike. Far from being failures, the Grange and the Greenback-Labor Party turned out to be mere first steps toward agrarian and labor revolt in Arkansas.

II. BUILDING THE FOUNDATIONS OF REBELLION

BY THE END OF 1882, Arkansas Democrats believed that the third-party challenge to their dominance was dead and buried. The *Fayetteville Weekly Democrat* sardonically wondered about the continued existence of "the few greenback papers scattered about in Texas and Arkansaw [*sic*]," since "they have no party."[1] While that statement bore a large measure of truth, such smug complacency on the part of Arkansas Democrats was nevertheless ill founded. For during 1882, Arkansas farmers and laborers set in motion a working-class rebellion that, had the democratic process itself not been thwarted in the state in the years that soon followed, most certainly would have rewritten the state's history. As events transpired, this rebellion of farmers and laborers still left a legacy of working-class protest in the state that would reverberate into the twentieth century, and it also provoked some of the most shameful misdeeds in Arkansas—and perhaps even American—history on the part of those determined to crush it.

The discontent of Arkansas farmers in the early 1880s, as well as their dissatisfaction with the Grange, manifested itself in the independent creation of farmers' organizations in two different parts of the state in 1882. A small group of farmers in Prairie County, located just to the west of the fertile east Arkansas Delta, formed the Agricultural Wheel, while the Brothers of Freedom emerged in northwestern Arkansas's Johnson County, home of the emerging coal mining communities of Spadra and Coal Hill. These organizations would quickly prove to be more radical and less reticent about engaging in independent politics than their predecessor, the Grange.

The relatively short, but certainly eventful, history of the Agricultural Wheel began on February 15, 1882, when nine men met "in an old log school-house, eight miles southwest of the town of Des Arc, in Prairie County, Arkansas." (Only seven of the nine men would be considered founders of the organization, as two from neighboring Lonoke County "took no part in the proceedings.")[2] One of the founders of the Wheel, W. W. Tedford, later said, "The question has often been asked, what gave rise to the Wheel? The question is as easily answered as asked, *Monopoly!*" More specifically, Tedford pointed to the anaconda mortgage (the crop-lien system), repossessed farms, and falling crop prices.[3] Furthermore, the weather, always potential friend or foe to farmers, had most decidedly been the latter in Prairie County during the year preceding the formation of the Wheel. In 1881, a severe drought had ruined crops, and then in January and February 1882, torrential rains caused the White River to flood a lot of the farmland in a county whose name describes its terrain.[4]

On February 22, 1882, the organization, not yet named, met again and adopted a constitution and bylaws. The organization took the name Wattensas Farmers' Club, and its constitution declared, among other points, that the club's "objects shall be the improvement of its members in the theory and practice of agriculture and the dissemination of knowledge relative to rural and farming affairs" and that "the members shall consist of such persons as will sign the constitution and by-laws and who are engaged in farming." Provisions of the bylaws included a stipulation that "the chaplain shall open the meetings with prayer" and another that two sentinels (whose annual election was provided for by the constitution) "shall . . . see that the hall is properly guarded." Within about a month of its founding, the organization adopted a secret ritual (as had the Grange), increased its membership to twenty, and changed its name to the Agricultural Wheel. Secret rituals were common among farmer and labor organizations in this era, and they consisted of practices such as certain grips, handshakes, and passwords in order to prevent outsiders from infiltrating their ranks.[5]

The odd new name carried a purpose. Tedford explained, "No machinery can be run without a great drive wheel, and as that wheel moves and governs the entire machinery, however complex, so agriculture is the great wheel or power that controls the entire machinery of the world's industries."[6] Yet the economic status of most farmers in Prairie County hardly befitted such a central position. In 1880 Reuben CarlLee, who later became an important figure in the Wheel, told a census taker that 90 percent of the county's farmers relied upon credit for obtaining their supplies (i.e., the much-maligned anaconda mortgage).[7] Tedford also explained that the name reflected the founders' belief that "we are surrounded by 'rings' of many kinds, especially political rings," or cliques that dominated political affairs to the detriment of democracy. The name also drew upon the biblical imagery of the prophet Ezekiel's wheel.[8]

In March 1882 the Agricultural Wheel adopted a platform that expressed the beliefs of its small body of members in clearer, more tangible terms:

> The general condition of our country imperatively demands unity of action on the part of the laboring masses, reformation in economy, and the dissemination of principles best calculated to encourage and foster agricultural and mechanical pursuits, encouraging the toiling masses, leading them in the road to prosperity, and providing a just and fair remuneration for labor, a just exchange of our commodities and best mode and means of securing to the laboring classes the greatest amount of good.[9]

The platform reflected the influence of the Grange in urging farmers to save their meat and bread and raise more corn and grains and less cotton, although it offered no advice to farmers as to how they could actually do that when many creditors demanded that farmers grow cotton as collateral. The preamble condemned monopolies as "dangerous to the best interests of our country, tending to enslave a free people and subvert . . . the great principles" of the nation's Founding Fathers. The preamble also declared that while "the laboring classes of mankind are the real producers of wealth, . . . they are gradually becoming oppressed by combinations of capital, and the fruits of their toil absorbed by a class who propose not only to live on the labors of others, but to speedily amass fortunes at their expense." The preamble reiterated the Wheelers' belief in God, "the great Creator of all things," who "created all men free and equal, and endowed them with certain inalienable rights, such as life, liberty, and the pursuit of happiness."[10]

The Wheelers' notions of freedom and equality and other such republican ideals, however, suffered from the same limitations as those of the nation's Founding Fathers. The declaration of the objects of the Wheel limited membership to "white males who are engaged in the occupation of farming, [and] also mechanics who are actually engaged in farming."[11] For the most part, the Wheel's membership requirements did not become more inclusive until the organization's expansion into the National Agricultural Wheel during the summer of 1886. The words "male" and "white" were then omitted from the membership requirements, with the stipulation that "colored farmers" would be organized into separate lodges. (Subsequently, white Wheel lodges would, at least in some instances, allow black Wheelers to come to their meetings as visitors.)[12] In 1887, the National Agricultural Wheel further loosened its membership requirements to allow the admission of "all mechanics who are engaged in their respective trades," provided that they not employ more than three workers.[13]

Recruiting white male farmers and mechanics who were "actually engaged in farming," the Agricultural Wheel spread rapidly across central Arkansas. The organization filed articles of incorporation at the Prairie County circuit clerk's office on August 22, 1882. By the following spring, enough subordinate Wheels (local chapters) existed that Wheelers were able to create a State Wheel organization on April 9, 1883. The State Wheel held its first meeting at Goff's Cave on July 18, 1883, which drew delegates from most of the thirty-nine subordinate Wheels that had been organized by then. By the time the State Wheel held its second meeting, at Stony Point on January 9, 1884, the number of subordinate Wheels had increased to 114, and the organization's membership stood at about five thousand, despite the fact that the organization had passed a resolution at Goff's Cave banning the organization of subordinate Wheels "within the limit of incorporated towns."[14]

The Brothers of Freedom

Also in 1882, probably shortly after W. W. Tedford and his compatriots organized their small farmers' club in Prairie County—the exact date is uncertain—two men in Johnson County, Isaac McCracken and Marion Farris, began forming a secret organization of farmers "for the avowed purpose of enabling them to obtain a just reward for their hard labor, and to incite a proper rivalry among merchants and dealers." Inspired by the Revolutionary War–era Sons of Freedom, they named their organization the Brothers of Freedom.[15] Farris did not become prominent in the state, but McCracken became the leading figure in the Arkansas agrarian revolt.

Born in Huntington, Canada, in 1846 to Scottish-Irish parents, McCracken spent the first eight years of his life there until his family moved to Lowell, Massachusetts. His parents apprenticed him to a block cutter, but in 1860 the teenager signed on as a "common seaman before the mast in a whaling vessel, and during three years he followed the sea," visiting Cuba, St. Domingo (Haiti), Jamaica, the Bermudas and Western Islands, and also the coast of Central America. He then returned to Lowell and became an apprentice to a machinist. He subsequently worked as a machinist in Lowell and Fall River, Massachusetts; Sparta and LaCrosse, Wisconsin; and Minneapolis and St. Anthony, Minnesota. Married in 1867, he and his wife moved to a farm in Johnson County, Arkansas, in 1870, but he took a job as a machinist in the Iron Mountain Railroad shops in Argenta (now North Little Rock). He joined the blacksmiths' and machinists' union but left the job after two years and began operating his farm. He later joined the Knights of Labor, which had not quite reached Arkansas when he and Farris started the Brothers of Freedom.[16]

In some ways the Brothers of Freedom seemed quite similar to the Agricultural Wheel. In fact, although no connection has been established between the founding of the two organizations, much of the preamble of the Brothers' Declaration of Principles matches the Wheel's preamble verbatim, which certainly suggests that such a connection may have existed.[17] The similarity in the rhetoric espoused by the two organizations extended beyond their official pronouncements. While a member of the Brothers of Freedom accused lawmakers of bowing to big business and enacting legislation that made "labor subservient to capital and monopolies," Wheeler W. Scott Morgan railed against "the infamous trusts that have become an incubus upon our body politic."[18] The Brothers also resembled the Wheel in advising farmers to avoid the credit system and in resolving that "the 'all-cotton' idea be buried in the grave with our forefathers," although this advice was just as impractical coming from one organization as the other.[19] Both organizations, however, made a more practical effort to help their members through cooperative enterprises, like the Grange before them. The Brothers contracted with local merchants to buy needed goods for farmers at reduced prices, and the organization established a cooperative store at Doddsville in Marion County that in 1884 was reported to be operating at "full blast . . . and giving all concerned good satisfaction."[20] In Sebastian County, the Fort Smith *Elevator* reported in 1885 that the Brothers were conducting "an extensive and very satisfactory co-operative trade with the business houses of St. Louis."[21] In July 1885 the Arkansas State Wheel took steps "to buy farm implements and machinery direct[ly] from manufacturers," which would save money for members by eliminating the role played by retailers as middlemen.[22]

The two organizations were not similar in every respect, though. While the Brothers, like the Wheel, did not admit women or African Americans, and did not admit merchants, bankers, and lawyers—all of whom the Brothers viewed as class enemies of the farmer—they did admit mechanics and industrial laborers. "The Brothers," according to the most authoritative historian of the organization, "intended that [their Declaration of Principles] lay the foundation for an organization open to oppressed laborers."[23] This may explain why the organization attracted some of the more radical old Grangers, such as Charles E. Tobey, who moved into the organization as the Grange declined and the Greenback-Labor Party disappeared. In 1884 Tobey explained how the "three great monopolies"—financial institutions, corporations, and railroads—used the two major parties to exploit farmers and laborers alike.[24]

If the Brothers' acceptance of mechanics and industrial laborers from the organization's inception indicated a sharper or at least broader sense of class consciousness than the Agricultural Wheel initially displayed, then the organization's origins in northwestern Arkansas may have been the reason why. This was the poorest region of the state. Most farmers who joined the Brothers of Freedom were probably landowners, but small landowners. The postbellum spread of "King Cotton" into the region made many of them poorer, not wealthier, as cotton prices declined each year.[25] In sixteen northwestern and western Arkansas counties where the Brothers of Freedom is known to have been active, farms tended to be smaller and less valuable (as measured by value of land, fences, and buildings) than the statewide average and equipped with fewer farm implements and machines. The value of livestock on farms in most of these counties also fell below the state average, and these farms were more likely to be cultivated by their owners. The rocky soil in this part of the state meant that these farms were below the state average in cotton production with a higher than average ratio (substantially higher in some counties) of corn bushels to cotton bales. In contrast, among fourteen counties in Arkansas where the Agricultural Wheel is known to have been active, only seven had an average farm value lower than the state average, and most had a lower-than-average corn-to-cotton ratio and a below average percentage of owner-cultivated farms. Geographically, the Wheel was more widely dispersed across the state than the Brothers of Freedom; three of these fourteen Wheel counties lay in the fertile Delta region of eastern Arkansas.[26]

The Knights of Labor

While the Agricultural Wheel and the Brothers of Freedom were both organizing farmers (who constituted the vast majority of the Brothers' ranks even though mechanics and industrial laborers could join), the state's labor movement was progressing much more slowly in 1882. In Little Rock, a threatened strike by the Brotherhood of Locomotive Engineers on the Iron Mountain led to what the *Arkansas Gazette* later recalled as "the first written agreement [in the nation] governing hours and wages between a railroad company and its employees." A committee of engineers from Little Rock negotiated the agreement with two of famed railroad magnate Jay Gould's top managerial figures, H. M. Hoxie and A. A. Talmage, both of whom would later figure prominently in the Southwest Railroad Strikes of 1885 and 1886. Not only did the contract accord recognition to the Brotherhood of Locomotive Engineers, but it also essentially created a closed shop for the union.[27] This proved to be a much easier and more amicable settlement of differences between railroad employees and management than what would soon follow in Arkansas and elsewhere in the region.

At the end of 1882, however, a larger national labor organization entered Arkansas and, although it never equaled the Brothers of Freedom or the Agricultural Wheel in membership in the state, it became just as significant, and certainly more so among the state's black population. The Knights of Labor (officially named the Noble and Holy Order of the Knights of Labor, and often referred to simply as "the Order") began in Philadelphia in December 1869, formed by nine men who had belonged to the dissolved Garment Cutters' Association of that city. Like its contemporary farmers' organizations and other fraternal orders of the day, the Knights created a secret ritual, and the Order remained so shrouded in secrecy that until 1882 members were forbidden from even using its name in public; in printed documents, five stars or asterisks were used in place of the name.[28] The Knights of Labor grew slowly during the 1870s, mostly among miners and mostly in and near Pennsylvania.[29] In the wake of the Great Railroad Strike of 1877, however, the Order held a convention—the first of its annual General Assembly meetings—in Reading, Pennsylvania, with the goal of creating a national labor organization. It adopted a preamble and platform (known thereafter as the Reading platform) that called for "the thorough unification of labor" in the face of the "recent alarming development and aggression of aggregated wealth" that if left unchecked would "lead to the pauperization and hopeless degradation of the toiling masses."[30] The platform drew upon previous antimonopoly, labor, and Greenback platforms while, as historian Robert C. McMath has noted, setting a model for the agrarian reform platforms that followed later in the nineteenth century.[31] Major specific goals of the Reading platform included the creation of federal and state bureaus of labor statistics; the establishment of cooperative enterprises; the "reserving of the public lands . . . for the actual settler"; worker safety laws; the abolition of the contract-labor and convict-lease systems; equal pay for equal work for both sexes; an eight-hour workday; and the Greenback doctrine of "a purely national circulating medium . . . issued directly to the people, without the intervention of any system of banking corporations, which money shall be a legal tender in payment of all debts, public or private."[32]

The Reading General Assembly appointed Uriah S. Stephens, one of the Order's founders, as the first Grand Master Workman. Stephens appointed organizers, including four in the South: one in Georgia, one in Florida, and two in Alabama. The organizer in Florida failed to form any local assemblies (the Knights' term for what would later be called union locals), but the Knights chartered locals in Alabama in 1878 and one in Georgia (albeit short-lived) in 1879. The Knights also chartered locals in Tennessee and South Carolina in the late 1870s, but the organization of the first locals in the Southwest took longer: not until 1882 would the Knights enter Louisiana, Texas, or Arkansas.[33]

The genesis of the Knights of Labor in Arkansas occurred on the evening of November 22, 1882, when "seven determined men," also described as "hard-worked clerks and carpenters," met in a blacksmith shop in the city of Hot Springs (whose population in 1880 was 3,554). Since the Order had yet to send an organizer into Arkansas, the seven men had to engage in "a great deal of correspondence and the exercise of proper patience" before they could actually form a local assembly. The official founding of Hot Springs Assembly No. 2419 (or, in Knights' shorthand, LA [Local Assembly] 2419) occurred on December 30, 1882, meaning that Arkansas barely joined its neighboring states of Texas and Louisiana in the ranks of Knighthood that year.[34] LA 2419 was a "mixed" local assembly, consisting of members of various occupations, as opposed to a "trade" local. The Knights' rather egalitarian membership requirements meant that anyone eighteen or older could join, with the occupational exceptions of lawyers, doctors, stockbrokers, professional gamblers, bankers, and liquor dealers, all of whom the Knights labeled as "social parasites" in the "interdicted classes," although the ban on doctors was lifted in 1884.[35] The Knights also excluded Chinese people from membership and supported the passage of the Chinese Exclusion Act of 1882, which was of little relevance in Arkansas since the US Census of 1880 counted only 133 Chinese people in the entire state.[36]

On the date of its official founding, December 30, 1882, twenty-one men, all white, became members of LA 2419 in Hot Springs.[37] The key figure, who probably carried on most of the aforementioned correspondence needed to form the local, was Dan Fraser Tomson. Born on April 23, 1850, in Hardeman County, Tennessee, Tomson moved with his family to Miller County, Missouri, in 1860. At the age of fourteen, he joined the Union Army, serving as a drummer boy in the Civil War. By 1871 he was working as a ward master at a US Marine hospital in St. Louis, and the following year he married Elizabeth Catherine Melton, with whom he would have five children. By the early 1880s, he and his family had moved to Hot Springs, where he began farming. During the 1880s, he would be the most important leader of the

Knights of Labor in Arkansas.[38] He also served as the first Master Workman of LA 2419.[39]

Although all the members of LA 2419 were white, the Knights of Labor as an organization did not exclude African Americans. Terence V. Powderly, who succeeded Uriah S. Stephens as the Order's Grand Master Workman in 1879 and held that position until 1893, informed a white Knight of Labor in Alabama in 1880 that "under the laws of our Order, a brother no matter what his color is can visit any Local in the Order if he is clear and in good standing."[40] In practice, however, most local assemblies in the South were racially segregated; locals that consisted of blacks as well as whites existed but were the exception rather than the rule.[41] Apparently Tomson and other members of LA 2419 helped organize the second Knights local in Arkansas—its first black local—Freedom Assembly No. 2447 in January 1883. This local evidently got off to a sluggish start; in May 1884, a charter member of LA 2419 wrote a letter to the Knights' national newspaper, the *Journal of United Labor*, in which he reported, "Our colored brethren [of LA 2447] have had a poor existence so far, but they are 'turning a new leaf' and manifesting more interest, and their meetings are better attended than heretofore, and it is to be hoped that they will build up a prosperous and useful Assembly." The letter also reported that Tomson and other members of LA 2419 "frequently visit them and encourage and help them along."[42] Privately, though, Tomson, in a letter to Powderly four months earlier, had offered a more blunt (and condescending), if still hopeful, assessment of the black local assembly's difficulties. "I am and have been all along doing for them what I could," he wrote, "but they got a bad start and it is so hard to get competent men among them, that the case many times seemed desperate and I almost despaired, but 'hard tugging' has pulled them through the worst I trust."[43] LA 2447 existed until at least 1886, a respectable lifespan for a Knights of Labor local assembly, although less enduring than LA 2419, which lasted until at least 1893.[44]

Unlike the Brothers of Freedom and, until 1887, the Agricultural Wheel, the Knights of Labor admitted women to membership, although, as historian LeeAnn Whites has noted, "The name of the organization, the *Knights* of Labor, makes one think of *men* as the honorable defenders of labor."[45] Still, at the Knights' apex in 1886, some sixty-five thousand women belonged to the organization.[46] Southern women, however, do not appear to have had the easiest path to membership. In 1888, Mrs. Ira Campbell of Jemison, Alabama, wrote in a letter to the *Journal of United Labor* that she was "ashamed to confess" that she lived "in a community where it is considered not lady-like for [women] to become members."[47] Such sentiments may have been less common in Arkansas, though. A local assembly organized in Malvern (Hot Spring County) in 1885 included women as well as men, and in March 1886 Tomson reported the organization of an all-female local in Pulaski County, which took the name Martha Washington Assembly and included housekeepers, salesladies, seamstresses, dressmakers, and bookbinders. In October 1886, Van Buren Assembly No. 6307 (named after the Arkansas town where it was organized six months earlier) amended its bylaws so that women would only have to pay half the two-dollar initiation fee required of men. Of the 202 local assemblies of the Knights of Labor that are known to have existed in Arkansas between 1882 and 1899, at least fifteen are known to have included women. At least five of those locals included black women. Twenty-one of those 202 local assemblies are known to have been black locals; as well as can be determined, none of them were racially integrated.[48]

Although the extant evidence is unclear, it seems quite likely that at least some of the housekeepers organized by the Knights of Labor in Arkansas were African Americans, who constituted the bulk of the domestic workforce in the South during the late nineteenth century and for decades thereafter. Few aspects of the Knights' activity in the South could be considered bolder than organizing black domestic workers. No group of free laborers in the South worked for less.[49] The audacity of the Knights in organizing these workers throughout the region alarmed or at least antagonized many whites. In 1886 the *Charlotte* (North Carolina) *Home-Democrat* responded to these efforts by warning, "White people had better begin to practice waiting on themselves more than they have been doing, for when most of the colored servants join the Knights of Labor . . . it will be almost impossible to get along with them."[50] For Knights organizers like Tomson, their willingness to recruit black domestic workers carried a certain irony, since it risked alienating many of the working-class whites who made up the majority of the Order's membership; even they could afford poorly paid black domestic help.[51]

The Knights of Labor grew slowly and unsteadily in Arkansas. In May 1884, a charter member of LA 2419 reported to the *Journal of United Labor* that he believed the two local assemblies in Hot Springs to be "the only ones in the State today. There was one in the country among the farmers some months ago, but I am told it has lapsed; also, one at Pine Bluff, but it has also passed out of existence, I am informed."[52] Tomson told the story of the Knights' slow start in Arkansas in a letter to the *Journal of United Labor* in March 1886. The Knights added only one local assembly in Arkansas during the first eleven months of 1884—South Hot Springs Assembly No. 3303. "So that for the first two years, with Pine Bluff lapsed," Tomson recalled, "the Order flourished only and was but little known except at Hot Springs." Then in December 1884, "Some brother, I suppose from Missouri or Kansas, dropped down into our extreme northwestern boundaries and founded a [Local] Assembly at Rogers and one at Fort Smith." Tomson became an officially commissioned Knights of Labor organizer during the winter of 1885, and this as well as other developments played a role in the chartering of fourteen local assemblies in Arkansas that year.[53]

While the Knights of Labor survived without flourishing during its first two years in Arkansas, working-class protest mounted in the state outside of the Order's ranks, particularly in the two industries whose workers had already demonstrated such proclivities: railroading and coal mining. In April 1883, brakemen on the Iron Mountain Railroad in Little Rock, who had struck for higher wages with some success nearly two years earlier, struck again after the company reduced the number of brakemen per train from three to two, laying off the one-third of the workforce that would no longer be utilized. The strikers attempted to block rail traffic just north of the city. The company retaliated by immediately firing all of the strikers—ultimately, about sixty to seventy-five of them lost their jobs—and a Pulaski County deputy sheriff arrested six strikers, a total that reached about fifteen by the time the strike ended. Police and railroad detectives succeeded in crushing the strike within a couple of days, and without any bloodshed, but this strike foreshadowed more serious conflict that would soon follow in the state's railroad industry.[54] The burgeoning Arkansas coal-mining industry, meanwhile, experienced in 1884 the second strike in three years by miners in Spadra seeking higher wages, which evidently failed since they struck again for the same reason one year later.[55] Trade unions continued making progress in the state as well; Little Rock typographers had belonged to Local 92 of the International Typographical Union (originally the National Typographical Union) since 1865, and in February 1884 Little Rock cigar makers formed Local 151 of the New York–based Cigar Makers' International Union. The *Arkansas Gazette* reported that "every cigar-maker in the city has joined the new organization," adding that "this is the only union south of St. Louis of this kind."[56]

While the Knights of Labor and the labor movement in general grew slowly in Arkansas from 1882 to 1884, the farmers' movement grew more rapidly. As the membership of the Agricultural Wheel reached about five thousand by the beginning of 1884, the Brothers of Freedom grew even faster. While no membership figure for the Brothers in 1884 seems to have survived, estimates place membership at thirty to forty thousand by the autumn of 1885, at a time when Wheel membership had grown to about ten thousand.[57] Along with the growth of the two farmers' organizations came the possibility that they might engage in independent or third-party politics, even though the founders of the Wheel were all Democrats and the Brothers initially prohibited partisan political discussions in lodges.[58] The Knights of Labor, too, claimed to be nonpartisan. In 1880, Grand Master Workman Terence V. Powderly proclaimed, "Our Order is above politics." When Powderly made this statement, though, he was serving as the mayor of Scranton, Pennsylvania, having been elected on the Greenback-Labor ticket.[59]

The Elections of 1884

Perhaps, then, given the political, class-oriented nature of the platforms of these organizations, it came as no real surprise to observers of Arkansas politics when all three of them entered the partisan fray in 1884. In May the *Arkansas Democrat* reported, "The 'Brothers of Freedom' of Franklin [C] ounty have put a full ticket in the field."[60] Meanwhile, the *Arkansas Gazette* published a letter from a Wheeler in Judsonia (White County) reporting that the county Wheel had voted 26–23 to nominate a county ticket.[61] In Pope County, the former Greenbacker and Arkansas State Grange officer Charles E. Tobey led the Brothers of Freedom down the independent political trail. As the vote in White County suggests, not all Wheelers or Brothers supported this course of action. The Russellville *Democrat* reported a stinging rebuke by a loyal Democratic member of the Brothers who suggested that his independent-leaning brethren should "go on all fours, have their ears spliced and learn to bray, as a disguised ass is dangerous to his neighbors."[62] In Sebastian County, the Brothers of Freedom County Council refused "to put a ticket in the field," and the members of Fairview Lodge No. 376 affirmed that decision by a vote of 15–3.[63]

Overall, however, the political insurgents held the upper hand in most counties where either one (or both) of the farmers' organizations was active, and even the Knights of Labor threw its hat into the ring in the one county in Arkansas where it had any significant presence at the time. Within the Brothers of Freedom, the debate over nominating independent candidates for office essentially ended when the organization's president and cofounder, Isaac McCracken, not only voiced his support for doing so but

3. The Leaders of the Knights of Labor, with Terence V. Powderly in the center. Kurz & Allison, Copyright Claimant. Ca. 1886. Lithograph. Retrieved from the Library of Congress, accessed March 20, 2018, https://www.loc.gov/item/2012648823/.

also announced that he would be an independent candidate for the state legislature as a representative from Johnson County. The Grand State Wheel met at Sulphur Springs in July, representing by this point six or seven thousand members, and while insufficient records or reports of the meeting exist to make clear what political issues were discussed, the Arkansas press reported that the Wheelers rejected the overtures of a "triumvir" of Little Rock–Conway Republicans who offered the Wheel $20,000 "for the purpose of [Republicans and the Wheel] entering into an unholy alliance." The Wheelers did not, however, reject the possibility of fielding independent tickets, which some county Wheels already had decided to do.[64] As for the Knights of Labor, in the one county in the state (Garland) where the Order had much (if any) presence, members persuaded their leader, Dan Fraser Tomson, to "make the race on the 'Working man's' ticket for the state legislature" in the autumn.[65] Ironically, just eight months earlier, Tomson had noted in a letter to Terence V. Powderly that some Knights in Massachusetts were trying to drum up support for the Greenback-Labor presidential candidacy of "old Ben Butler," a Union general during the Civil War and erstwhile Radical Republican congressman. "As this order is not a political machine," wrote Tomson, "I suppose of course that you will 'nip it in the bud,' so far as the K. of L. is concerned?" One can only wonder if Tomson was aware of Powderly's own connections with the Greenback-Labor Party, but given Tomson's opposition to Knights in Massachusetts supporting Butler's campaign, it might be viewed as either ironic or fitting that his own bid for the Arkansas state house of representatives fell short on election day.[66] The inconsistency that Tomson displayed in 1884 regarding Knights of Labor involvement in independent or third-party politics would reappear in the years that followed.

As the campaign approached, the Democratic press of Arkansas tried (predictably) to keep Brothers and Wheelers (all of whom were white) from supporting independent candidates. For example, the *Arkansas Gazette* charged that "all of the old enemies of the Democratic party . . . who know that under their true name, Republicans, they could never come to the front, are now zealous and loud mouthed 'Brothers' and 'Wheelers.' Let nobody be deceived by them."[67] Apparently many Brothers and Wheelers did not believe this partisan rhetoric, however, for the Brothers' candidates "swept all the offices by sizeable majorities" in Johnson, Newton, and Van Buren Counties. The outcome in Franklin County differed only in that the Brothers' candidate for county treasurer lost. The Brothers' tickets won partial victories in three other counties—Perry, Pope, and Searcy. In Scott County the Brothers fused with the Republicans (that is, jointly nominated a ticket), and the fusion ticket won every office except representative and county clerk. A Brothers-Republican fusion ticket fared even better in Crawford County, winning all but "one minor position . . . on the swing vote of disgruntled Democrats who probably were Brothers."[68] In Conway County, the entire Democratic county ticket went down in defeat, although the exact composition of the opposition is unclear. Berton E. Henningson Jr., who has examined the Brothers of Freedom more closely than any other historian, suggested that the Brothers' ticket in Conway County was "probably . . . fielded jointly with the Wheel." On the other hand, Kenneth C. Barnes, in his examination of Conway County from 1861 to 1893, deemed it "unclear if the farmers and Republicans had a fusion ticket or completely separate slates" in 1884. "What is clear," Barnes asserted, "is that with the highest voter turnout ever seen in Conway County, the farmers and Republicans defeated the Democrats for every county office, with most of the winners appearing to be Republican." Brothers of Freedom tickets lost to Democratic tickets in the counties of Logan, Yell, and Sebastian (where the Brothers of Freedom County Council's initial decision not to run a ticket obviously did not stick) and in Faulkner County, where the Brothers' ticket was probably put forth jointly with the Agricultural Wheel. Wheel tickets won in Prairie and White Counties.[69]

In all, according to Dan Fraser Tomson, 15 of the 127 members of the Arkansas state legislature "were elected through the direct influence of the 'Brothers of Freedom' and the 'Agricultural Wheel'—organizations of farmers and laboring men—themselves members of these orders."[70] While this figure obviously represents minor success, nevertheless the Brothers and the Wheel, in their first campaigns and with many members of both orders opposed to independent political action, elected more than double the number of legislators that the Greenback-Labor Party did when it elected seven (its highest total ever in Arkansas) in 1878, two years after the first Greenback convention in Arkansas.[71] The campaign of the agrarian orders in 1884, therefore, suggested the possibility of a greater challenge to the Democratic Party in Arkansas in the years ahead, particularly since the Brothers of Freedom and the Agricultural Wheel were still growing and the Knights of Labor had barely established its presence in the state. (The Knights did, however, expand into the state's coal-mining region by forming a mixed local assembly in the Sebastian County town of Fort Smith in December 1884).[72] Moreover, fusion between the farmers' groups and the Republican Party proved, at the county level, more widespread and effective than it had during the Greenback-Labor Party's campaigns.

If the Brothers' and the Wheel's independent insurgency in 1884 hinted at future campaigns to come, however, the same could be said of how Democrats in Arkansas responded. After the success of the agrarian or fusion tickets at the county level in September, Democratic newspapers increased their rhetorical attacks. Ignoring the real grievances of many Arkansas farmers, the *Arkansas Gazette* instead chastised those who had voted against the Democratic Party by conjuring up the supposed horrors of Reconstruction, charging that Republican schemers were behind the insurgent tickets. Arkansas Republicans, the *Gazette* insisted, "are shrewd enough to know that all roads leading from [D]emocracy lead to [R]epublicanism even though by a roundabout course; and, depend upon it, . . . they have not yet relinquished the hope of restoration to power, that the reign of misrule, ended in 1874, may be resumed."[73] Democrats in Conway County, having been actually defeated and dislodged from power by some combination of Republicans and members of the Brothers and the Wheel, responded in stronger and more ominous ways. In early 1885, as if they were turning back the calendar to 1868, they reformed the Ku Klux Klan (or, at least, donned the regalia of the Klan) and began a violent and terror-filled campaign of night riding. In a county where, according to the census of 1880, African Americans constituted 25 percent of the population, the Klan declared that it would force all of them to move to the southern part of the county, south of the railroad tracks. Klansmen conducted night rides and raids on a nearly daily basis during the latter part of winter and early spring. At least twice they raided the farm of the new Republican county sheriff, a white man named Pleasant H. Spears, damaging his property and killing an African American farm laborer. The campaign of Klan terror continued in Conway County through the summer, and the sheriff and other Republican county officials proved powerless to bring the Klansmen to justice. African Americans finally formed their own military company during the summer for self-defense.[74]

Convergence among Reformers

The political activity of the Brothers of Freedom and the Agricultural Wheel in Arkansas in 1884 not only helped to underscore the similarity between the two organizations but also brought them into closer contact in some counties and increased the likelihood that members of each were aware of the other. When the State Wheel met at Sulphur Springs in July 1884, by which time the Wheel and Brothers had stepped into the realm of electoral politics, the convention appointed a committee "to confer with the Brothers of Freedom with a view to affecting the consolidation of the two Orders." The convention also took "steps . . . toward the organization of a National Wheel and extending the influence of the Order into other states." By then, according to a contemporary account, the Wheel already had "rolled into the State of Tennessee."[75] In 1885 the Brothers of Freedom, which by then had chartered lodges in Texas and Alabama, began "serious merger negotiations" with the Wheel.[76]

As indicated by his report to Terence V. Powderly about the electoral success of the Brothers and the Wheel in September 1884, Dan Fraser Tomson was well aware of both organizations. He also thought that their antimonopolist, producer-oriented rhetoric closely resembled that of the Knights of Labor and that the three organizations should be working together. In that same letter, Tomson informed Powderly, "I am in correspondence with 'Hon. Isaac McCracken,' Clarksville, Ark., one of the leaders [of the] B. of F[.]' and with 'A. Walter, Esq[.]' of the 'Ag. Wheel,' Beebe, Ark., endeavoring to turn these bodies into the K. of L." Tomson described the organizations to Powderly thusly: "The 'Brothers of Freedom' in the Northwest, and the 'Agricultural Wheel' in the North Central portion of the state—organizations among the farmers, control some eight or ten counties and are spread in about between thirty and forty counties of this state." Tomson asked Powderly to write to McCracken and Walter to assist him in his efforts to bring the Brothers and the Wheel into the Order of the Knights of Labor, and Powderly instructed one of his lieutenants to do so.[77] While Tomson may seem to have been overly ambitious in his efforts to expand the Knights of Labor, considering how miniscule the Order was in Arkansas compared to the Brothers and the Wheel, it is worth remembering that the Knights of Labor was a national organization with over seventy thousand members by July 1884.[78]

At the same time that Tomson was trying to enlist Powderly's help in merging the Brothers and the Wheel into the Knights of Labor, he also bemoaned the Knights' lack of growth in Arkansas. "We have progressed very slowly here [in Hot Springs] and nothing has been attempted in other portions of the state at all," he informed Powderly. Tomson also voiced a complaint commonly made by Knights of Labor leaders in the South when he pointed out that "not a single call has been made within our borders from any of our leaders or even any of our brothers whatever from abroad." Tomson suggested that this neglect factored significantly in the Knights' sluggishness in the state. The working people of Arkansas, he declared, were "ready and willing to take hold and there might be an organization [local assembly] effected at nearly every town in the state, in my opinion[,] and at Little Rock, Fort Smith, Texarkana and other cities two, three, or four."[79] Powderly responded to the complaints of Tomson and other southerners in early 1885 by embarking on a lecturing and organizing tour of the region that was to include visits to twenty-four cities and towns in thirty-six days, and he accepted invitations to speak before the state legislatures of Tennessee and Arkansas. Powderly became ill during this grueling tour, however, and two days before he was scheduled to arrive in Little Rock, Tomson received a telegram from Jackson, Mississippi, informing him that illness had forced Powderly to return home to Pennsylvania.[80]

Even as Tomson was fretting about the interminably slow growth of the Knights of Labor in Arkansas, however, events were already underway in the railroad industry, inside and outside of the state, which would soon cause membership rolls to expand rapidly. In October 1884 Jay Gould's Southwestern Railway system cut wages by 10 percent, and the affected workers included hundreds employed by the Iron Mountain branch of the Missouri Pacific line in Arkansas. Not well organized, and caught off guard, workers in Arkansas and elsewhere on the Southwestern system submitted to the wage cut, but the episode spurred many of them to begin organizing into local assemblies of the Knights of Labor. In Arkansas, though, the first local of railroad workers would not be organized until five months later, after yet another battle with Gould had begun.[81] The unscrupulous Gould personified the Gilded Age term "robber baron." In 1869, he and James "Diamond Jim" Fisk Jr. helped cause a stock market crash by trying to corner the gold market.[82] Gould's business rival Robert Garrett once dryly remarked, upon leaving Baltimore on a train, "Watch Jay Gould while I am gone or he will steal Maryland."[83]

As for Tomson's efforts to absorb the Brothers of Freedom and the Agricultural Wheel into the Knights of Labor, they came to naught, at least in an absolute sense. The Brothers of Freedom merged into the Agricultural Wheel in 1885, and the Wheel in turn later merged into another agrarian order, the Southern Farmers' Alliance.[84] The Knights of Labor, meanwhile, never merged with any of these organizations. Yet Tomson's efforts paid off in other ways. In the years that immediately followed, the Knights of Labor would work closely with the Agricultural Wheel in Arkansas, and Powderly and McCracken would correspond with each other as well.[85] American labor's "Great Upheaval" of the mid-1880s was about to begin, and Arkansas would not be left out, as the state's farmers, railroad workers, miners, and other laborers launched what would become the most inclusive and broad-based working-class revolt in the state's history.

III. THE GREAT UPHEAVAL

AMERICAN LABOR HISTORIANS USE THE term "the Great Upheaval" to refer to different periods of massive labor unrest during the Gilded Age. The first was 1877, when the Great Railroad Strike paralyzed railroads in many parts of the nation and spread beyond that industry, but a longer one occurred during the mid-1880s, when a wave of major strikes occurred and labor political tickets, often led by or affiliated with the Knights of Labor (or, in Arkansas, the Knights and farmers' groups) vied for office throughout the United States.[1] The first Great Upheaval skipped Arkansas, but the state became just as engulfed in the second Great Upheaval as did practically any other, and the wave of unrest unfolded—sometimes spinning out of control—in railroad towns and coal-mining communities, on plantations, and at the ballot box. By 1888 the strike wave was receding in Arkansas, as in much of the rest of the nation, but the political revolt was reaching a crest.[2]

Since the railroad industry was the nation's largest during the Gilded Age and had been at the heart of the first Great Upheaval, its central role in the second Great Upheaval could not have surprised contemporary observers.[3] In contrast to the relatively brief turbulence of the Great Railroad Strike of 1877, which lasted for about two weeks, a wave of major railroad strikes occurred between 1884 and 1886. Arkansas would eventually become a key battleground state in these railroad strikes. Later during the Gilded Age, in 1894, the Pullman strike would affect railroad lines across much of the nation as well, albeit with less impact in Arkansas than the railroad strike that had hit the state eight years earlier.

In 1884, the Knights of Labor waged two successful strikes against the Union Pacific Railroad. The first strike, which occurred in May, began in Denver when shopmen struck against a 10 percent wage reduction. The second strike occurred in August and began when the company cut wages by 10 percent for fifteen first-class machinists in Ellis, Kansas, and fired twenty shopmen in Denver who had played important roles in the May strike.

Neither of these strikes reached Arkansas, where the Union Pacific was not a part of the railroad network, but they led to membership growth for the Knights of Labor, particularly among railroad shopmen. "The Knights of Labor," as one historian has noted, "absorbed much of the praise [for the two victorious strikes] and the Order was soon substantially represented on the Union Pacific and many neighboring roads." The Order's official national membership figure rose from 51,914 in July 1883 to 71,326 in July 1884 to 111,395 in July 1885.[4]

When hundreds of railroad employees on the Iron Mountain line in Arkansas saw their wages cut by 10 percent in October 1884 as part of a wage reduction made across Jay Gould's Southwestern Railway System, they did not strike. Nevertheless, the wage cut certainly made them more receptive to joining the Knights of Labor, which still had a scant presence in Arkansas at that time.[5] In March 1885, Dan Fraser Tomson received an organizer's commission from Terence V. Powderly, and from the 12th to the 21st he organized four local assemblies. The first, LA 3646 in Little Rock, was organized with thirty charter members, either all or most of them railroad workers of various kinds. Before the year was over, it would report sixty-two members, and in 1886 its membership would reach at least two hundred. In Texarkana, Tomson organized LA 3663, a mixed local assembly with forty-two charter members; that total would rise to ninety-two later in the year. (At the same time that Tomson organized this local assembly in Texarkana, Arkansas, another Knights organizer founded a local assembly across the state line in Texarkana, Texas, with twenty-seven charter members, according to Tomson.) Next Tomson organized a local assembly in Hope, Arkansas, LA 3669, another mixed local with eighteen charter members, which would report thirty members before the year was over. Tomson organized his fourth local assembly in the ten-day span, LA 3674, at Malvern with twenty charter members, even though "it rained all day and all night" while he was there. Although the ranks of charter members of this mixed local apparently did not include any women, some joined later, and the local's membership doubled within the year.[6]

The letter in which Tomson told Powderly of these accomplishments brimmed with the enthusiasm that helped make Tomson the most important leader of the Knights of Labor in Arkansas during the 1880s. Now that the Order was finally growing substantially in the state, Tomson expressed eagerness for the trend to continue. "The locals I have founded here," he proudly informed Powderly, "will stand and be a credit to themselves and the Order, else I am deceived in the material." Still clearly hoping for a visit from Powderly one month after illness had forced the cancellation of the Grand Master Workman's planned visit to Arkansas, Tomson told him, "So now when you come this way you will be met by the Order everywhere." Tomson was also clearly eager to form a Knights of Labor district assembly in Arkansas. (District assemblies were higher ranking bodies that could coordinate activities among their member local assemblies and serve as a liaison between those locals and the national Knights of Labor General Assembly.) "There are nine [local assemblies] in the state," Tomson noted, "and one just over the [state] line at Texarkana, making ten. Can we not form a district assembly of all these locals with headquarters at Little Rock, provided all will petition for it?"[7]

For all his ebullience, however, Tomson also provided Powderly with insight into some of the problems confronting the Arkansas Knights of Labor. Regarding his founding of LA 3669 in Hope, Tomson reported that he would have initiated "many more" than eighteen charter members "if the men had had the money to pay [the] membership fee." Tomson explained how pecuniary problems were hindering his organizing efforts in other ways as well. "If I had means to travel," he told Powderly, "I could fairly organize the state in a couple of months I believe." The men whom he was initiating into the Order were of limited help. "At Little Rock and Texarkana they paid me fully," Tomson wrote, "but at Hope + Malvern nothing, not even a cent, and I was as a matter of course out four or five dollars of money—hotel and incidental expenses."[8] Powderly could certainly relate to Tomson's misfortune; Powderly biographer Craig Phelan noted that when the Knights' leader was traveling to visit Knights' assemblies and organize new ones, he often found the rank-and-file indifferent to his expenses, which meant that he would find himself "stranded in out of the way places while [General Secretary-Treasurer Frederick] Turner forwarded funds."[9] Tomson succinctly summarized the financial difficulties that stood in the way of more rapid expansion of the ranks of Knighthood in Arkansas: "The great barrier here is poverty and but few places are able to raise more than enough to barely pay for charter and such supplies as are absolutely necessary for the successful carrying on of the local."[10]

The First Southwest Strike

Fortuitously, by the time that Tomson began organizing local assemblies in the face of such monetary obstacles, events were once again underway in the railroad industry that would aid the growth of the Knights of Labor in the region and nationally. In February 1885, the Wabash Railroad—like the

Southwestern Railway lines four months earlier (both were in receivership at the time, but still under Jay Gould's management)—announced wage cuts that would take effect on the 26th of that month. On the morning of the 26th, about two hundred Wabash shopmen went on strike in Springfield, Illinois; the strike rapidly spread across the Wabash and into the Southwestern system. In addition to extending through much of Illinois, the strike also spread into Missouri, Kansas, and Texas. Many of these strikers were not unionized when the strike began, but local assemblies of the Knights of Labor began appearing "all along the lines." While the Knights did not play a direct role in the settlement of the strike, which occurred in the middle of March, that settlement was nevertheless favorable for the workers. The Missouri, Kansas, and Texas Railroad and the Missouri Pacific Railroad, which included the Iron Mountain Railroad in Arkansas, rescinded the wage cuts of the previous October, and the Wabash immediately followed suit. The two Southwestern lines also pledged that in the future wages would not be reduced without a thirty-day notice. The strike and its settlement, according to one study, "provided the perfect atmosphere for the unprecedented rate of growth of the Knights of Labor."[11] Tomson organized railroad workers into LA 3646 in Little Rock just before the strike ended.[12]

This strike, often referred to as the first Southwest (or Southwestern) strike even though it began on the Wabash, proved to be a prelude rather than an end to the most significant conflicts between the Knights of Labor and Jay Gould's railroad empire. In April and May 1885, the Wabash laid off employees who belonged to the Knights, and then on June 16 the railway closed its shops in Decatur and Springfield, Illinois; Fort Wayne, Indiana; and Moberly, Sedalia, and St. Louis, Missouri. Two days later the company reopened the shops, but management demanded that workers sign "yellow dog" contracts (anti-union pledges) before returning. Most of the 1,600 affected members of the Knights of Labor refused. The executive board of District Assembly (DA) 93, based in Moberly but representing workers across the Wabash railway, deemed this ultimatum the equivalent of a lockout and asked the national Knights' General Executive Board (GEB) for arbitration services and strike funds. The GEB proved both unwilling and unable to offer financial assistance. Wabash general manager A. A. Talmage, for his part, refused to negotiate. First he refused to meet with DA 93's executive board in late June, and then in late July he rebuffed what the historian Norman J. Ware characterized as "a weak attempt" by Terence V. Powderly to see him.[13] Finally, on August 18 the GEB called all of the Wabash's workers out on strike and declared that if the strike remained unsettled six days later,

"All Knights of Labor in the employ of the Union Pacific and its branches and Gould's Southwestern system, or any other railroad, must refuse to repair or handle in any manner Wabash rolling stock until further orders from the General Executive Board, and if this order is antagonized by the companies through any of its [*sic*] officials, your Executive Committee is hereby ordered to call out all Knights of Labor on the above system without further action."[14] This announcement forced Gould and his lieutenants to the bargaining table. Gould and Talmage met with Powderly and the GEB in New York on August 26, and Powderly and Frederick Turner met with Talmage again in St. Louis eight days later. The negotiations produced a settlement that stated that the Wabash would no longer discriminate against members of the Knights of Labor and that all employees who had been locked out on June 16 or had subsequently gone on strike would be reinstated by October 1 and before any new workers were hired. Powderly pledged that in the future, the Knights of Labor would not strike against Gould's railroads without first meeting in conference with railroad officials.[15]

This settlement further bolstered the reputation of the Knights of Labor among working-class Americans, and membership began to soar after it was announced. The *St. Louis Chronicle* declared, "The Wabash victory is with the K. of L. . . . No such victory has ever before been secured in this or any other country."[16] Still a bigger conflict between the Knights and Gould loomed ahead in the near future, though, one that would bring Arkansas directly into the fray.

In the midst of these railroad strikes in 1885, the Knights of Labor grew steadily in Arkansas. Fourteen new local assemblies received charters that year, more than in the previous three years combined. Eight charters went to locals in Pulaski County; after Tomson organized LA 3646 in March, four more locals in Little Rock would be founded by the year's end, plus three in the railroad shop community to the north, Argenta. LA 3646, which expanded into Argenta, included railroad workers, and other locals in Pulaski County probably did as well. Not all of them did, though; for instance, one of the locals in Argenta consisted of white women, and another was a mixed local assembly of black women. Of the four locals founded in Little Rock in 1885 subsequent to LA 3646, two of them were mixed local assemblies of black men, and another was a mixed local assembly of black women. By the end of 1885, three of the five local assemblies in Little Rock and four of eight in Pulaski County consisted of African Americans. The Knights of Labor also chartered a mixed local assembly of African Americans in the small city of Pine Bluff, where a white mixed local assembly with eighty members already existed, and a white mixed local assembly in Marianna, the small county seat of Lee County, in 1885.[17]

In October 1885, Dan Fraser Tomson wrote to Knights of Labor General Secretary-Treasurer Frederick Turner, asking if the local assemblies of Arkansas could form a state assembly. Turner replied in the affirmative, albeit with the stipulation that the state assembly could not be chartered until the following January. Thus on November 25, 1885, fourteen delegates representing twelve Arkansas local assemblies and, according to Tomson, one thousand members met in Little Rock for two days to organize a Knights of Labor State Assembly. The assembly elected a complete slate of officers, headed by Little Rock Knights in the top two positions, State Master Workman and State Worthy Foreman. The term served by the initial group of officers would be only temporary, however, since the state assembly agreed to hold a second meeting in Little Rock on January 6, 1886, by which time it could be chartered. That three-day session elected E. H. Ritchie of Pine Bluff as State Master Workman, although Knights from Pulaski County claimed four of the seven officer positions. "All of the [Local] Assemblies of the State," reported Tomson, "are attached to the State Assembly except the one on the State line at Texarkana and the two so isolated in the northwest [at Fort Smith and the Benton County town of Rogers], and we feel that they will cheerfully come in as soon as it is possible to reach them with the proper explanations." "The railroad employees of the several [Local] Assemblies," Tomson noted, "have been permitted to attach themselves through proper representation to District Assembly 101, in order to perfect the thorough organization into one body of the Gould southwestern system."[18] Undoubtedly many Pulaski County Knights, therefore, went into DA 101 along with Southwestern employees from other states as well.

The Merger of the Agricultural Wheel and the Brothers of Freedom

As the Knights of Labor finally started to gain some traction in Arkansas, Tomson continued to look to the Agricultural Wheel as a kindred organization. He also maintained hope for the possibility of consolidating the Wheel into the Knights of Labor. In December 1885 Tomson, perhaps having forgotten that he had informed Powderly of the Wheel in 1884, wrote in a letter to the Grand Master Workman, "We have an order called the 'Agricultural Wheel' in this state, claiming to number 40,000 members. By our state organization [the new Arkansas Knights of Labor State Assembly] we shall be able eventually to thoroughly cooperate and perhaps get them into our Order."[19] In fact, the Agricultural Wheel had recently engaged in the process of merging with the similar Brothers of Freedom. The grand councils of the Brothers and the Wheel had met at Springfield (Conway County) in early December 1884 in an attempt to initiate the merger. Some Wheelers who did not favor independent political activity expressed misgivings because of the greater level of independent activism that the Brothers of Freedom had engaged in, but the negotiations nevertheless continued throughout 1885. Finally, on October 15 of that year, the merger occurred at a specially called meeting of the Arkansas State Wheel at Greenbrier in Faulkner County. The Brothers of Freedom, despite having a much larger membership (estimated at between thirty and forty thousand) than the Wheel (about ten thousand) agreed to drop its name; thus the consolidated organization would be known as the Agricultural Wheel. On the other hand, the convention elected Isaac McCracken, the president of the Brothers of Freedom, to the position of Grand President of the now considerably enlarged Wheel. "A new Constitution and By-laws," noted Wheeler W. Scott Morgan, "in substance similar to the old one, and a new secret work were adopted." "The Order," he added, "now had assumed an importance which bid fair to accomplish much good." Rapid growth soon followed not only in Arkansas but also in other southern states.[20]

Meanwhile, even as some Wheelers looked warily upon the merger with the Brothers of Freedom due to the latter organization's supposed greater involvement in politics, the Wheel seemed to be moving in that direction itself. In July 1885, at a session at Mount Carmel (Lonoke County), the State Wheel passed resolutions calling upon the state government to establish an agricultural college and experimental farm as well as a state mining, manufacturing, and agricultural bureau "for the promotion and benefit of practical and scientific agriculture, and encouraging the mining and manufacturing interests of this state."[21] Two months later the Des Arc Wheel—the founding chapter of the organization—adopted the following resolution, which it submitted to other Wheel lodges throughout the state for their consideration:

> Resolved, that we will not support any man as a candidate for the state or national legislature who is not a farmer, and publicly pledged to the support of the farmers' interests as against all other interests, and publicly pledged to labor, and to vote for the enactment into laws of any measure which may be recommended by the Grand [State] Wheel or by a majority of the Wheels of his county or congressional district.

In a characteristically hostile editorial, the *Arkansas Gazette* retorted, "There are not three counties [in Arkansas] in which the farmers cannot control the local conventions held by either of the two political parties. Especially is this true of the [D]emocratic party, composed almost exclusively of white men, who can exercise just as large an influence in the party councils as they choose to exercise." The editorial claimed that this Wheel resolution would "practically disfranchise and proscribe all classes who do not till the soil" and attempted to link the resolution to the supposed political inequities of the years from 1865 to 1874 in Arkansas by reminding readers that "during the days of [R]econstruction large classes were disfranchised."[22] When a Wheel lodge in Sevier County rejected this resolution, the *Gazette* of course praised those Wheelers for being "solid" and "sensible."[23]

The Second Southwest Strike and Politics

The Great Upheaval of 1886 came to Arkansas not through the Agricultural Wheel, however, but rather through the same organization as in much of the rest of the nation: the Knights of Labor. On March 1, 1886, the Knights began a second strike against Jay Gould's Southwestern Railway system in Texas. The causes of the strike remain disputed, even among historians. The first historian to examine the strike closely, Ruth Allen, suggested that in 1885 Gould "had accepted a Fabian failure [a reference to the Roman general Fabius, who avoided decisive contests until circumstances were favorable for victory] that he might triumph the more completely" in 1886.[24] More recently, Craig Phelan has concurred that Gould "set about precipitating a conflict to rid himself of the nuisance of a feisty work force."[25] Theresa Case's most recent study of the strike, on the other hand, attributes more agency to the rank and file of the Knights of Labor in its outbreak, deeming the event "a logical, even inevitable outgrowth of railroaders' struggle to win a permanent voice with management."[26] The strike began in Marshall, Texas, after a Texas and Pacific shop fired Charles A. Hall, the Master Workman of a local assembly of railroad shop employees, for taking three days off to attend a session of DA 101 in that town. Hall had received permission from his foreman to attend the meeting, however, and, according to Allen, his firing "can be explained only as crass ineptitude or as the expression of a desire to affront the workers with the serious possibility of forcing them to revolt."[27]

Once Hall's local assembly struck on March 1, the Master Workman of DA 101, Martin Irons of Sedalia, Missouri, telegraphed all of the local assemblies under his jurisdiction and requested that they vote on whether to extend the

4. The great railway strike—attempt to start a freight train, under a guard of United States marshals, at East St. Louis, Illinois. Nebinger, G. J., artist. 1886. Wood engraving. Printed in *Frank Leslie's Illustrated Newspaper*, April 10, 1886, p. 121. Retrieved from the Library of Congress, accessed March 20, 2018, https://www.loc.gov/pictures/item/90707123/.

strike across the whole Southwestern system. Irons, a native of Scotland, was about fifty-five years old at the time. He came to the United States when he was fourteen, and he became a machinist after serving an apprenticeship in New York City. He eventually migrated to Missouri, and for a time served as the Master of a large Grange chapter. By the early 1880s he had found work in the railroad shops in Sedalia. In 1884 or 1885 he joined the Knights of Labor, and he helped unite the locals in Gould's Southwestern system into DA 101.[28]

When the votes from the local assemblies came in, Irons tabulated them and then called for the Knights of Labor to strike against the entire Southwestern system beginning on March 6, 1886. Here, too, however, the circumstances remain shrouded in mystery. Within days of signing and issuing the strike order, Irons began hearing reports from within DA 101 that the strike vote had been "dishonestly reported." Irons called a meeting of the DA 101 executive board in St. Louis to investigate, but as he privately told Terence V. Powderly later that month, an unidentified man forced him at gunpoint to sign an affidavit reaffirming the validity of the strike order. Powderly only revealed this story decades later in his autobiography, which was not published until after his death, but he presented it without any skepticism about its truthfulness. Ruth Allen and Craig Phelan both accepted the veracity of the story; Allen deemed it "a crucial moment in the history of labor in the Southwest," and Phelan called it "an inauspicious start to such a critical battle."[29] Theresa Case, on the other hand, has plausibly suggested that Irons fabricated the story as something of a face-saving measure at a point when the strike was clearly going badly for the Knights of Labor: "He had reason to despair over the decision to order a walkout, a decision in which he had played a key role and one in which DA 101 had not included Powderly or the GEB."[30]

Notwithstanding the lingering questions surrounding the firing of Charles A. Hall and Irons' claims about reaffirming the strike order under duress, many Texas Knights of Labor working on the Southwestern lines had complaints that the strike of 1885 had failed to settle. In January 1886, for example, a local assembly in Baird, Texas, composed a statement of grievances against the Texas and Pacific that called for a daily wage of $1.50 for unskilled workers instead of the $1.15 that they were being paid, a speedier settlement of discharges, and the firing of Chinese workers. The Baird Knights of Labor accused the company of paying higher wages to Chinese workers than to white workers along the western end of the railway, but according to Case, Chinese railroad workers actually received considerably less pay than whites. Other Knights of Labor local assemblies of railroad workers in Texas also demanded $1.50 per day for unskilled workers.[31]

On March 6, 1886, the day that the strike was to begin across the entire Southwestern system, some 250 Knights of Labor employed by the Iron Mountain Railroad in Little Rock walked off the job at ten o'clock in the morning. "The principle cause of the strike at Little Rock," according to a close examination by the historians Ralph V. Turner and William Warren Rogers, "was the Knights' acceptance of Irons' directives," but Turner and Rogers also acknowledged other factors, such as demands for higher wages among some workers and the Knights' desire to gain union recognition, which the settlements with Gould in 1885 had not produced. On March 11, Irons prepared a statement of grievances and demands on behalf of the strikers and sent it to H. M. Hoxie, one of Gould's lieutenants. The demands included $1.50 per day for all unskilled labor, including section laborers, trackmen (who were only being paid $1.10 in Little Rock), and crossing watchmen; payment to all bridgemen at the rates of $2.00, $2.25, $2.50, or

$2.75 per day, "according to the nature of the work performed by them"; and the abolishment of convict labor throughout the Southwestern system, among other points.[32]

The number of strikers in Little Rock soon reached approximately three hundred. The strike would last for about two months. When the strike began, J. E. DeLay, the chairman of the State Executive Board of the Arkansas Knights of Labor, told railroad officials that the strikers would not damage railroad property, and in fact the Knights even convinced Sheriff Robert Worthen to deputize seven of them so that they could help prevent any such damage. But the Knights' determination to shut down freight traffic on the Iron Mountain—which they succeeded in for several weeks—led to conflicts when management tried to run the trains. At least two incidents involved the exchange of gunfire, leaving a Knight wounded in the leg in one instance and a deputy seriously but not fatally wounded in the other, and eventually strikers hijacked locomotives and allegedly burned several railroad trestles. Sheriff Worthen revoked the deputy commissions that he had given the seven members of the Knights of Labor, and, as the strike spread to other railroad cities and towns in Arkansas, Governor Simon P. Hughes sent state militiamen to Texarkana. In Little Rock, the number of arrests associated with the strike reached nine; three men received indictments and two were fined. A court injunction named 241 strikers who were prohibited from "molesting the Iron Mountain's employees or interfering with the running of trains, passenger or freight."[33]

Powderly and the Knights of Labor General Executive Board made numerous attempts at negotiation with Gould and other Southwestern system executives, but to no avail. By the end of April 1886, the Southwestern system was operating at nearly full scale thanks to strikebreakers and many skilled workers who had never joined the strike. A congressional committee, investigating the strike at Powderly's urging, convinced him to call it off on May 4, the same date, coincidentally, as the infamous Haymarket riot in Chicago that resulted in the deaths of seven policemen and at least four workers. The strike ended in total defeat for the Knights of Labor. Not only did the strikers win no concessions from Gould, but most of them lost their jobs. In Little Rock, by mid-May, an estimated 95 percent of strikers had not returned to their jobs even though many of them had applied. Powderly and the GEB raised over $86,000 (probably the rough equivalent of at least $2 million today) for the assistance of strikers across the Southwestern system, which stretched across Texas, Arkansas, Missouri, Kansas, and Illinois. In

Arkansas, the Knights of Labor State Assembly and local assemblies did what they could to provide assistance to the strikers, but their efforts fell short of meeting the strikers' needs.[34]

As many historians have pointed out, the Southwestern strike of 1886 dealt a major blow to the Knights of Labor. The outcome of this and other strikes that the Knights of Labor lost in 1886, as well as the Haymarket riot, helped send the Order's membership from its official peak that year of 729,677 into a decline from which it never recovered. (The membership figure fell to 548,329 in one year.)[35] Yet the strike served to bring farmers and laborers closer together in many of the areas where it took place, and it also helped spur a farmer-labor political alliance in those areas. These effects became apparent almost immediately in Arkansas, where Knights of Labor membership actually continued to grow after the strike.[36]

On April 3, 1886, while the strike was still underway, the Johnson County lodges of the Agricultural Wheel held a convention at the hamlet of Belle Grove. The short career of the Brothers of Freedom had begun in this county four years earlier, and in 1884 the Brothers nominated a ticket that swept the county offices and sent Isaac McCracken (by now the president of the Wheel) to the state legislature. According to the hostile *Arkansas Gazette*, the purpose of this county Wheel convention was to discuss "the propriety of putting a ticket, both county and district, in the field in the coming campaign." "We understand from reliable sources," the report added, "that they resolved to put out a full-fledged people's ticket, as they call it."[37] Later that month McCracken circulated a letter, published by at least one Agricultural Wheel newspaper (probably more), in which he "call[ed] the Grand Wheel of the State of Arkansas to convene at the Hall of Big Rock Wheel No. 440, near Little Rock, on Wednesday, the 9th day of June, 1886, at 10 o'clock a.m., for the purpose of nominating a state ticket, and transacting such other business that may come before the same."[38]

On May 14, 1886, shortly after the Southwestern strike ended, the Pulaski County Wheel held a meeting at Mabelvale, a small train station town ten miles south of downtown Little Rock. The *Arkansas Gazette* reported that "while the proceedings were secret, it has been learned that they [those assembled] considered county and state politics." The Greenback-Labor Party, it will be recalled, had fared quite well in Little Rock, where its successes included the election of the former slave Isaac T. Gillam to the state legislature in 1878. The Wheel meeting at Mabelvale hosted a committee of five members of the Knights of Labor from Little Rock—two white men and three black men. In spite of the alleged secrecy of the proceedings, the *Gazette* was able to report that "the Wheel—the political end—appointed a committee to confer with the Knights of Labor committee with a view to forming a coalition between the Wheel and Knights of Labor for the purpose of putting out a county ticket." At some point in 1886, probably after this meeting, the Knights of Labor formed a local assembly in Mabelvale that included farm and sawmill hands and teamsters (which then meant one who drove a team of animals).[39]

On June 8, 1886, nearly four weeks after the meeting at Mabelvale, the Pulaski County Wheel and the Knights of Labor met in a joint "secret session" in the hall of the Brotherhood of Locomotive Engineers in Little Rock. The *Arkansas Gazette* boasted of getting a reporter into the hall, since he "could not afford to be left to look through a keyhole." The reporter called the gathering of about 110 men "as queer [peculiar] an assembly as could well be imagined." "There were colored men, Wheelers, and Knights of Labor," he noted, not oblivious to the existence of "colored Wheels" and black local assemblies of the Knights of Labor but apparently believing that the black men in attendance should be singled out for their race, not atypically in that era. The reporter observed that "the greater part of the Knights of Labor were [R]epublicans, and a majority of the Wheelers were [D]emocrats, while it was hard to say what the colored men were." Isom P. Langley, a self-described "Democrat-Greenbacker-Republican-Wheeler-Knight of Labor-farmer-preacher-lawyer-editor" from Hot Springs, presided over the meeting. The reporter said that Langley made speeches in which he "damned the [Democratic] party from top to bottom . . . and said it was time to organize a new party, composed of white and black Knights of Labor and Wheelers." The reporter claimed that Langley also said the purpose of the meeting was "to have a conference between the Wheelers and Knights of Labor about putting out a county ticket," but this seems like a questionable statement when some of the delegates (including Langley) came from counties other than Pulaski. Another column in that day's edition of the *Arkansas Gazette* reported that the State Wheel convention would meet in Little Rock on the day after the Wheel–Knights of Labor conclave, followed a day later by the Republican state committee. "This fits in very nicely," the staunchly Democratic newspaper sardonically commented, "and gives our old-time radical friends their golden opportunity."[40]

McCracken presided over the State Wheel meeting on June 9 in his role as the organization's president. He, Langley, and two other "political

Wheelers"—Grand Secretary R. H. Morehead and the chairman of the State Wheel executive committee, Reuben B. CarlLee, both of Prairie County—exercised the most influence at the convention. Not only had McCracken been elected to the state legislature in 1884 on a Brothers ticket, but CarlLee had won election to the legislature in 1882 and 1884, apparently as "a rebel from the Democratic party." McCracken and his allies called for a vote on a resolution to nominate a ticket of candidates for the forthcoming state elections, which carried by a vote of 47–30; the meeting also approved "an agrarian-reform platform that harked back to the Greenbackers and forecast the populist program of the future," in the words of historian F. Clark Elkins.[41] The *Arkansas Gazette* published a number of letters and resolutions from Arkansas Wheelers that made it clear, however, that not all of the organization's members approved of this course of action. The Clark County Agricultural Wheel, for example, passed a resolution that stated that "we as a County Wheel will not hold ourselves bound to support a state ticket if one is put out by the State Wheel; but for the good of the order beg said convention [of the State Wheel] to desist from so doing."[42] Even the Little Rock *State Wheel-Enterprise* warned, "The nomination of a state ticket would be the funeral dirge of the Agricultural Wheel."[43]

As noted by Elkins, the platform that the State Wheel adopted at Little Rock included demands that were either identical or similar to those previously made in the platforms of the Greenbackers (and, in many cases, the Knights of Labor as well) such as the reservation of public lands "for actual settlers," that the government "issue its own money" that would be "legal tender in payment of all debts, public and private" and "in sufficient quantities to transact the business of the country on a cash basis," the "free and unlimited coinage of silver and gold," "the enforcement of the constitution of our state in regard to . . . unjust discriminations [by railroads] in freight and passenger rates," and the establishment of a graduated income tax. The platform ended by declaring the Agricultural Wheel's opposition to "the present system of working the convicts of the state, and . . . the bringing of convict labor into competition with the honest or legitimate labor of farm, shop and manufactory."[44] Some form of the convict-lease system (whereby convicts were forced to work for companies or private employers) had existed in Arkansas since 1873, and in 1883 the state adopted the same system that existed in other southern states, which involved lessees of convicts paying the state for the right to work them while also bearing all expenses associated with the confinement and care of the convicts.[45]

The ticket that the State Wheel put forth in Little Rock in June 1886 featured John G. Fletcher as the nominee for governor. Fletcher was a Confederate veteran and businessman who in 1875 cofounded the first cottonseed-oil mill in Little Rock. He was also a Democratic politician and, although he initially accepted the Wheel's nomination, he changed his mind the next day, apparently caving in to pressure from Democrats. After Fletcher withdrew from the Wheel ticket, so did the rest of the candidates. Subsequently, the State Wheel waited until early August, after both the Democrats and Republicans had held their state conventions, to put forth another state ticket—albeit incomplete this time—headed by the veteran Granger and Greenbacker Charles E. Cunningham of Little Rock.[46]

The Pulaski County Plantation Strike and the Elections of 1886

The Knights of Labor, meanwhile, kept the Great Upheaval alive in Arkansas even after the railroad strike ended in May 1886. Not surprisingly, the strike created some difficulties for the Knights of Labor in Arkansas; four months later, State Master Workman E. H. Ritchie of Pine Bluff wrote that the strike and "the attendant excitement throughout the State, shook us as a mighty earthquake from center to circumference, and for a time we were almost in a state of confusion. This drained the treasuries of our Locals and materially crippled us, so that we are not even yet recovered from this terrible shock." Nevertheless, by June the indefatigable Dan Fraser Tomson began to organize African American farmworkers on the plantations in southern Pulaski County (south of Little Rock). "This was a new departure for the Order," wrote Ritchie, "but the work was not undertaken without deliberation and a careful survey of the field."[47]

As was most likely anticipated, Tomson's efforts immediately met stiff resistance from planters, who "were so bitterly opposed to the project that they refused the poor fellows their rations and circulated threats of violence." Tomson then procured the assistance of a black Knight, G. W. Merriman, who had served two terms as the Master Workman of LA 4225 of Argenta. Ritchie described Merriman as "a very intelligent and honorable colored brother" who "not only proved himself as an apt student and competent for the work [of helping Tomson organize black farmhands], but far above average in the exercise of proper judgment where the souls of men are put to the test." Ritchie rendered this judgment after about thirty of the farmhands, men and women, went on strike on Thursday, July 1, 1886, at the

Tate plantation, demanding a raise from seventy-five cents to one dollar per day "until the [cotton crop] was out of the grass" and payment in cash rather than scrip. Members of the Knights of Labor from Little Rock brought meat, flour, and meal to the strikers as they remained on the plantation over the weekend. On Monday, July 5, at five o'clock in the morning, Sheriff Robert Worthen—already acquainted with the Knights of Labor due to the railroad strike—came to the plantation with several deputies. The officers approached the house of one of the strike leaders, Hugh Gill, "called him out of bed and to the door," and then one of the deputies shot him with a double-barreled shotgun, wounding him in both arms. When this news spread throughout Pulaski County, about 250 black men, many of them armed, came to the scene. Worthen and the deputies remained inside Gill's house and sent out word for a posse to be sent from Little Rock. When the posse of twenty-seven men arrived on the evening of July 5, some of its members fired shots. Some newspaper accounts reported that the strikers fired shots as well, but Ritchie claimed that the strikers, under the guidance of Tomson and Merriman, who also arrived on the scene, "refused to return fire, . . . preferring death rather than to violate the law or resort to violence." No one was seriously hurt that evening, but the posse succeeded in dispersing many of the black men on the scene. On July 7, the strike ended, as most of the strikers returned to work without their demands being met.[48]

The failure of the strike apparently did not dissuade African Americans in Arkansas from joining or remaining in the Knights of Labor. More than two months after the strike ended, Ritchie reported the existence of "a dozen or more" local assemblies of African Americans in the state, "numbering, perhaps, a thousand men. . . . No one appreciates the Order more than they."[49] Ritchie's use of the word "men" failed to acknowledge the facts that women had participated in the Tate plantation strike and that at least four local assemblies in Pulaski County included black women. After the strike, the Knights of Labor organized local assemblies of African American farmers or farm hands in at least three more Arkansas counties: Jefferson, Little River, and Lonoke.[50] Hugh Gill, the strike leader who had been shot by one of Sheriff Worthen's deputies, faced the charge of assault with intent to kill the sheriff. The *Arkansas Democrat* observed that "the colored people and Knights of Labor are watching the trial . . . with a good deal of interest. Some say he is being tried for letting the deputy shoot him."[51] Gill's date in court came swiftly—on Friday, July 9, 1886, the day after the strike ended—and the judge declared, "I don't think a jury would convict the accused on the evidence before me, and I therefore discharge the defendant." The *Arkansas Democrat* noted that "quite a crowd of colored people and a few Knights of Labor had assembled in the circuit court room when the decision was made [and] . . . were jubilant over the verdict."[52] The Arkansas Knights of Labor State Assembly subsequently asked the Order's General Executive Board "for assistance to prosecute the sheriff and deputy of Pulaski County, Ark., for the shooting of Hugh Gill," but the board, beleaguered with all sorts of requests for help amid the Great Upheaval, did not grant the request. At the Knights of Labor General Assembly convention in Minneapolis in 1887, where the board issued its report denying that request, an African American schoolteacher, Mrs. Cassie M. Hollensworth of Pine Bluff, represented the Arkansas Knights of Labor State Assembly.[53]

Although the Tate plantation strike was far smaller, shorter, and more localized than the Southwestern strike of the previous winter and spring, it too would have political implications as local, state, and congressional elections approached. On the evening of July 7, 1886, pursuant to a call by Sheriff Worthen for men "who would be willing to serve as deputies, if necessary, to quell any more trouble with the colored men at the Tate plantation and vicinity," a crowd of white as well as black men packed a courtroom in Little Rock. As Worthen reported rumors of a planned black uprising on the plantations of Pulaski County, the white planter Colonel Anderson Mills arose and denounced the meeting as "entirely out of place and uncalled for" and "simply a political scheme." Another white man, Dr. F. M. Chrisman, expressed agreement with Mills. When a black man, E. A. Fulton, also concurred and added that "there was [*sic*] politics in the trouble that had taken place on the Tate plantation," Worthen interrupted and denied all charges of any political motives on his part, dramatically announcing that he would not seek reelection to the office of county sheriff.[54] Dan Fraser Tomson would later charge that Worthen and his deputies had committed "outrages" at the Tate plantation "in the hope that the colored people, being organized, would resist, and that this would serve as a pretext to break up organization among them." Shortly before the county elections, which occurred in September, the Pulaski County Republican Party composed and adopted a platform that, as one historian has noted, undoubtedly resonated with railroad strikers and Tate plantation strikers alike in its denunciation of Democrats who had "sent officers to harass and disturb good, honest working people" and "sent armed troops among us and protected them by mock trials from punishment for assaults and attempted murders committed on the inhabitants of this state and county."[55]

The Pulaski County Republican Party nominated Dr. F. M. Chrisman for county judge, and another prolabor Republican, Colonel W. S. Oliver, ran for sheriff. Both of these candidates received Knights of Labor endorsements, especially from African American Knights, although some white Knights of Labor publicly denounced these endorsements. Chrisman and Oliver both lost to Democratic opponents—in the latter case, Robert Worthen, who ran for reelection despite publicly announcing in July that he would not. In Young Township, which included the Tate plantation, Worthen defeated Oliver by only forty-seven votes, though, and reports of black voters being denied access to the polls in Pulaski County suggest that Republican candidates may have had more support than the official tallies indicated. Chrisman, in fact, told a reporter from the *Arkansas Democrat* that he and the other defeated Republican county candidates would contest the election results, although apparently they never did.[56]

The Knights of Labor's endorsement of Republican candidates for county offices in Pulaski County apparently scuttled the plans that Wheelers and Knights had reportedly made in the weeks following the Southwestern strike to nominate a joint Wheel-Knights county ticket. Elsewhere in the state, however, such tickets did materialize; an independent ticket that was jointly nominated by the two organizations won control of the county offices in Carroll County.[57] A ticket described by a Wheel newspaper as "a combination of Wheelers and Republicans" did likewise in Independence County.[58] In Nevada County, the *Arkansas Gazette* reported, "A combination of Republicans, so-called independents, Knights of Labor, Greenbackers, soreheads, chronic kickers and communists overwhelmed the Democracy and carried the county by a considerable majority." F. M. Thompson of Hope (Hempstead County), whom the *Gazette* identified as a Republican, won election to the state senate district that included Nevada County, replacing an old Greenback holdover, Charles M. Norwood. Two other Republicans also won state senate seats, as did two men whom the *Gazette* identified as Wheelers—George Martin of Sulphur Rock (Independence County) and John Dunaway of Conway (Faulkner County). Democrats won twenty-seven seats in the state senate. The number of Wheelers elected to the state house of representatives is unknown. One Wheel (but anti-Wheel ticket) newspaper listed ten Wheelers plus two Greenbackers as having won seats, but other newspaper reports suggested that the Wheel had elected at least one candidate to the legislature in at least nineteen of the state's seventy-five counties. Charles E. Cunningham claimed that "thirty or thirty-five" Wheel candidates won election to the state legislature in 1886.[59]

The incomplete Agricultural Wheel state ticket, headed by Cunningham, also included another prominent former Granger and Greenbacker, Charles E. Tobey of Pope County, for state land commissioner. When the executive committee of the State Wheel put forth the ticket in early August 1886, the *Arkansas Gazette* labeled it the "Labor Ticket," insisting that the ticket did not represent the Agricultural Wheel but rather only the handful of men who ran the executive committee, such as Isaac McCracken and "the Hon. Boomerang [Reuben] CarlLee."[60] When Cunningham subsequently referred to himself in a public address as the gubernatorial candidate of the state ticket of the Wheel, the *Gazette* reiterated its position that the executive committee was "wholly without authority to speak for the State Wheel" and therefore "the 'labor ticket'" had "no more claim for support on the Wheelers than on the Republicans or Democrats."[61] Ironically, Cunningham published a campaign pamphlet in which he stated that he had been nominated by the State Wheel executive committee as "a labor candidate," but clearly this was meant not to dissociate himself from the Wheel but rather to appeal to the vote of the Knights of Labor and laboring men in general.[62] Given his candidacy for Congress four years earlier as a member of the Greenback-Labor Party, the "labor candidate" label certainly did not seem incongruous.

On the other hand, the *Gazette*, for all of its blatant hostility to the Wheel ticket, was not incorrect in its assertion that the ticket did not have the support of most Wheelers. Even the *Columbia Banner*, the official organ of the Columbia County Wheel, expressed disapproval of the Wheel ticket and urged readers to "vote as one man for the nominees of the Democratic party."[63] The *New York Times*, which was not hostile to the Wheel ticket, reported that "the ticket is not likely to receive a united support, yet Wheelers who are posted claim at least 20,000 votes for it."[64] This prediction proved fairly accurate, as the official returns credited Cunningham with 19,169 votes (approximately one-third of the Arkansas Wheel's membership), as compared to 90,650 for Democratic incumbent Simon P. Hughes, former Worthy Master of the Arkansas State Grange, and 54,063 for Republican Lafayette Gregg of Fayetteville. According to Cunningham, the shortfall between the prediction of the *New York Times* and the actual vote could be attributed at least in part to an unfair, inaccurate vote count in three counties, especially "the capital county," Pulaski. (He did not identify the other two counties in his letter to the *Gazette* in which he made this charge.) Even the official results indicated growing dissatisfaction on the part of Arkansas voters with the Democratic Party, though; the 55.3 percent of the vote garnered by Hughes was the smallest percentage of the vote received by a Democratic gubernatorial candidate since the party "redeemed" the state and recaptured the governor's office in 1874. In fact, Democrat Augustus H. Garland ran unopposed in the general election that year, winning 100 percent of the votes cast, as did Democrat William R. Miller in 1878. The *New York Times* suggested that, notwithstanding Cunningham's third-place showing, "enough is shown . . . to prove that the Wheelers hereafter are to be an important political factor in the State, and politicians are already beginning to show signs of alarm."[65]

The less than overwhelming showing of Agricultural Wheel candidates in the Arkansas state elections in September 1886 did not dissuade "political Wheelers" from entering the fray in three of the state's five elections for seats in the US House of Representatives. (Democratic incumbent Poindexter Dunn of Forrest City won reelection without opposition in the First District, as did Democratic incumbent Samuel W. Peel of Bentonville in the Fifth District.) Wheel candidates challenged Democratic incumbents in the three other districts, as did Republican candidates in two. Reuben CarlLee ran against Democratic incumbent Clifton R. Breckinridge and Republican D. D. Leach in the Second, L. H. Hitt of Nevada County ran against Democratic incumbent Thomas C. McRae (also of Nevada County) and Republican J. C. Ray in the Third, and Isom P. Langley ran as the sole challenger to Democratic incumbent John H. Rogers of Fort Smith in the Fourth District.[66]

As Wheel candidates facing candidates of both major parties, CarlLee and Hitt stood no realistic chance of being elected to Congress. CarlLee had won election to the Arkansas state legislature as a representative from Prairie County in 1882 and 1884, where he helped secure passage of a law that reduced the crime of selling mortgaged property from a felony to a misdemeanor. He also introduced bills to increase appropriations for public institutions for the deaf, blind, and insane. Despite these accomplishments as a legislator, CarlLee finished a distant third in the congressional race with only 18 percent of the vote. Of the sixteen counties in the Second District, he only carried one, Van Buren, where the Brothers of Freedom's ticket had won the county elections two years earlier. CarlLee came in second place in eight other counties, but of those he was truly competitive only in Prairie County.[67] Hitt, a thirty-one-year-old native of Mississippi who became a resident of Arkansas in 1879, was a Baptist minister and a farmer. A Nevada County "convention of Wheelers and laborers" that was reportedly called for by the old Greenbacker Rufus K. Garland nominated Hitt in September;

later that month a self-proclaimed (but anonymous) Wheeler in the Third District called Hitt "a so-called nominee of the Wheelers" and suggested that Hitt would "try to combine the Republican, Greenbacker and Knights of Labor votes" but would still not get three thousand votes. Hitt was sometimes referred to as a Greenbacker, and indeed, during the campaign he advocated the issue of greenback currency and the reduction of tariffs.[68] But a man whom the *Arkansas Democrat* described as "a leading Greenbacker and Wheeler of Hot Spring County," J. Frank Williams, who also was a Knight of Labor, declared that in the Democratic incumbent McRae "the labor organization[s] and labor element of the Third District have all they can ask or can hope to expect from one man." "He stands firm on the land question, the silver question and the tariff question," Williams opined, while also being "a strong advocate of the proper control and regulation of the railroads, that they may be made a blessing to subserve the interest of a growing and prosperous people, and not a monopolizing curse that resolves itself into a mighty oppression and a tax-gatherer." Williams went on to cite McRae's opposition to the importation of contract labor and his advocacy of "proper adjustments of the convict labor" as additional reasons for his support of the congressman.[69] Hitt received only 15 percent of the vote in the Third District, carrying none of its nineteen counties, and while he finished second place in seven of them, only in his home county of Nevada, a center of third-party strength since 1880 and home to two local assemblies of the Knights of Labor, did he finish a strong second.[70]

Isom P. Langley, on the other hand, seemed to have a better chance than his fellow Wheel candidates in his congressional bid in the Fourth District. Not only did he not have to contend with a Republican candidate, but also the district included Pulaski County, a Knights of Labor stronghold with thirty-seven local assemblies in 1886, a center of the railroad strike during the previous spring, and the place where the Knights of Labor had waged the strike of African American farmhands during the summer. Furthermore, Langley's Democratic opponent, incumbent John H. Rogers, had staunchly opposed a federal labor arbitration bill that the Knights of Labor had lobbied for as the railroad strike had begun to collapse. Langley, on the other hand, was not only a prominent member (and the chaplain) of the Arkansas State Wheel, but he also belonged to the oldest Knights of Labor local assembly in the state, Hot Springs Assembly No. 2419, which he joined in 1885. In 1886 he became the editor of the official newspaper of the Arkansas State Assembly of the Knights of Labor, the *Industrial Liberator*. In fact, despite his prominence in the Agricultural Wheel, he was nominated for Congress by "a labor convention" by one account, and modern guides to congressional elections list him as a "labor" candidate.[71] In September 1886 the *Arkansas Wheel* newspaper stated that he was nominated "by the Wheelers and Knights of Labor."[72]

Evidence suggests that Langley indeed received support from, but not limited to, workingmen; according to one account, he "polled more than twice the labor votes of his district."[73] The one known surviving minute book from an Arkansas Knights local assembly in 1886, that of Van Buren Assembly No. 6307 in Crawford County, reports that Langley's campaign speech there was attended by most of the assembly's members, who included tobacco factory workers, farmers, a railroad conductor, and men who worked as general laborers for the city. Shortly thereafter, members of the assembly began discussing partisan politics at one of their meetings—a violation of the Order's rules but one that occurred frequently—and most of the Knights who were present declared their allegiance to labor candidates. In the contest against Rogers, Langley received 42 percent of the vote in Crawford County (which had four local assemblies of the Knights of Labor in 1886), marginally better than the 38 percent that he received in the district as a whole. He carried Pulaski County, however, with 56 percent of the vote, and he also carried Saline County, a rural county that included three mixed local assemblies of the Knights of Labor, one of which included stoneware manufacturing workers. Langley and Rogers each received 714 votes in Johnson County, birthplace of the Brothers of Freedom, home of two mixed locals of the Knights of Labor that included coal miners, and the site of miners' strikes in 1884, 1885, and 1886. In Garland County, home of Hot Springs Assembly 2419, Freedom Assembly 2447 (the state's first African American local), and one other mixed Knights local, the official count gave Rogers an edge of only fifteen votes.[74]

Partisans versus Nonpartisans in the Knights of Labor and Agricultural Wheel

Just as some Arkansas Wheelers opposed their organization's plunge into partisan politics, so did some Knights of Labor, including not only J. Frank Williams but also the Order's state organizer who had run unsuccessfully as a candidate for the state legislature in 1884, Dan Fraser Tomson. Two months after the congressional elections, the State Assembly of the Arkansas Knights of Labor met in Pine Bluff, where, according to Tomson, "the [white] delegates . . . formed combinations with the colored delegates prejudicing their minds with partisan politics to elect the officers of the State Assembly, and succeeded." "Brother John W. Howell of South Hot Springs LA # 3303, a bitter partisan leader, office holder + seeker, chairman [of the] Co. [County] Republican Committee of Garland County for years—a real professional politician," Tomson reported to Terence Powderly, "was elected State Master Workman over myself, the Republicans including the devious far outnumbering the Knights present." Most of the other officers elected by the State Assembly, Tomson noted, were "colored men elected by combination." As a result, he claimed, "the [local] assemblies all over the state are applying to withdraw from the State Assembly in order that they may be able to form D.A.'s [district assemblies]." "Something must be done," Tomson beseeched Powderly, or "else the State Assembly, and, I believe, the Order will go to pieces."[75]

While Tomson was a founding father of the Knights of Labor in Arkansas and the most important figure in the Knights' history in the state, in this case his dismay seems to have overcome his usually sound judgment. He was correct in that Arkansas local assemblies did begin forming district assemblies; during the twelve months ending in October 1887, the Knights chartered district assemblies in Texarkana, Arkansas, and in Hot Springs. During the next twelve-month period, new district assemblies blossomed in the state: one in Paragould, two in Brinkley, two in Little Rock, one in Pine Bluff, and one in Fort Smith.[76] Nevertheless, Tomson's prediction that "the Order is going down here" unless the partisan takeover of the state assembly was "stopped" seems far less accurate. The Knights of Labor chartered forty-two local assemblies in Arkansas in 1887, and according to official figures, the Order's membership in the state rose to 5,385 by the middle of that year, compared to 2,986 one year earlier. The number of active local assemblies increased from 56 to 139 during that same period. Perhaps the fact that the Republican Howell defeated Tomson for the exonerated post of State Master Workman contributed to the latter's bitterness and gloom, despite his strong assertions to the contrary. "I want you and everyone to understand," Tomson told Powderly, "that I am not 'one bit sore' *personally.* I care nothing—not a fig for my defeat even though it was by a bitter personal enemy through combination etc. . . . *This is not it by any measure or means.*"[77] Despite his personal consternation in this instance, which his ardent protestations to the contrary only seemed to confirm, Tomson would nevertheless remain steadfast in his efforts to keep the Arkansas Knights of Labor out of partisan politics in the years ahead.

The growth of the Knights of Labor in Arkansas in 1887 came, not surprisingly, in the face of continued opposition. Shortly after the organization of a local assembly in Augusta (Woodruff County), which consisted primarily of tenant farmers and sharecroppers but was led by a butcher as Master Workman, the county "ring," according to Tomson, organized a boycott against the butcher. "Threats of violence against me were also frequent," reported Tomson, who organized the local assembly. While he was able to report that "our oppressors have ceased their persecutions openly in a very great measure," he nevertheless added that "the hireling press and extremists of the State continue to slander us."[78]

Much of the Knights of Labor's growth in the state in 1887 occurred among farmers, and the delta county of Woodruff became a Knights of Labor stronghold, with no less than thirteen local assemblies during the late 1880s. Many of these assemblies consisted of tenant farmers, sharecroppers, and farmhands. Some of the assemblies probably consisted of African Americans, who outnumbered whites in Woodruff County, though the incomplete records of the Knights of Labor fail to confirm this.[79] One local assembly in Augusta won "what may be considered a victory," wrote its recording secretary in the fall of 1887, in challenging the owners of the cotton gins in the community. "The owners . . . were charging us $4 per bale for ginning, and as they own all the machinery we are compelled to pay it." In keeping with the fourth article of the Knights of Labor platform—"the establishment of cooperative institutions, productive and distributive"—the members of the local assembly informed the cotton gin owners that "rather than pay that amount we would erect a gin on the cooperative plan and do our own work." Consequently, the gin owners reduced their prices to a range from $3.00 to $3.50 per bale, which the Knights judged to be "a more reasonable figure."[80] This victory hardly solved the financial problems of all farmers in the county, however, be they members of the Knights of Labor or the Agricultural Wheel. Later in 1887 the Knights and Wheelers in the county jointly "petitioned the landholders for a reduction of land rent of 25 percent per acre." The Knight who informed the *Journal of United Labor* of this development, the recording secretary of a local assembly of tenant farmers and sharecroppers, added that "we earnestly request all members of the Order to stay away from here, and counsel others to do so until further notification."[81]

The Agricultural Wheel continued to grow in Arkansas (and beyond) in 1887 as well. The National Agricultural Wheel chartered State Wheels in Mississippi, Alabama, Texas, Missouri, and Indian Territory that year, and at the fifth annual meeting of the Arkansas State Wheel in Hollywood (Clark County) in July, "Nearly all the counties in the State were represented," according to W. Scott Morgan.[82] The growing ranks of Arkansas Wheelers now included African Americans; delegates at the State Wheel meeting voted to seat a group of African American members from St. Francis County. Later that year, African American Wheel organizers established chapters in the old Greenback-Labor stronghold of Hempstead County, as well as in other counties.[83] The Wheel also continued to form cooperative enterprises in Arkansas. Around the beginning of February, Lonoke County Wheelers established at Cabot a "Wheel Trade Union," which the *Arkansas Gazette* reported "will do a mercantile business . . . on the cooperative plan." The company started with a capital stock of $10,000, divided into shares of $25 each. The *Gazette* reported that ninety-four Wheelers invested in shares, and that "the stockholders are all farmers who will share in the profits of the store after all expenses are paid."[84]

By this point, though, many of the leaders of the Arkansas Wheel seemed more concerned with politics than with cooperative enterprises. The "political Wheelers" who had supported the organization's candidates in 1886 soon discovered, however, that their small delegation in the state legislature could not exert much impact. While the legislature passed four laws relating to the regulation or taxation of railroads in 1887, it rejected a proposal to create a state railroad commission and also failed, to the disappointment of the Knights of Labor as well as Wheelers, to create a bureau of agricultural and labor statistics. "In the eyes of the Wheelers," concluded historian F. Clark Elkins, "the distress of the farming majority had not been materially relieved."[85] Perhaps not surprisingly, then, by midsummer a newspaper in rural Dallas County, where both the Agricultural Wheel and the Knights of Labor were active, suggested that if members of the two organizations could not win desired reforms through the Democratic Party, then "let them seek relief through the organization of a third party."[86] This notion seemed to be spreading among Wheelers as the organization itself expanded across much of the South; earlier that summer an Agricultural Wheel newspaper in northern Alabama, the *Alabama State Wheel*, expressed itself more forthrightly when it editorialized, "The Knights of Labor, Wheelers, Farmers' Alliance, Grange, Patrons of Husbandry [*sic*—the latter two organizations were one and the same] and all of the trades unions are striving for the self-same object—that is, the abolition of class legislation, stop[ping] the importation of pauper labor, the elevation of the toiling masses, the education of the rising generation, the equalization of taxation and the entire obliteration of the misnamed Democratic and Republican parties."[87]

At the same time that these newspapers were suggesting that the Wheel proceed further down the partisan political path, the Arkansas State Wheel, at its meeting in Hollywood, seemed to be heeding the advice. The State

Wheel's committee on demands composed a lengthy list of tasks for the federal government to tend to, including the purchase of all unoccupied Indian lands, the reclamation of all unearned land grants made to corporations, the unlimited coinage of silver, a graduated income tax, and the prohibition of dealing in futures on all agricultural products. The committee also resolved to "present these demands to all candidates for office and ask them for a pledge to support them," and to publish the names of candidates along with their avowed approval or disapproval of Wheel demands.[88] When the National Agricultural Wheel met in McKenzie, Tennessee, in November 1887, the organization approved a list of demands that resembled that of the Arkansas State Wheel, contending that their enactment would "secure to our people freedom from the shameful abuses that the farmers and mechanics are now suffering at the hands of arrogant capitalists, powerful corporations, and the seemingly insatiable greed of Shylocks." The National Wheel also resolved to "not support any man for Congress, of any political party, who will not pledge himself, in writing, to use all his influence for the formation of these demands into laws."[89]

By 1887 the Great Upheaval, in terms of strikes, seemed to be fading following the turbulence of 1886, but the discontent that had sparked the strikes remained strong.[90] In his study of the Knights of Labor and American politics, Leon Fink compiled an incomplete list of 189 towns and cities in which the Knights of Labor fielded political tickets from 1885 to 1888, and he suggested that this wave of electoral activity "may still stand as the American worker's single greatest push for political power."[91] In Arkansas, however, the close ties between the farmers' movement and the labor movement, exemplified in many ways by the Knights of Labor itself, meant that that "greatest push" would begin at the end of that period. As the Great Upheaval of the mid-1880s winded down in Arkansas, the working-class political revolt had only just begun. In a state where farmers, for many of whom engaging in strikes was not an option, far outnumbered industrial laborers, this revolt would in many ways be an agrarian revolt. Nevertheless, the Arkansas Knights of Labor, with farmers, miners, railroad workers, and many other categories of workers in its ranks, would play a critical role in leading what would prove to be a serious challenge to the political status quo in the state. Just how serious this revolt became would be evidenced by the incredibly drastic measures that Arkansas Democrats would resort to in order to meet the challenge to their power.

IV. THE UNION LABOR PARTY

IN HIS STUDY OF RACE relations in Arkansas after the Civil War, John William Graves wrote that the state "was the most solidly Democratic state in the solid South." In support of this assertion, Graves noted that from 1836, the year that Arkansas entered the Union, through 1860, Democrats had carried the state in every presidential election, had similarly monopolized the governor's office, and had even held all of the state's congressional seats with the exception of one Whig congressman in 1847.[1] Republicans assumed control of the governor's office in 1864 when a state constitutional convention appointed Unionist Isaac Murphy as provisional governor, and a "rump election" supervised by Union troops, in which only twelve thousand Arkansans voted, made him a full-term, four-year governor.[2] Republicans held on to the governor's office for ten years, but when Augustus H. Garland became the governor of Arkansas in 1874, the Democratic Party began a nearly century-long stranglehold on the office that finally ended with the election of Republican Winthrop Rockefeller in 1966.[3] The story of how the Democratic Party avoided the end of that long run of dominance of the state's highest office during the middle of its second decade, however, paints a disturbing portrait of Gilded Age Arkansas in which the constitutional rights of many citizens, as well as democracy itself, were violated and betrayed.

The challenge to the Democratic Party's dominance in Arkansas began on a serious level, following the Greenback-Labor and farmer-labor efforts of 1878 through 1886, with the formation of the Union Labor Party (ULP). A gathering of approximately 450 reformers—among them old Greenbackers and members of the Knights of Labor, the Farmers' Alliance, and the Agricultural Wheel—convened in Cincinnati on Washington's Birthday (February 22) in 1887 and launched the ULP, composing a platform that clearly reflected the influence of the Knights' Reading platform and the old Greenback platforms while foreshadowing the Populist platforms of the 1890s. Among other demands, the ULP called for a graduated land tax "on all large estates";

governmental ownership of the means of communication and transportation; the issue of a sufficient quantity of full legal tender directly from the federal government to the people, which might also be "loaned [to] citizens upon ample security at a low rate of interest"; the free coinage of silver; a graduated income tax; a constitutional amendment establishing direct popular election of US senators; the continuation of the national ban on Chinese immigration; the abolition of convict leasing; and the prohibition of "the employment of bodies of armed men by private corporations," five years before the lack of such a national law would become quite apparent at the Homestead steel mills in Pennsylvania. Due undoubtedly to the presence of women's suffragists at the convention, the platform also demanded women's suffrage, a demand that the Populist Party would omit from its Omaha platform in 1892 at the insistence of southern delegates. Every state in the Union except California, Louisiana, Maine, Nevada, South Carolina, and Vermont sent at least one delegate to this Cincinnati conference, which was dubbed the Industrial Labor Conference.[4] Arkansas delegates included R. P. Bailer, Charles E. Cunningham, O. S. Jones, and R. H. Morehead. Cunningham could probably boast of the strongest third-party credentials of any man in Arkansas at this time. Morehead was also a well-established "political Wheeler," and Jones, a property-owning farmer and blacksmith from the third-party stronghold of Nevada County, would later serve as a ULP state legislator and candidate for state auditor.[5]

Nationally, the ULP never amounted to much, and its primary significance would be to serve as a bridge between the loosely organized farmer-labor political activity of the mid-1880s and the Populist Party.[6] In Arkansas, however, the party continued a decade of political insurgency that had begun with the Greenback-Labor Party and been carried on by the Brothers of Freedom, the Agricultural Wheel and, to a lesser degree, the Knights of Labor. As was the case in some of these previous efforts, the campaigns of the Arkansas ULP would benefit from cooperation or fusion with the Republican Party.

The Emergence of the Arkansas Union Labor Party

Since 1887 was neither a national election year nor a state election year in Arkansas, the ULP showed no signs of life in the state that year.[7] By early 1888, however, Wheelers and Knights were getting the party off the ground. The fervor of at least some Arkansas Knights for the ULP seems to have been the motivating factor for the hanging in effigy at Forrest City in February of Dan Fraser Tomson, who had gone from running for the state legislature in 1884 as an independent labor candidate to denouncing what he saw as the baneful impact of partisan politics upon the Order by 1887. About two weeks after the occurrence, Knights of Labor LA 7978 of Forrest City passed a resolution unanimously and submitted it to the local newspaper for publication. The resolution declared that "we do fully and freely indorse the action of those Knights (to us unknown) who hanged in effigy Dan Fraser Tomson, the so-called State Master Workman of the Knights of Labor of Arkansas, and that the *East Arkansian* be requested to publish the same to the world."[8] Tomson subsequently stated in a letter to the Knights' national newspaper that the man most responsible for the spectacle was "a professional ring politician and ballot-box stuffer."[9] By then the *Arkansas Democrat*, the political leanings of which were totally in keeping with its title, could already see what was happening in the state, warning, "The men who are too good Democrats to associate with Wheelers and Knights of Labor, who want to drive out instead of call in new recruits, are the men that we have to fear in this campaign."[10]

One week after the publication of this worried editorial, R. H. Morehead, chairman of the state executive committee of the ULP of Arkansas, issued the call for the first state convention of the party to meet in the hall of the state house of representatives in Little Rock on April 30. The call read as follows:

> All persons who indorse the demands of the national and state Wheel, the demands of the national Farmers' Alliance, the declaration of principles of the Knights of Labor, and all true reformers who believe in political action independent of the old parties and desire to have justice done to the industrial masses, and to perpetuate the blessings of liberty, are invited to take part in the election of delegates to said convention, the basis of representation being the same as the number of members in the lower house of the legislature from each county.[11]

The *Arkansas Gazette*, no less fervent than the *Arkansas Democrat* in its support for the Democratic Party, cried, "'Union Labor' is the fraud our political frauds will adopt as their rallying cry this year. It is an alleged organization controlled by a few tenth-class politicians and political humbugs who can no longer get anything from either of the old political parties, and are therefore ready to lead any movement that promises to keep them before the people."[12]

Even before the Arkansas ULP held its first state convention, reports began to emerge of Knights of Labor, Agricultural Wheel, and independent political nominations. From the small Dallas County community of Fordyce, where the local newspaper had suggested during the previous summer that the Knights and the Wheel organize a third party if they could not get desired reforms from Democrats, came news days after Morehead's call for the state ULP convention that the Knights of Labor had "put out a full municipal ticket."[13] In early April, the *Fayetteville Democrat* reported that "the Knights of Labor took an active interest in the city election and the men they endorsed were elected in every instance." The newspaper added that the Knights "had endorsed the Democratic ticket except for mayor," but the mayoral candidate that the Order endorsed, Colonel J. H. Van Hoose, was an independent who defeated the Democratic incumbent, E. B. Wall, by a vote of 284–147.[14] Later that week, word came from Jonesboro, a then small town in northeastern Arkansas, that members of the Agricultural Wheel had held a meeting and nominated State Wheel President L. P. Featherston for Congress.[15] The *Marianna Index* presented a less certain account—"We have received disputed statements as to whether such selection of Mr. Featherstone [*sic*] was by way of nomination or merely of recommendation"—while also reporting that the convention was not strictly a Wheel meeting but rather "a kind of joint convention of Wheelers and Knights of Labor."[16] The fact that Featherston had indeed been offered a nomination became apparent, however, by April 16, when the *Arkansas Democrat* reported that "Featherston has accepted the Wheel nomination, and declared himself an independent candidate for Congress from the First Congressional District."[17] Ultimately, however, Featherston would run for the congressional seat as a Union Labor candidate. The Mississippi native, who lived in Tennessee before moving to Forrest City in 1881, owned far more land than most Wheelers—reportedly sixteen thousand acres, though he only farmed about 2 percent of that—but on the campaign trail in the fall of 1888, he spoke the Wheel language in his denunciation of trusts, banks, monopolies, and the anaconda mortgage.[18]

The first state convention of the Arkansas ULP convened as scheduled on April 30, 1888, in Little Rock. Some fifty delegates attended the convention, representing twenty-two of the state's seventy-five counties. "The Arkansas party's ranks," wrote historian Clifton Paisley, "were so filled with 'political Wheelers' that the leadership was scarcely distinguishable from that of the Agricultural Wheel of Arkansas." Prominent political Wheelers at the convention included Reuben CarlLee, Isom P. Langley, and Isaac McCracken, who presided as chairman. Three or four black delegates attended, all but one of whom were reportedly Knights of Labor from Pulaski County. The convention wrote a platform advocating "legislation as will secure the reforms demanded by the Agricultural Wheel, the National Farmers' Alliance and the Knights of Labor."[19]

The convention nominated a state ticket headed by former state senator Charles M. Norwood, a one-legged Confederate veteran, for governor. Norwood had long resided in Lafayette County, where his family owned a sizable amount of land, but by this time he was "a physician [residing] in the Greenback stronghold of Nevada County."[20] The *St. Louis Post-Dispatch* reported that the candidate was "regarded as a strong man," while the bitterly partisan *Arkansas Gazette* characterized him as "probably the most ignorant man who ever aspired to high position in Arkansas."[21] The convention also selected six delegates to the national ULP convention to be held in May in Cincinnati. These delegates included CarlLee, Charles E. Cunningham, and a black Knight of Labor from Little Rock, P. M. E. Thompson. Thompson, a Little Rock police captain, played an important role at the state convention even though less than a month earlier he had served as the chairman of a meeting of Republicans of the city's Third Ward that met to select delegates to the party's county convention. The state ULP convention instructed the delegates to support A. J. Streeter of Illinois for the presidential nomination and Terence V. Powderly as his running mate.[22] Powderly, however, seemed unlikely to accept that nomination, and the national ULP instead nominated Streeter while choosing Cunningham as his running mate.[23]

Norwood seemed to understand the frustrations of many Arkansas farmers and laborers, and he articulated them well on the campaign trail. He urged working-class voters to "strike decisive blows for the emancipation of enslaved labor in the upcoming campaign." He condemned capitalists and their allies in government for "withholding from the honest producer and laborer the full and just reward of their toil and sweat."[24]

Fortuitously, perhaps, for Norwood, since the discontent of the Great Upheaval seemed to have dissipated after 1886, signs of labor unrest in the state reemerged in 1888. Miners in Coal Hill struck twice that year. The first strike began on Monday, April 2, 1888, on the heels of an investigation that revealed horribly brutal treatment (including several murders) of convict laborers at the mines of the Ouita Coal Company. After the gruesome revelations became a major news story, the Arkansas Penitentiary Board took the convicts away from the mining company, which was actually subleasing the convicts from the Arkansas Industrial Company. The free miners employed by Ouita sent a committee to the company's superintendent, however, demanding that the company make an agreement to "not give employment to any of the late employees of the Arkansas Industrial Company." When the superintendent refused, the miners struck. About one month later, workers who were building the Pulaski County Courthouse threatened to strike if convict laborers were utilized for loading stone onto wagons for hauling. The Arkansas ULP platform, put forth just before the threatened strike in Little Rock, called for "a change in the convict system, the abolition of the contract system [which allowed immigrants to come to the United States in exchange for a year of their labor after arriving] and the working of the convicts within the walls of the penitentiary at Little Rock." The platform also called for "a law regulating mining and proper ventilation for same."[25] Other workers in Arkansas had problems, too. In Newport, where the ranks of the Knights of Labor included carpenters, mill hands, and farmhands, J. H. Robertson (later a leading figure among the Knights and the Populists in the state) reported that "many men are idle" and that some members were considering a move to the Washington Territory in search of land or employment.[26]

Certainly plenty of tillers of the soil in Arkansas were faring no better than industrial or mechanical toilers at this time. In Jefferson County, a member of the Knights of Labor bemoaned high rents for land and mules, as well as the credit (crop-lien) system.[27] In June the State Assembly of the Arkansas Knights of Labor issued a platform that demanded the passage of "an act declaring a yearly rental on real estate exceeding 15 percent of its taxable value [to be] usury."[28] During the same month, the Knights' State Executive Board issued an appeal to the local assemblies in behalf of State Master Workman Dan Fraser Tomson "to keep his homestead from being sold at mortgage sale."[29] Later that year a report from the Knights' State Statistician, H. H. Dill of Van Buren, indicated that a survey of the membership revealed that farmhands were being paid an average of only $0.65 per day, as opposed to $1.10 a day for members who worked in shops.[30]

When the State Assembly of the Knights of Labor met in Forrest City in July 1888, the assembled officers and other delegates did not endorse the ULP state ticket.[31] At about that same time, General Master Workman Powderly informed the readership of the Knights' national newspaper, "There is no Knight[s] of Labor ticket in the field anywhere in the United States."[32] Yet evidence exists of Knights of Labor support for the ULP in the Arkansas campaigns of 1888. In June the *Journal of United Labor* reported, "Two [Knights of Labor] district assemblies will be organized in Arkansas within the next 30 days—one in the first and one in the third congressional districts."[33] These were districts located, respectively, in eastern and southern

Arkansas, in which the ULP fielded candidates in the congressional elections that year—L. P. Featherston in the First District and J. A. Ansley in the Third.[34] The minutes book of Van Buren Assembly No. 6307, the only Arkansas Knights of Labor minutes book known to be extant for 1888, clearly shows support for the third party. At a meeting of the local assembly in February, H. H. Dill delivered a speech before his brother Knights in which he accused the two major parties of allowing "corners on produce [and] money" and showing "indifference . . . to the laboring people." Dill concluded his speech by declaring that "he would neither support the Democrat[ic] or Republican party," to which Master Workman W. F. Stocker replied, "Amen."[35] Members of the Van Buren Assembly who were inclined to support a third-party candidate in their Fourth District congressional race that fall had a viable option: Isaac McCracken, cofounder of the Brothers of Freedom and president of the National Agricultural Wheel, ran as the lone challenger to Democratic incumbent John H. Rogers. McCracken apparently ran as an independent rather than a Union Labor candidate, but the distinction meant little as he was one of the most ardent political Wheelers.[36]

The Agricultural Wheel held its annual state convention in Little Rock at the same time that the Knights of Labor State Assembly was in session at Forrest City. The political Wheelers, as reported by the *Arkansas Gazette*, were divided as to the organization's course of action regarding politics. Former state legislator and past Wheel congressional candidate R. B. CarlLee, whom the *Gazette* derisively called "the Hon. R. Boomerang," predicted to a reporter that the Wheel would "take some political action," adding, "Don't you think it ought to after having its demands ignored by one party and indorsed by another? I think we will indorse the Union Labor ticket and support it." McCracken, on the other hand, told a reporter, "I am here to oppose the indorsement of any party by this body. This is the Agricultural Wheel and it can't do anything of that kind." The State Wheel, McCracken suggested, "might pass a resolution acknowledging the compliment paid it by having its demands indorsed by the Union Labor party, but I think that is far enough." This attitude would seem to explain why McCracken did not campaign as a Union Labor candidate in his bid for Congress that year, and his position of official nonpartisanship for the Wheel won out over CarlLee's unabashed partisanship, as the State Wheel followed the exact course that McCracken had predicted: the convention thanked the ULP for "endorsing its demands upon the state legislature" but did not make an endorsement.[37] On the other hand, McCracken's refusal to have the State Wheel endorse the

ULP seemed hollow in light of his challenge to Rogers in the Fourth District that year, as did, for that matter, his status as an independent rather than ULP candidate. Moreover, while Wheel candidates could run as independents or on Wheel tickets in local, county, and even congressional elections in Arkansas in 1888, at the state level the only alternative to the status quo would be the ULP ticket.

At the local and county levels, Arkansas Wheelers were putting forth tickets even before the State Wheel convention met in late July. In White County, Wheelers decided in April to nominate a county ticket.[38] A Wheel lodge in Ashley County passed a resolution endorsing the candidacy of Wheeler J. H. Callaway for the state legislature, a race that he would lose to a Democrat.[39] In early June, a disapproving rural Arkansas newspaper reported that representatives of the subordinate Wheels of Mississippi County had held a meeting that led the editor to "surmise that the 'polititianers' [*sic*] who have crept into the organization made an attempt to secure an endorsement, if not a pledge to support, those candidates who are more than willing to sacrifice the old parties in order to ride into office over the 'felloes' [*sic*] who ought to be guardians of the hubs and spokes of their Wheels."[40] In mid-June, the *Arkansas Gazette* published details of a convention in Craighead County attended by representatives of twenty-three subordinate Wheels, including one "colored Wheel," as well as representatives of a local assembly of the Knights of Labor who also "engaged in the proceedings." The convention nominated a complete county ticket and endorsed the congressional candidacy of L. P. Featherston, "though," reported the hostile *Gazette*, "with no great enthusiasm."[41] Days later the *Hot Springs Sentinel*, in the town where the first two Arkansas assemblies of the Knights of Labor had been organized, reported that the Garland County Wheel had put forth what the newspaper derided as "a very weak" ticket.[42]

Democratic newspapers in the state were also quick to point out that not all Arkansas Wheelers favored third-party or independent tickets. The *Gazette* reported that the action of the Craighead County convention of Wheelers and Knights of Labor did not meet with the approval of "a great many of the leading and influential farmers of the county who are members of the Agricultural Wheel . . . who have always been Democrats, [and] say they intend to remain Democrats and are having nothing to do with this political move." "They will not," the newspaper approvingly noted, "vote the Wheel ticket."[43] Of course, "leading and influential farmers" did not make up the majority of the Wheel's membership, and even the leading political Wheelers were not men of considerable wealth. Isaac McCracken had turned to farming after working as a machinist in the Iron Mountain Railroad shops in Little Rock. Isom P. Langley's self-description of "Democrat-Greenbacker-Republican-Wheeler-Knight of Labor-farmer-preacher-lawyer-editor" hardly seems to suggest the lofty socioeconomic status of a planter, and in fact his tenures as a lawyer and newspaper editor were brief. Wheeler W. Scott Morgan's biographical sketch of Reuben CarlLee in his lengthy *History of the Wheel and Alliance, and the Impending Revolution* suggests a hard-scrabble upbringing and, following service in the Confederate Army that resulted in "several severe wounds," an unprosperous adulthood in which he supported himself by farming and engaging in the real estate and insurance businesses. CarlLee's greatest success in business seems to have occurred after he joined the Agricultural Wheel in 1883 and eventually became the state business agent and manager of the Arkansas Wheel's St. Louis-based cooperative exchange.[44]

Even though "the leading and influential farmers" could not legitimately be seen as spokesmen for the Arkansas Wheel, dissent among Wheelers in Craighead County continued to simmer as the summer of 1888 passed. In mid-August the *Arkansas Gazette* gleefully reported that a Wheel lodge in the eastern district of Craighead had "surrendered its charter on account of the efforts to force it into politics by the bosses." These disgruntled erstwhile Wheelers, the newspaper reported, "say they joined the Wheel as an agricultural and not as a political institution."[45] About two weeks later the *Gazette* jubilantly noted further disruptions among Craighead County Wheelers, reporting that twenty-seven members of a lodge called the Philadelphia Wheel had dropped out "on account of the leaders trying to force politics on the order and admitting negroes into the State and National Wheels." According to the report, this mass exodus cost the lodge more than half its membership. The twenty-three remaining members then voted on whether to endorse the Wheel county ticket, and the endorsement passed by the slimmest margin possible.[46]

That those Wheelers who so staunchly supported the Democratic Party would also declare their opposition to the admission of African Americans into the Agricultural Wheel hardly seems surprising. Black men in Arkansas had tended to vote against the Democratic Party since getting the right to vote in 1868; even through the 1880s, after the Democrats had begun a long period of dominance of the state government, black voters favored the GOP by a margin of about two to one.[47] The Greenback-Labor Party had fared well among black voters in Little Rock, where black members of the Knights of Labor subsequently had been involved in independent or third-party politics since 1886. While the Knights of Labor was playing an important role in laying the foundations for a third party, the Order claimed only slightly more than three thousand members in Arkansas by the summer of 1888.[48] The Agricultural Wheel, with about seventy-five thousand members in the state at that time, obviously could mobilize many more voters than the Knights. Just how many of these Wheelers were African Americans is unknown, but the two hundred "colored Wheels" that existed in the state in 1888 exceeded slightly more than 10 percent of the 1,947 Wheel lodges.[49] African American Wheelers, therefore, may have constituted only about 10 percent of the organization's membership, but their lack of ties to the Democratic Party made them particularly important to the third-party effort. In Little River County, where the Knights of Labor had organized a local assembly of black farmers, white Wheelers were reportedly "opposed to putting out a Wheel ticket" in May 1888 while black Wheelers were "decidedly in favor of it."[50] During the same month, Wheelers and Knights of Labor met in joint convention in Woodruff County and nominated a full county ticket. The six-man slate included two African Americans, one of them, John Brandon, as a candidate for the state house of representatives.[51]

The importance of African Americans to the hopes of the third-party cause in Arkansas in 1888 became even greater when the Republican State Central Committee met in Little Rock on July 18 and endorsed Charles M. Norwood for governor. The Republicans explained this decision by declaring that the Arkansas Democratic Party "has robbed the state treasury and boasts of bulldozing voters and stuffing, destroying, changing and burning ballots and ballot boxes and poll books, for which no one has ever been prosecuted in the courts." In contrast, the Republicans described Norwood's ULP as one that "proclaims that officers have no right to rob the state treasury and that there can be no good, honest government without honest and fair elections."[52] This assessment, particularly of the Arkansas Democratic Party, would soon prove to be more prophetic than the Arkansas Republicans who wrote it probably realized at the time.

Predictably, Democratic newspapers in Arkansas reacted to the Republicans' endorsement of Norwood with indignation and outrage. "All disguises have been at last removed," charged a melodramatic editorial in the *Arkansas Gazette*. "The mask has been torn off, and the authors of the crimes of the Reconstruction era stand forth in bold relief."[53] The *Mountain Echo*, published in Marion County, struck a less hysterical but equally resolute note in declaring that "we can't think that many sensible Democratic farmers and mechanics will lend their aid to a candidate who makes war on the party that redeemed Arkansas from misrule," referring of course to the alleged "crimes" mentioned by the *Gazette.* If the phrase "sensible Democratic farmers and mechanics" referred to white men, as it undoubtedly did in overwhelmingly white Marion County, the state's Democratic press was well aware of the threat that black voters posed to the success of the Democrats' state ticket.[54] Under the headline, "They Will Not," the *Lonoke Democrat* asked, "Will the colored people allow the few colored Republicans about Little Rock to turn them over, like so many sheep to the butcher, to Dr. Norwood[?]"[55]

Obviously, the Republicans' endorsement of Norwood magnified the importance of the black vote to his and the ULP's chances of success. Arkansas Democrats would therefore respond to this threat with more than just a revival of Reconstruction-era racist rhetoric. They would also revive the use of mob violence that had undermined black voter turnout and Republican strength during Reconstruction. Democrats in Conway County already had done this in 1885, donning the robes of the Ku Klux Klan and engaging in acts of terror and violence after they had been defeated by a combination of Republicans, Brothers of Freedom, and Wheelers. In the summer of 1888, Democrats elsewhere in the state showed that they too were willing to return to the use of such methods. In Crittenden County, armed white Democrats literally ran black Republican officeholders (among them some members of the Knights of Labor) out of town on a railway bound for Memphis, and when the black men appealed to Democratic governor (and former Grange leader) Simon P. Hughes for assistance and justice, he refused to help. In fact, he subsequently appointed white Democrats to fill the vacant offices. Not only were black Republican officeholders forced to leave in this coup d'etat, but other prominent black leaders of the anti–Democratic Party insurgency were chased away too, among them York Byers, a Wheeler who owned two hundred acres of land and had been a candidate for sheriff.[56]

Furthermore, white skin did not guarantee the safety of those who opposed the Arkansas Democratic Party. In 1868 Klansmen killed a Freedmen's Bureau agent in Little River County.[57] About two weeks before that year's presidential election, Republican congressman James Hinds and another prominent white Arkansas Republican, Joseph Brooks, were shot by local Democratic leader and Klansman George Clark in Monroe County while traveling to a rally for Republican presidential candidate Ulysses S. Grant. Brooks survived the attack, but Hinds did not.[58] Twenty years later, this pattern of Democratic violence against the party's political opponents resurfaced in Arkansas. On July 18, 1888, Captain Jim Blackwood, described by the *Arkansas Gazette* as "a prominent farmer . . . and a candidate for [Woodruff] county and probate judge on the Knights of Labor [actually Union Labor] ticket, was shot to death by one John Lookingbill, who is also a prominent citizen of that section and a brother-in-law of L.D. Snapp, of Snapp's post office at which place the shooting occurred."[59] The *Arkansas Democrat*, which identified the assassin as Jasper Luckenbill, reported that "the difficulty was the outgrowth of an old feud," but the rural *Osceola Times* reported that the "cause" of the killing was "politics."[60]

"Counted Out": The Elections of 1888

Despite these ominous signs, Union Labor leaders expressed high hopes for Arkansas as the state election approached. In July, days before the Arkansas Republican Party endorsed Norwood, Union Labor vice presidential candidate Charles E. Cunningham gave a speech in Milwaukee in which he predicted that "Arkansas would surprise the old parties in November."[61] At the beginning of August, the national ULP executive committee, meeting in Chicago, resolved to "give special attention to Arkansas until the September [state] election." Presidential candidate A. J. Streeter, Cunningham, and six other national party leaders stumped the state for Norwood in August. One party leader stated, "We will carry Arkansas for the Union Labor Party if we can get a fair count, and we are taking steps to secure a fair count."[62]

Notwithstanding the refusal of the Arkansas Knights of Labor State Assembly to endorse the ULP, many Arkansas Knights continued their involvement in the party. For example, in Little Rock, the Pulaski County ULP held its convention at the Knights of Labor Hall in mid-August. Not surprisingly, members of the Knights of Labor, including Isom P. Langley, figured prominently in the proceedings of the interracial convention, which nominated a county ticket. The ticket included an African American for the position of circuit clerk and another as one of its four nominees for the state house of representatives.[63]

Just before the state election, the Knights of Labor became the subject of newspaper coverage in Arkansas for a reason other than political activities. For the second time during 1888, Knights of Labor miners at Coal Hill went on strike. The *Arkansas Gazette* reported that the strike, which began at Stiewel's Mines and spread to the Ouita Coal Company, stemmed from a demand for an increase in wages from $0.80 per ton to $1.00 per ton.[64] A notice

5. National campaign poster of the 1888 Union Labor Party, featuring Alson J. Streeter for president and Charles E. Cunningham for vice president. Kurz & Allison, Copyright Claimant. Ca. Aug. 31, 1888. Print. Retrieved from the Library of Congress, accessed March 20, 2018, https://www.loc.gov/pictures/item/2003656923/.

in the *Journal of United Labor*, however, sent to the national Knights of Labor newspaper by a committee of strikers, reported that the strike began due to "the unwarranted discharge of some of our men," while also noting the demand for $1.00 per ton starting on September 1, 1888. "One of our brothers was discharged for refusing to work in bad air, and another for taking time in which to bury his deceased brother," according to the notice. "In slavery days the slaves had the privilege of half a day [off] each week, and sufficient time to bury their dead, but the miners here are granted no such favors." Referring to a superintendent as "a tyrannical brute," the notice urged "brother miners everywhere [to] keep away from Coal Hill," declaring it "not a place for white men to live in."[65] Here in Johnson County, where, according to the Census of 1890, 96 percent of the population was white, even the limited racial egalitarianism that the Knights of Labor displayed elsewhere in the state apparently did not resonate with the membership, particularly when those members associated African Americans with the convict labor they had struck to keep out of the mines after its removal earlier in the year.[66]

Amid the reports about the strike in Coal Hill, the Arkansas state election took place on Monday, September 3, 1888, drawing more voters than any previous election in the state's history. According to historian Clifton Paisley, "The political Wheelers and Republicans charged fraud before, during and after the election," but it was only one month later that ULP presidential candidate A. J. Streeter claimed that while in Arkansas "a day or two before the [state] election," he "was plainly told by leading Democrats that they were going to carry the state, fairly if they could, but violently and fraudulently if they had to resort to such measures to seat their candidate." The official returns indicated 99,214 votes for the Democrat, James W. Eagle, as opposed to 84,213 for Union Laborite Charles M. Norwood. As Paisley has pointed out, however, since the charges of election fraud made against Arkansas Democrats "were never given a full hearing one cannot be sure the count was accurate."[67] More recent studies have concluded that the count was indeed not accurate; one even suggests that Norwood "would probably have won the governor's office had not election fraud prevented him."[68]

Election fraud was certainly not uncommon in Arkansas (or elsewhere in the South) at this time. Each political party would print tickets featuring, as one historian has explained, "distinctive shapes, symbols, or colors [that] made it easy for even illiterate voters to make their choices." This system also made ballot box stuffing possible, however, and the theft of ballot boxes occurred frequently as well.[69]

One man who had no doubt at the time that election fraud had prevented Norwood from winning the governor's office was, not surprisingly, one of the most ardent political Wheelers, Reuben CarlLee. On September 14, 1888, while in St. Louis, CarlLee wrote a letter to an acquaintance in New York City, G. W. Pike. Pike subsequently gave the letter, with its author's consent, to the *New York Press*, which published it on September 18. CarlLee minced no words in his damning indictment of Arkansas Democrats and their illegal, immoral, and fraudulent actions during the campaign and election:

> I am just from Arkansas. If the people of the United States only knew half [of] how we have been treated Congress would wipe out the fraudulent State government of Arkansas and grant us a republican form of government as guaranteed by the federal constitution.
>
> In Arkansas county they robbed us of the ballot box at two townships with over 500 majority for us. In Union county Gov. Hughes armed the Democratic

> clubs with the State Winchesters on the night before the election (Sunday). They paraded over the county and whipped over twenty colored men, some of them so badly that they had to keep [to] their beds. On Monday they shot and killed seven Union Labor men and wounded over 20 more, and at Eldorado, the county seat, they took the poll books away from the judges and burned them before the eyes of the people and then held a new election at which no Union Labor men were permitted to vote.

CarlLee's letter also detailed alleged violent or fraudulent methods by Democrats in eighteen other counties: Conway, Crittenden, Garland, Howard, Jackson, Lafayette, Lee, Lincoln, Little River, Lonoke, Miller, Mississippi, Monroe, Pope, Pulaski, St. Francis, Saline, and Woodruff. "We undoubtedly carried the state," he insisted, "and have been counted out." Only the federal government, he concluded, could ensure Arkansas "an honest election. Until then, the shotgun and Winchester rifle in the hands of [D]emocratic clubs, backed by the State officials, . . . rule in Arkansas and not the people."[70] Streeter repeated many of these charges in an interview in St. Louis about three weeks later, and he referred to the election as "one of the greatest outrages in American history." CarlLee and Streeter both predicted that Norwood would contest the results of the election.[71]

As might be expected, Democratic newspapers in Arkansas reacted to CarlLee's charges with indignant outrage. The *Arkansas Gazette* labeled him "an utterly unscrupulous defamer of Arkansas, with an apparently unlimited capital of a lively and utterly depraved imagination."[72] Democratic governor Simon P. Hughes also publicly responded to CarlLee's charges by writing a letter to the *New York Press*, which was also sent to Arkansas newspapers. "CarlLee seems ambitious to become notorious as an untruthful and unscrupulous defamer and enemy of the State of Arkansas, of which he is a citizen," wrote Hughes, in language that a writer for the *Gazette* apparently borrowed. "In his letter are statements I know to be false, and without the semblance of truth." Hughes went on to dispute many of the specific charges made in CarlLee's letter, most notably that Democrats had killed seven white Union Labor men in Union County. According to the governor, "One man only was killed in Union county on the day of the election, and . . . he was accidentally killed."[73]

Despite the fraud and violence that undoubtedly depressed Norwood's vote tally, the official returns nevertheless reveal some areas of significant support for the ULP in the state election. Norwood carried most counties in southwestern Arkansas, including three counties carried by Greenback-Labor gubernatorial candidate W. P. "Buck" Parks in 1880: Hempstead, Lafayette, and Nevada. In addition to being bastions of Greenback-Labor support, all three of these counties became, considering their relatively scant population, Knights of Labor strongholds in the mid-1880s, with multiple local assemblies in each. Norwood also carried a number of counties in northern Arkansas that were predominantly or almost entirely white, including Searcy, another county that Parks had carried in 1880. Finally, Norwood also defeated Eagle in several black-majority plantation counties in the eastern Arkansas Delta. In St. Francis County, where the Knights of Labor had anywhere from three to six active local assemblies at the time, Norwood won by a margin of slightly more than 3–2. In Phillips County, where former slave Bryant Singfield had organized black farmhands after the Civil War and where the Knights of Labor organized black and white local assemblies, Norwood won 74 percent of the vote. In Crittenden County, where African Americans constituted 85 percent of the population according to the Census of 1890, and where Democrats had expelled black officeholders during the previous summer, Norwood received 54 percent of the vote. In Pulaski County, where the Knights of Labor and labor unions in general were more prevalent than anywhere else in the state, Norwood drew 52 percent of the vote. In all he carried twenty-three of the state's seventy-five counties.[74]

As Reuben CarlLee and A. J. Streeter had predicted, Norwood contested the results of the election. The same state election had resulted in thirteen Republicans and nine Union Laborites winning seats in the state house of representatives. Two Union Laborites retained seats in the state senate that they had won as Agricultural Wheel candidates in 1886, and three Republican holdovers remained in the senate as well. On January 23, 1889, one of the Union Labor representatives, Jasper W. Dollison of Clay County—Master Workman of a Knights of Labor district assembly in northeastern Arkansas—introduced a nineteen-page petition, signed by Norwood, calling for an investigation of the gubernatorial election. The state house of representatives consented, but the state senate added an important provision. As another member of the Knights of Labor from Clay County put it, the senate "resolved that before the State should proceed to investigate the fraudulent election of the Rev. Mr. Eagle, Mr. Norwood put up $40,000 to pay all expenses of the contest in the event that the Democratic committee should determine to count him out regardless of evidence in the case." With that provision came the end of Norwood's fight for the governorship.[75]

The ULP's campaign in Arkansas did not end, of course, with the state election in September. Two months later the presidency would be up for grabs, as well as all of the seats in the US House of Representatives. The fact that Arkansan Charles E. Cunningham was the running mate of A. J. Streeter meant that the Union Labor ticket was of more interest in Arkansas than in most other states, but no one realistically expected that ticket to capture the nation's executive branch. The congressional races, however, seemed to offer the Arkansas ULP more opportunity for victory. The party fielded candidates in the First District (L. P. Featherston), the Third (J. A. Ansley), and the Fifth (John Gates). Isaac McCracken apparently ran as an independent candidate in the Fourth District, but undoubtedly many voters associated him with the Agricultural Wheel, the Knights of Labor, and the ULP. In every district except the Fifth, only two candidates ran, one of them a Democrat in each case. In the Fifth District, incumbent Samuel Peel faced two challengers: one a fellow Democrat (E. P. Watson) who ran as an independent, and the other the Union Labor candidate, Gates of Carroll County, where the Knights of Labor and the Agricultural Wheel had previously experienced electoral success at the county level. In the Second District, the Republican Party nominated John M. Clayton to challenge the Democratic incumbent, Clifton R. Breckenridge. Clayton was the younger brother of former Republican governor Powell Clayton, and from 1876 until 1886 he served as the sheriff of Jefferson County. Norwood endorsed Clayton as the election approached, and the *Faulkner County Wheel* newspaper averred that "a matter of common fairness would suggest that we vote for Clayton as the Republicans supported the Union Labor ticket in the state election and are now supporting our candidates for congress in the First, Third and Fourth districts, and have even sent some of their ablest speakers into these districts to work for their election."[76]

That the races in the First and Second Districts would be the most competitive was foreshadowed by the much greater coverage that the *Arkansas Gazette* gave to those two contests compared to the other three.[77] Less than a week before the election, the *Gazette* published a report that Powell Clayton, by now the chairman of the Republican State Central Committee, and L. P. Featherston "are working hand in hand."[78] In response to this report, the *Gazette* editorialized, "The leaders of the Union Labor Party have contracted to sell out to the Republicans. They are making common cause with the authors of the devilish measures which disgraced and degraded Arkansas from 1868 to 1874."[79] Of course, the Democratic press found it even easier to tie the Second District challenger to his older brother, who had served as governor from 1868 to 1871. In late October 1888, the *Gazette* reprinted a short piece from the *Lonoke Democrat* charging that "John M. Clayton assisted his brother

Powell to reconstruct Arkansas. He was a state senator, and the mouthpiece of his delectable [*sic*] brother in the legislature." The *Democrat* added that if John M. Clayton defeated Clifton R. Breckenridge, "It would not only be defeating a distinguished Democrat with a national reputation, but he would feel it as a Clayton vindication. Let every Democrat, Wheeler and Union Laborer see to it that no such disaster shall befall the Second District."[80]

As in the state election in September, Arkansas Democrats had more than the influence of the press at their disposal in the congressional elections. Perhaps not pausing to consider that the latter could be contested before the US House of Representatives or perhaps simply determined to maintain power at all costs, white Democrats once again resorted, certainly in the state's First and Second Districts, to undemocratic, illegal, and violent measures to vanquish those who had the audacity to challenge them. The extent of these measures would become apparent when the candidates in those two districts, who were declared to have lost their bids for office, courageously took their cases to the lower chamber of Congress.

The official returns indicated Democratic victories in each of Arkansas's congressional districts. Union Laborite Ansley and the "independent" candidate McCracken each made respectable showings, receiving 40.3 and 42.2 percent of the votes in the Third and Fourth Districts, respectively. The Democrats prevailed by much smaller margins in the first two districts though: 15,576–14,228 votes in the First and an even closer count of 17,857–17,011 in the Second. Within about a week of the election, both Featherston and Clayton announced their intention to contest the results.[81]

As with the gubernatorial election, the dubious veracity of the official returns in the congressional elections does not negate their value in revealing areas of strong opposition to the Democratic Party. In the First District, the original certified returns showed Featherston winning the counties of Chicot, Crittenden, Desha, Lee, Mississippi, Phillips, and St. Francis. According to the Census of 1890, these were all black-majority counties. Furthermore, the Knights of Labor was active in all of these counties with the possible exception of Mississippi. In the Second District, the original returns credited Clayton with carrying four counties: Arkansas, Jefferson, Lincoln, and Monroe. Except for, on both counts, Arkansas County, these were black-majority counties with multiple local assemblies of the Knights of Labor. Jefferson County, where Clayton had served as sheriff, was one of the state's Knights of Labor strongholds with a total of sixteen local assemblies known to have been in existence between 1886 and 1893. In the Third District,

Ansley won three counties: Hempstead, Nevada, and Little River. The Census of 1890 reported all of these counties as being more than 50 percent white, and the Knights of Labor had organized local assemblies in all of them, including a local of black farmers in the Little River County hamlet of Red Bluff in 1886. Hempstead and Nevada Counties had both been Greenback-Labor Party strongholds. Isaac McCracken carried only one county in the Fourth District, receiving 60 percent of the vote in Pulaski County, where the Knights of Labor still had at least thirteen local assemblies at the time, as compared to 37 percent in the rest of the district. John Gates failed to carry any counties in the Fifth District, being the only Union Labor candidate to face two other candidates, a Democratic incumbent and an independent Democrat.[82] Statewide, the Streeter-Cunningham ticket received 10,613 votes in Arkansas, its fourth-best showing in the nation behind Kansas, Texas, and Missouri.[83]

Dangerous Democracy

Featherston and Clayton both hired a lawyer named John McClure to represent them in their contested election cases. One of the state's leading Republicans, McClure had been the chief justice of the Arkansas Supreme Court during Reconstruction. In the case that Featherston brought before the US House of Representatives, he charged Democrats in the First District with having committed "conspiracy, violence, intimidation, and fraud." He claimed that voter fraud, in many cases ballot-box stuffing, had occurred in fifteen of the district's seventeen counties, and that because of threats of bodily harm, he and his representatives could take testimony from witnesses in only four counties.[84]

The outcome of Clayton's investigation into the methods by which Democrats stole the election from him showed that Featherston and his representatives were wise to heed such warnings. In Conway County, Democrats intimidated black voters on Election Day and stole and burned a ballot box and poll books in a precinct with many black voters. Clayton went to the scene of the most flagrant abuses—the small town of Plumerville (population: 214 [1890])—without any bodyguards, against the warnings of several advisers. Four days later, on January 29, 1889, Clayton died as the result of a shotgun blast that nearly severed his head from his body. The question "Who killed John Clayton?" would remain an unsolved mystery in Arkansas, but more than one century later historian Kenneth C. Barnes would convincingly pin the crime on prominent Conway County Democrats. Clayton's brothers, William H. and Powell Clayton, hired the Pinkerton Detective Agency to investigate the assassination when it became apparent that county and state law enforcement officers were not making much of an effort to do so. On March 30, 1889, a black investigator named Joseph P. Smith became the second fatality in the case when he too was shot in Plumerville, apparently for being on the verge of solving the Clayton case. Constable Richard J. Gray, described by Barnes as "a well-educated mulatto physician and a leader of the black community," and Deputy Sheriff Tom McGee captured and arrested Smith's killer, but the killing was ultimately ruled to be a justifiable homicide.[85]

John McClure continued to pursue John M. Clayton's contested election case, as well as Featherston's, after Clayton's assassination. In the meantime, however, William H. Cate took the seat in the US House of Representatives from Arkansas's First District, and the incumbent Clifton R. Breckenridge kept his seat in the Second. Ultimately, the US House ruled that Featherston had defeated Cate by eighty-six votes, and the Union Labor candidate took his seat on March 5, 1890, during the middle of the first session of the Fifty-First Congress. The US House also later ruled Clayton to have been the winner in the Second District and therefore declared the seat to be vacant on September 5, 1890, shortly before the end of the first session. This meant that on November 4, 1890, two congressional elections were held in Arkansas's Second District: a special election to fill the seat for the remainder of the Fifty-First Congress and another to determine who would hold the seat during the Fifty-Second Congress.[86]

The national shock and outrage over the Clayton assassination at least proved helpful in righting a wrong carried out by Democratic officials in Pulaski County during the state and local elections of the previous September. On the night after the elections, burglars had raided the courthouse in Little Rock and broken into a safe from which they stole "several ballot boxes from what unofficial tally sheets showed to be heavily Union Labor–Republican districts." The four candidates of the ULP for the state house of representatives took their case to the Pulaski County Election Board. When that body refused to provide any justice, even Little Rock's Democratic newspapers, the *Arkansas Democrat* and the *Arkansas Gazette*, sided with the Union Labor candidates. These men then took their case to the Arkansas General Assembly. In the wake of the slaying of Clayton, which had occurred just three weeks earlier, the legislature removed the four Democratic representatives from Pulaski County from office, and the Union Labor candidates replaced them. One of the newly installed legislators, Green W. Thompson, became one of only eight African Americans in the Arkansas General Assembly at that time.[87]

The assassinations of John Clayton and the investigator Joseph Smith did not, however, mark the end of politically motivated violence in Arkansas. St. Francis County had gone the ULP's way in every election in 1888: Norwood and Featherston both won the county even by the dubious official tallies, and a fusion ticket of black Republicans and white Union Laborites swept Democrats out of the county offices, although the white sheriff, Agricultural Wheel member D. M. Wilson, was an incumbent who had been elected twice as a Democrat. At 2:00 a.m. on September 4, 1888—hours after the end of the state and county elections—a violent episode occurred in Franks, a predominantly African American township in St. Francis County. One or more unknown assailants fired shots at a group of men who were guarding the building where the ballot box was being kept. No fatalities occurred, but among the seven wounded men, according to a newspaper account, were some of the "best [white] citizens of the county." The *Arkansas Gazette* suggested that the assailants were African Americans who were trying to steal the ballot box, which the newspaper claimed contained mostly Democratic votes (an ironic charge given the widespread theft by Democrats of ballot boxes in Union Labor–Republican precincts throughout the state that year). The wounded men fired back to apparently unknown effect, and so the episode ended. Eight months later, however, a far more serious matter of politically and racially motivated violence occurred at Forrest City, the county seat of St. Francis. Tensions over a forthcoming school board election, particularly fear among white citizens that African Americans were on the verge of taking over the school board that controlled the public schools for both races, exploded in the form of two days of bloody conflicts that became known as the Forrest City Riot. Four men were killed: a Democratic city marshal, Sheriff Wilson, a Union Labor deputy county clerk, and a black Republican school board member. All except the Democratic marshal were members of the Agricultural Wheel. Many African Americans, including some elected officials, subsequently left town due to threats or fears for their safety, as did some white Wheelers, among them L. P. Featherston. White Democrats went on to sweep the school board election.[88]

Dissent after Defeat

The two supposedly nonpartisan organizations that had created the ULP in Arkansas—the Agricultural Wheel and the Knights of Labor—both suffered as a result of political dissent stirred within their ranks by the campaigns of

1888. After the state election, but before the congressional and presidential elections that fall, Arkansas Knights of Labor State Statistician H. H. Dill of Van Buren wrote in a letter to the *Journal of United Labor*, "Politics nearly ruined us in this State, but I think we will get over it and be better by having the experience."[89] Dill, it will be recalled, had vowed at a meeting of his local assembly in February 1888 to support neither the Democratic nor the Republican Party. Just before the federal elections, a member of the Knights from Newport, John H. Robertson, wrote in a letter to the same newspaper that "politics has done the Order great injury in this State." After the elections had passed, Robertson wrote in another letter to the *Journal*, "Now that the political war is over and the smoke of battle about cleared away, I want to ask those members who neglected their duties and dropped out of their Assemblies and became 'political fanatics' and 'partisan cranks,' what have they gained by the operation?" Robertson went on to chide those "fanatics" and "cranks" for "neglecting and trying to make your organization subordinate to some 'political party.'" Ironically, Robertson, while serving as the Knights' State Secretary-Treasurer, would also be the assistant secretary of the Arkansas People's Party campaign committee in 1892 and an Arkansas delegate to the party's national convention in 1896.[90] In a letter to Terence V. Powderly signed by all the members of the Arkansas Knights of Labor State Executive Board in early January 1889, the board members complained that "partisan politics" and "designing demagogues . . . [in] our Assemblies" had done significant damage, and that of 158 local assemblies and 3,750 members "nominally" existing in the state, "only 30 Assemblies, with an aggregate membership of 806[,] reported and paid per capita tax to the State Assembly" by the first of October 1888.[91] This problem was not unique to the Arkansas Knights of Labor; the national Order's General Secretary-Treasurer, John W. Hayes, claimed that the Knights' involvement in the political campaigns of 1888 led to a reduction in membership of some 55,000, or more than one-fifth of the reported mid-1888 total of 259,518.[92]

The Agricultural Wheel, too, lost members amid the campaigns of 1888. Two historians who closely examined the Wheel and the ULP in Arkansas have suggested that only about one-third of the seventy-five thousand Wheelers in the state supported the third party that year.[93] "Encouraged by Democratic leaders," notes Carl H. Moneyhon, "many local Wheel groups bolted the state organization and returned their charters because of the organization's new political stance." Many of those Wheelers who left then joined either of two branches of the Farmers' Alliance: the Farmers' Alliance of

Arkansas, which was affiliated with the Texas-based Southern Farmers' Alliance, or the independent Farmers' Cooperative Alliance of Arkansas, which was based in the Sebastian County mining community of Greenwood. The Texas-based Alliance entered Arkansas in December 1886 when organizer James Madison Perdue chartered chapters in Miller County. The Farmers' Alliance, split into two branches, grew slowly in Arkansas, but in 1888 it began to pick up disaffected ex-Wheelers. In December 1888, the Southern Farmers' Alliance and the National Agricultural Wheel held a joint meeting at Meridian, Mississippi, where representatives of the two orders agreed to a merger, although it would not be consummated until three-fourths of the state chapters of each organization had given their approval. This merger alienated some Arkansans who belonged to the Farmers' Alliance of Arkansas, some of whom subsequently shifted their affiliation to the independent Greenwood County–based state organization.[94]

Under the terms of the merger agreement between the Southern Farmers' Alliance and the National Agricultural Wheel, the Wheel would lose its name. Wheel president Isaac McCracken would become the vice president of the consolidated organization. The Wheel would give up more than just its name in the merger. Unlike the Wheel, the Southern Farmers' Alliance still had a whites-only membership clause, and this was retained in the merger, despite the "efforts of a minority of the merger committee, including the Arkansas representatives, to oppose . . . [the] clause and protect the colored Wheels." Ultimately, and not surprisingly since the Wheel began in Arkansas and was larger than the Alliance there even in the face of some defections, Arkansas was the last state where the merger won approval. Not until February 1890 did the two rival State Alliance organizations in Arkansas consolidate into a body attached to the Southern Farmers' Alliance, and one year later, on February 14, 1891, the Arkansas Farmers' Alliance and the State Wheel finally approved the merger that ended the separate existence of the latter. Once that happened, African American Wheelers "were . . . left to pursue an independent course or to . . . work their way into the Colored Farmers' National Alliance." The Colored Farmers' Alliance had begun in Texas in 1886, and it would reach Arkansas later in 1891 with infamous results.[95]

Yet despite the damage done to both the Knights of Labor and the Agricultural Wheel by the campaigns of 1888, neither organization fell into a rapid decline in Arkansas in the aftermath of the elections. The organizing efforts of the indefatigable Dan Fraser Tomson helped to restore the Knights of Labor's membership in the state by the summer of 1890 to about 3,500, or nearly the same figure as two years earlier.[96] In February 1889 the Arkansas Knights of Labor State Executive Board, in session in Little Rock, organized a "Co-operative Exchange" in order to "better the financial condition of the members by purchasing goods from the manufacturer and delivering them direct[ly] to the consumer at the actual cost of handling." By then Knights of Labor miners were on strike yet again in western Arkansas, this time in the small Sebastian County community of Hackett City. A notice in the *Journal of United Labor* reported, "The price paid for digging coal is only 1½ cents per bushel, and there are crowds of idle men in the vicinity. Those who are working can scarcely earn enough to feed themselves and families."[97] During the spring, miners at Coal Hill walked off the job again in response to a 10 percent reduction in wages and the practices of a company store, which the miners referred to as a "pluck-me store."[98] (Miners across the United States used this derisive term to describe these commissaries that often charged more than independent retailers for goods of lesser quality.)[99] Nor did the Agricultural Wheel seem to lose much momentum in Arkansas in 1889. The fact that some staunch Democrats had left by then may have strengthened the influence of Union Laborites in the organization, and in March the executive committee of the State Wheel reaffirmed its commitment to the ULP and fusion with the Arkansas Republican Party. Following its meeting in Little Rock, a member of the executive committee told a reporter of plans for "a consolidation of Republicans, Wheelers and Union Labor men to defeat the corrupt Democracy. . . . The people are heartily tired of ballot-box stuffing, fraud and assassination, and propose now to have some honesty and integrity in the government."[100]

While spokesmen for the Arkansas Knights of Labor were more circumspect about that order's political intentions in 1889—State Executive Board member J. W. McSlarrow of Independence County insisted in a letter to the *Arkansas Gazette* that "the Knights of Labor are not a party, but are strictly non-partisan and non-sectarian"—letters from Arkansas Knights to the *Journal of United Labor* continued to promote political insurgency.[101] "A late Democratic convention of our State," wrote a Knight from Clay County during the summer, "was formally presented with the demands of the Knights of Labor and Agricultural Wheel and [was] requested to indorse either the whole or any part of them. That request was treated with scorn, and the demands of the noble Order of the Knights of Labor were spurned from that convention as if each one of them had been a miniature devil."[102] Weeks later, J. Frank Williams, a Knight from the Hot Spring County railroad town of Malvern, declared, "It is a mystery to me how any Republican or Democratic Knight expects the legislation asked by the Knights of Labor, when they are voting men into power on a platform of principles diametrically opposed to our platform."[103] Three years earlier (as discussed in the previous chapter), Williams had endorsed Democratic incumbent congressman Thomas McRae over the Agricultural Wheel / Greenback candidate L. H. Hitt.

The reluctance of some white Democrats in Arkansas, and elsewhere in the South, during the Gilded Age to switch their political allegiance might seem odd to many Americans in the twenty-first century. White men in the postbellum South, however, faced enormous pressure to remain loyal to the Democratic Party. Milford W. Howard, who served as a Populist congressman from Alabama from 1895 until 1899, experienced the bitter split that abandonment of the Democratic Party could produce even between father and son. "My own father would not hear me speak and said he would rather make my coffin with his own hands and bury me," Howard later recalled, "than to have me desert the Democratic Party."[104] Even in Arkansas's neighbor to the west, Oklahoma, which did not become a state until forty-two years after the Civil War ended, Democrats immediately proved adept at preaching the doctrine of the Solid South. When Republicans opposed the ratification of the state's first constitution, noted the historian Dewey W. Grantham, "Democratic leaders derisively identified . . . [them] with 'the Carpetbagger, the Corporation, and the Coon.'"[105] In Arkansas the violence that opponents of the Democratic Party faced most likely made the decision of men like Williams to leave "the party of the fathers" all the more difficult.

Clearly, then, Williams and other former Democrats must have believed that they had compelling reasons to be supporting the ULP, especially after all the fraud, intimidation, and violence that Arkansas Democrats had unleashed against Union Laborites and Republicans alike during the state and congressional elections of 1888. Certainly Arkansas Democrats' continued rejection of the demands of the Agricultural Wheel and the Knights of Labor figured heavily in the ULP's persistence in the wake of what could have been a crushing defeat. In the state legislature that was elected in September 1888, "Third party men," notes historian Jason McCollom, "were . . . conspicuous in their efforts to address the concerns of farmers and wageworkers," but opposition from Democrats and, in some cases, Republicans prevented them from accomplishing much. Most Union Labor representatives in the legislature supported a bill to create "a railroad commission with the authority to set freight rates," but with Democrats divided over the bill and all Republicans in the state house voting against it, the bill failed. The best that Union Labor legislators could achieve in the specific interests of their farmer and labor constituents was the creation of the Arkansas Mining, Manufacturing, and Agriculture Bureau.[106] The Arkansas State Wheel had passed a resolution in 1885 calling for the establishment of this bureau "for the promotion and benefit of practical and scientific agriculture, and encouraging the mining and manufacturing interests of this state."[107] Similarly, the Knights of Labor's Reading platform of 1878 pledged "to arrive at the true condition of the producing masses in their educational, moral, and financial condition, by demanding from the various governments the establishment of Bureaus of Labor Statistics."[108] Arkansas's Union Labor legislators could claim little credit even for this minor victory, however, since Democratic legislators contributed to it after Governor Simon Hughes declared in 1888 that "the State should have an agricultural, mining and manufacturing bureau, which should be a bureau of statistics and immigration, also." Democrats did not, however, support the more proactive Union Labor demands that might have alleviated some of the burdens upon working-class Arkansans of farms and industry.[109]

Challenging Democracy: The Elections of 1890

The Arkansas ULP began its campaign for the state and congressional elections of 1890 on January 28 when its state executive committee met in a hotel in Little Rock. The committee only consisted of five men. Wheeler W. Scott Morgan of Hardy served as the chairman. Charles M. B. Cox of Rector, who had written the letter to the *Journal of United Labor* in August 1889 complaining about how a state Democratic convention had "spurned" the demands of the Knights of Labor and the Agricultural Wheel, also occupied a position on the committee. The committee decided that the party would "run full State and local tickets" and "make no compromise with either of the old parties."[110] The *Arkansas Gazette*, predictably, scoffed at the latter declaration, editorializing that "the Union Laborites will do exactly what Powell Clayton commands. They will jump when he cracks his whip. When he takes snuff they will endeavor to sneeze their little heads off."[111]

For all of the bias and hyperbole of the *Arkansas Gazette*, its claims bore some merit, as became evident during the following summer. In June 1890 the ULP nominated Napoleon Bonaparte Fizer, a Methodist minister from White County, for governor, and in July the Republican Party endorsed him, citing his commitment to free and fair elections. The Arkansas ULP platform also included demands for the free and unlimited coinage of silver, government loans on real estate to those engaged in farming, government ownership or control of the means of communication and transportation, and the passage of laws prohibiting the alien (foreign) ownership of land. In general, it espoused a tone of antimonoplism.[112] The *Gazette*, however, focused less on the ULP platform and more on the fact that the GOP was supporting Fizer: "In the Republican party is Fizer's only strength; and as no candidate can successfully avoid responsibility for the record of the political party he represents, Mr. Fizer must stand or fall on the record made by the Republicans in Arkansas," which the *Gazette*, not surprisingly, deemed to be "an infamous record."[113]

In contrast to the decline that the Knights of Labor was experiencing nationally by 1890, reports in both the *Journal of the Knights of Labor* and the *Arkansas Gazette* indicate growth for the organization in Arkansas that year. At around the end of 1889, M. S. Richey of Cushman, a member of the Arkansas Knights of Labor State Executive Board, reorganized a local assembly in nearby Alvis (Independence County) that included women and manganese miners. During the winter and spring of 1890, the Knights chartered new local assemblies in the Arkansas towns of Sleeth (Jefferson County), Jasper (Newton County), Cushman, Mount Nebo (Yell County), Jenny Lind (Sebastian County), and Kearney (Jefferson County), and reinstated or reorganized a local assembly of miners and farmhands in the Sebastian County community of Huntington. In June a Knights of Labor newspaper, the *People's Vindicator*, began publication at Pott's Station (now Pottsville) in Pope County.[114]

At the same time that the Knights of Labor seemed to be experiencing a revival in Arkansas, the Farmers' Alliance was clearly growing in the state. At the end of March 1890 the *Arkansas Democrat* reported, "The combined forces of the Wheel and Farmers' Alliance in Arkansas give it a membership of more than 100,000."[115] Earlier in the month the *Arkansas Gazette* had noted approvingly, "The agricultural organization known as the Farmers' Alliance, which is becoming strong in Arkansas, has determined to keep out of politics."[116] In the summer of 1890, however, the Arkansas Knights of Labor and the Arkansas Farmers' Alliance jointly issued a platform of demands upon the state legislature that included the adoption of the secret ballot, a law that would mandate weekly cash payment for miners and industrial workers, an anti–child labor law, an anti–convict labor bill, antitrust legislation, and railroad regulation. The platform also made demands of Congress, including "a law providing for government control of railroads, telegraphs and the express business," the abolition of the national banking system, and the "issue of money direct[ly] to the people, which shall be full legal tender for all debts, public or private."[117]

Later that summer, Arkansas Knights of Labor State Master Workman Dan Fraser Tomson, just as he had two years before, proclaimed the Knights' political neutrality at a meeting of the State Assembly of the Arkansas Knights of Labor: "Mr. Fizer is not a representative of the Knights of Labor, and we had nothing whatever to do with his candidacy, and will certainly not ratify him as a body."[118] At this meeting of its State Assembly, the Arkansas Knights of Labor created a legislative committee to work for the passage of the demands made jointly with the Farmers' Alliance, which largely resembled those of the ULP. The Arkansas Knights chose Michael Woods of Coal Hill as the chairman of this committee, and Woods also replaced Tomson as State Master Workman. Tomson had relocated to Tuscumbia, Missouri, by this point and declined to serve another term, although he did agree to represent the Arkansas Knights at the national Knights of Labor General Assembly meeting in Denver later that year.[119]

While the Arkansas State Wheel was on its way to being absorbed by the Farmers' Alliance, the political Wheelers remained active in the campaigns of 1890. Not only did W. Scott Morgan serve as the ULP's state chairman and deliver the opening address at the party's state convention in June, but Isaac McCracken, Isom P. Langley, Reuben CarlLee, and Congressman L. P. Featherston all participated in the convention as well. In addition to Featherston seeking reelection in the First District, Langley sought the vacant Second District seat (the one that the US House of Representatives ruled to have been won by John Clayton in 1888) in both the special election to fill the seat for the remainder of the Fifty-First Congress and the election for the Fifty-Second Congress, both of which would be held on the same day in November 1890.[120]

As in 1888, Union Laborites expressed concerns about whether Arkansas voters would be accorded "a free ballot and a fair count." In May 1890, John H. Robertson stated in a letter to the *Journal of the Knights of Labor* that an Arkansas Democrat had told him, "I will never compromise with a d____d nigger one iota. If we can't beat them any other way, we will bulldoze and scare them our way." This blunt if not exactly honest man also told Robertson, "The Democrats of this State want no secret ballot now, and, as we always have the majority in the Legislature, we can keep her down."[121]

In 1890 Arkansas Democrats adopted additional measures, too, in their efforts to meet the Union Labor challenge. They placed State Wheel vice president D. E. Barker on their platform committee and co-opted much of the third-party platform, including demands regarding land reform, railroad regulation, convict labor, free school textbooks, and, ironically, the secret ballot.[122] Voters who had been in the state long enough may have remembered, however, how the Democrats had adopted Greenback-Labor Party demands only to repudiate them after the elections had passed. Before Election Day even arrived, on September 1, 1890, events occurred that indicated that this election might be reminiscent of the fraudulent, violent elections of two years earlier. On August 31, according to the *New York Times*, "The man carrying the tickets [that would be dropped into the ballot boxes] for the Union Labor and Republican Parties of Conway County [was] reported to have been attacked by armed men when he got off the train at Morrilton," just a few miles from where John Clayton had been assassinated, "and the tickets were taken from him and destroyed."[123] Like the warning that Robertson had received from an Arkansas Democrat, this despicable occurrence proved to be a sign of things to come as, in the words of historian Carl H. Moneyhon, "Once again violence and intimidation were used to ensure a Democratic victory" on Election Day.[124] Kenneth C. Barnes, who unraveled the mystery of Clayton's assassination more than a century later, concurred that "Democratic violence . . . won out in the elections in September 1890." Barnes identified Democratic deputy sheriff Oliver T. Bentley, who was involved in the slaying of Clayton, as one of the ringleaders of the attack on the man carrying the opposition tickets on the day before the election.[125] The official results of the election, as dubious as they were, indicated an even larger voter turnout than the previous record set two years earlier, with Democrat James P. Eagle defeating Fizer in a count of 106,267 votes to 85,181. In terms of percentages, this 55.5–44.5 margin was slightly larger than that of Eagle's 54.1–45.9 victory over Norwood in the previous election.[126]

In the congressional elections two months later, only three of the state's five districts were contested, in contrast to 1888 when at least two candidates ran in every district. Democratic incumbents Thomas C. McRae (who became the governor of Arkansas in 1921) and Samuel W. Peel coasted to automatic reelections in the Third and Fifth Districts, respectively. In the Fourth District, incumbent Democrat John H. Rogers did not seek reelection, and Democrat William L. Terry easily defeated the Republican E. M. Harrison. The only two real contests came in the First District, where Union

Laborite L. P. Featherston, finally having been seated in March 1890, sought reelection, and in the Second District, which was vacant following the ruling of the US House of Representatives that the late John Clayton had won the election of 1888. In this district, Democrat Clifton R. Breckenridge, who had held the seat until the ruling of the House in September 1890, ran against the political Wheeler, Knight of Labor, and Union Labor candidate Isom P. Langley in both a special election to fill the seat for the remainder of the Fifty-First Congress and a simultaneous but separate election to hold the seat in the next Congress.[127]

Although Featherston had not been seated in the US House of Representatives until eight months before his bid for reelection, he nevertheless could point to a strong record of trying to help farmers during that brief stint. He introduced several bills to provide for agricultural relief and protection of farmers' products, another "to increase the volume of money on a real estate and gold and silver basis," and another calling for the direct election of US senators, which was a demand of the ULP, the Knights of Labor, and the Southern Farmers' Alliance. He also introduced petitions on behalf of the Arkansas Farmers' Alliance and Agricultural Wheel against the passage of the Conger Lard Bill, which many southern farmers opposed, since it would have placed taxes and restrictions upon the production of vegetable oil–based lard substitutes, including those using cottonseed oil.[128] Featherston supported, not surprisingly, the Lodge Election Bill, which would have facilitated federal supervision of presidential and congressional elections; predictably, this position led Arkansas Democrats to dub him "Force Bill" Featherston.[129]

Langley also publicly supported the passage of the Lodge Election Bill and rejected the pledge made by Arkansas Democrats at their state convention that year to enact a "separate coach" law that would segregate passengers by race on railroad cars. According to a newspaper account of a speech that Langley made at a barbecue in Prairie County in August 1890, he "contended there was no necessity" for such a law, "charging that even the Democracy did not want this."[130] Between 1887 and 1890, however, four southern states—Florida, Mississippi, Texas, and Louisiana—adopted Jim Crow laws for passenger trains, and Arkansas, Alabama, Kentucky, and Georgia followed suit in 1891. In his classic study *Origins of the New South, 1877–1913*, C. Vann Woodward suggested that the passage of these laws accompanied "the decline of the reactionary regimes of the Redeemers and triumph of white democratic movements," including the Farmers' Alliance, which was "making itself felt in the legislatures of these states."[131] A later scholarly examination of the introduction and passage of the "separate coach" law in Arkansas suggests a more complicated story in which Democrats exploited the racism of many white farmers as another means of retaining control of the state government and the state's congressional seats. "Faced with a serious Republican–third party menace," wrote John William Graves, "Democratic leaders were willing to propitiate the small white farmers by yielding to their demand for segregation laws designed to 'keep the Negro in his place.'" Furthermore, "By emphasizing the race question attention could be drawn from the troublesome economic issues which were dividing the white vote."[132] A recent study similarly asserts that a variety of economic and class-related factors, rising agrarian unrest, and the challenge that the biracial third party–Republican coalition posed to Democratic rule "forced the planter/merchant/business socioeconomic class into a more segregationist position in order to elevate the standing of the white farmer and maintain Democratic Party control over Arkansas."[133]

Newspapers across the United States paid close attention to the congressional races in Arkansas's First and Second Districts. As of the end of September, Arkansas Republicans had not formally seconded the ULP's nomination of Langley. The *Chicago Tribune* warned that if Republicans did not support Langley, then his Democratic opponent Clifton R. Breckenridge "will be elected from a strong Republican district by Republican folly, instead of by ballot-box stuffing and murder as before. Langley should be elected from that district by a rousing majority as a rebuke to the worst crime ever committed in Southern Democratic politics."[134] As duly noted two days later by the *San Francisco Chronicle*, an Arkansas Republican convention gave its endorsement to Langley as Powell Clayton "made a speech in which he said the State of Arkansas would never be cleared from the stain of the murder of John M. Clayton so long as Breckinridge remains in Congress."[135] (Actually, Breckenridge was not a member of Congress at that time, having been expelled nearly one month earlier.)[136]

As in 1888, the elections in the First and Second Districts on November 4, 1890, turned out to be extremely close. On the day after the elections, the *New York Times* reported, "Returns point strongly in favor of the election of Breckenridge in the Second, and to the defeat of W.H. Cate (Dem.) in the First."[137] The *Journal of the Knights of Labor* reported the next week that "returns . . . indicate the election of Langley . . . and Featherstone [*sic*]." The reports of both newspapers proved premature, however; four weeks later the *Journal* published a letter from an anonymous (but clearly Democratic)

Knight of Labor from Van Buren, Arkansas, that said of the newspaper's earlier report, "It is a mistake, for both named gentlemen were elected to stay at home, and Hon C.R. Breckenridge and Cate were elected by the true laborers to represent them in Congress, and are men who will oppose any such measures as the McKinley Bill [a tariff increase], the Force Bill, etc., and are in favor of the Australian [secret] ballot, furnishing school books to patrons by the State at actual cost of production, and many other measures for the benefit of the whole people."[138] James Cline, the recording secretary of a Knights local assembly in Potts Station, responded with a letter to the *Journal* in which he wrote, "I hope our Van Buren brother is a true Knight, but if so he is certainly woefully misinformed." Cline called Breckenridge and Cate "positively true Bourbon or bandana Democrats" who opposed "almost every principle advocated by labor men."[139]

Unfortunately for Featherston and Langley, the letter from the Knight in Van Buren proved correct, at least insofar as the results of the elections were concerned. The official returns gave Cate an even narrower victory over Featherston in the First District than had the original returns two years earlier, while Breckenridge defeated Langley in both the special election to fill what little time remained in the Fifty-First Congress and the election for the Fifty-Second Congress by margins that were practically identical to his narrow advantage indicated by the original returns in the election between himself and John M. Clayton in 1888.[140] As in that year, violence marred the elections in these districts in 1890, and Union Laborites and Republicans once again charged with likely justification that Democrats had won through fraudulent means, but this time neither Featherston nor Langley would file a contest before the US House of Representatives. While the fate of Clayton (as well as the fact that no one had ever even been arrested for his assassination) may have influenced Featherston and Langley in making that decision, the fact that the Democratic Party took back control of the US House in the elections of 1890 probably loomed larger.[141] Even though the official returns probably slightly underestimated Featherston's and Langley's support, both men did well in counties where the Knights of Labor remained active. In four of the five counties carried by Langley and in all six carried by Featherston, the Knights either still had functioning local assemblies in 1890 or at least had them in the late 1880s.[142]

If one believes that honestly conducted, fairly counted elections, in which voters are free to vote (and candidates are free to run) without the prospect of suffering bodily harm or death are vital to democracy, then what happened in Arkansas from 1888 to 1890 must be considered a tragic travesty and an affront to the very foundations of the American republic. The means to which all too many Democrats resorted in Arkansas during those years to maintain their party's grip on power in the state amounted to something of a reverse coup d'etat, in which the ULP was kept from taking control of the governor's office through violence—even murder—and fraud. While there is no way to know for sure how the ULP would have governed Arkansas, some reasonable assumptions can be made. For an example of what might have been, one may look to another ex-Confederate state, North Carolina. In 1894 a coalition of Republicans and Populists, not unlike the Union Labor–Republican coalition in Arkansas from 1888 to 1890, captured control of the state, "engineer[ing] a virtual revolution in North Carolina politics," according to one study.[143] During the four years that this Republican-Populist coalition held power in the Tarheel State, the state legislature capped interest rates at 6 percent annually, increased spending on public education, raised taxes on railroads and businesses, and enacted what one scholar deemed "probably the fairest and most democratic election law in the post-Reconstruction South."[144] North Carolina Democrats, however, ultimately crushed this coalition in 1898 by means that were quite reminiscent of what their brethren in Arkansas had done about a decade earlier: they mounted a campaign that relied heavily on white supremacist propaganda and also used violence and intimidation to regain control of the state legislature.[145]

If it is somewhat speculative to postulate how the Union Laborites and their Republican allies would have governed Arkansas had democracy been allowed to prevail in the state in 1888 and 1890, one can more clearly state what would *not* have happened. It seems most unlikely that the Union Laborites and Republicans would have passed the "separate coach" law (which also segregated waiting rooms in train stations) in 1891, which would be followed a dozen years later by a law segregating street cars.[146] Moreover, while Arkansas Union Laborites and Republicans, quite understandably, advocated voting reforms designed to ensure a "free ballot and a fair count," the "election reform" laws that the Democratic-controlled state government would soon enact were far from what men such as Charles Norwood and Napoleon Fizer had in mind. The rules of voting in Arkansas were about to change in ways that would make the continued strength of a biracial, farmer-labor coalition practically unsustainable. Nevertheless, as the early to mid-1890s progressed, economic conditions for farmers and laborers alike, in Arkansas and across the United States, would worsen considerably, and the state's farmer-labor revolt would in some ways be reinvigorated in spite of nearly overwhelming efforts to destroy it.

V. POPULISM AND THE DEPRESSION OF THE 1890s

AFTER TWO CONSECUTIVE CAMPAIGNS IN which Arkansas Democrats defeated the Union Labor challenge by dubious, despicable means, and with the victorious party turning its attention to segregation and "election reform" laws, some of the vanquished seemed to sense that their opportunity for reform had passed. Isom P. Langley, a lifelong Arkansan who had been active in politics for nearly twenty years, left the state in early 1891 to become the pastor of a Baptist church in Poplar Bluff, Missouri.[1] More generally, many African Americans in Arkansas became disheartened by the turn of events, as one might have expected, and many who were able to leave the state began to do so. "On account of the Separate Coach bill," reported the *Arkansas Gazette* in February 1891, "it is said that 300 colored families have left Pulaski and Lonoke counties in the past two weeks for Oklahoma; four families, of Conway, have departed for Liberia, and a few from St. Francis County for Oklahoma." The report added that "about forty families" would be leaving Jefferson County if the bill became a law, which it soon did.[2] Additional reports appeared in the *Gazette* that month about African Americans leaving the state, most of them for Oklahoma, but in April the newspaper claimed that "the negro exodus from Arkansas seems to have stopped," accusing the promoters of the movement of "fraud and deception" that had proven effective because "the great mass of negroes . . . are deaf to reason."[3] In fact, however, as Kenneth C. Barnes has shown, the political violence and fraud that Democrats brought to bear during the campaigns of 1888 and 1890 and the passage of the "separate coach" law helped spark what Arkansan African Americans called "Liberia Fever"—that is, a desire to participate in the "back-to-Africa movement" by migrating there. In early 1891 "a flood" of correspondence ensued from black Arkansans to the Washington, DC, office of the American Colonization Society. "The great majority of the letters the ACS received in the early part of 1891, in fact," notes Barnes, "came from black Arkansans seeking to emigrate."[4]

Other Arkansans who had been active in the Union Labor Party (ULP), the Knights of Labor, the Agricultural Wheel, the Brothers of Freedom, and in some cases even the Greenback-Labor Party and the Grange, remained undaunted though. The ULP had died at the national level—in truth, it had scarcely ever even existed—after the presidential election of 1888, and it came to an end in Arkansas in 1891. Or it did in name at least. Since 1889 political activists in the various Farmers' Alliances (Southern, Northern, and Colored) and the Knights of Labor had been taking steps toward the formation of a new, more significant national third party. In May 1891 a convention of more than 1,400 politically minded reformers, mostly midwesterners, met at Cincinnati "in order," in the words of historian Lawrence Goodwyn, "to erect the preliminary organizational scaffolding of the new party."[5] This party, which became the People's Party (also commonly referred to as the Populist Party), would absorb the remnants of the ULP in Arkansas.[6] The Populists would have more difficulty drawing votes in Arkansas than did the ULP, however, for a variety of reasons, not the least of which were disfranchisement measures enacted by Arkansas Democrats that would prevent many of the state's poor and uneducated men from voting at all. On the other hand, the continued economic struggles of many working-class Arkansans—farmers and wage earners alike—would become even more acute when a national depression of major proportions began in 1893. This economic calamity would spark another Great Upheaval in 1894, in Arkansas and elsewhere, and it would also help to further radicalize some of the state's agrarian and labor reform advocates.

As historian John D. Hicks noted, "few southerners attended" the Cincinnati convention of 1891; according to a tabulation that appeared in an Arkansas Farmers' Alliance newspaper, only 48 of the 1,417 delegates came from ex-Confederate states. Furthermore, some southerners who were present, such as Georgia Farmers' Alliance President and Congressman L. F. Livingston, came for the express purpose of preventing the formation of a third party. Texas sent by far the largest delegation of any state of the old Confederacy with twenty-six, led by third-party supporters. Arkansas's delegation of six was dominated by third-party men: W. Scott Morgan, who in 1890 was the state Union Labor Executive Committee Chairman and who served as the secretary of the Cincinnati conference; the former Granger, Greenbacker, Agricultural Wheel gubernatorial candidate (1886), and Union Labor vice presidential candidate (1888) Charles E. Cunningham, who served as the temporary chairman of the conference; and a trio whom the conference named as Arkansas's representatives on the People's Party national executive committee: former state and national Wheel President Isaac McCracken, former Congressman L. P. Featherston, and J. O. A. Bush, a newspaper publisher and former Union Laborite who had served as the county clerk of Pike County from 1886 to 1890.[7] When a delegate from Kansas, Congressman Jerry Simpson, had Morgan read a letter from Southern Farmers' Alliance President L. L. Polk of North Carolina urging the delegates to hold off on forming a third party, "The letter was received," according to the *Cincinnati Enquirer,* "with painful silence, which was broken . . . by a delegate from Arkansas moving that 'we sit down on that communication as hard as we can.' Great applause greeted the motion."[8]

Democratic newspapers in Arkansas reacted to the news from Cincinnati with predictable condescension and ire. "In Arkansas," scoffed the *Arkansas Gazette,* "it is the old crowd, who in 1888 wore the 'Union Labor' mask while working for the Republicans, and next year will be masked as the 'People's Party.' After 1892 they will assume a new disguise."[9] The *Morrilton Pilot,* the Democratic organ of the town about six miles from where John Clayton was murdered, said of the People's Party and its Arkansas representation on the national executive committee, "It is simply a lot of disgruntled non-descripts who want office and are anything for office."[10]

What these dismissive assessments of third-party activism overlooked was the considerable economic distress of so many Arkansans. Even before the national depression that began in 1893, conditions were worsening in Arkansas. During 1891–1892, crop prices continued to drop, "dragging the value of farm production," according to one study, "to a point even below the lamented lows of the eighties." At Little Rock cotton sold for about nine cents per pound during the late 1880s, but after the harvesting of a record crop in 1891, the price fell to about seven or eight cents, while farmers selling by the end of the season received something closer to six cents per pound. Farmers in outlying areas who had to pay higher transportation costs felt the pinch even more. According to a report in a Farmers' Alliance newspaper published in the western part of the state, cotton farmers were losing 1.75 cents on every pound of cotton sold. The Farmers' Alliance made efforts to alleviate the economic hardship of its rank and file, sponsoring cooperative activities such as stores, cotton yards, and a state purchasing agency. In February 1891 the State Alliance passed a resolution calling for the repeal of the crop-lien law. The state senate actually promptly passed a law that would have enacted that repeal, but the house voted to postpone the bill indefinitely just before the legislative session ended in March.[11]

Many industrial workers in Arkansas were struggling as well. Unrest in the coal mines of western Arkansas, a frequent scene of labor strife during the 1880s, reemerged in the spring of 1891. In April the *Fort Smith Call* published a vague report of "trouble with the coal miners" and "somewhat apprehensive" mine owners. Miners had held "a secret meeting" in Fort Smith "at which delegates were present from the various mines of Arkansas and the Indian Territory [Oklahoma]." The miners heard a speaker that the newspaper described as "a sort of lecturer and agitator" from Indiana named P. H. (Phil) Penna, a representative (and later the president) of the recently organized United Mine Workers of America. Penna told the miners that the members of the UMWA "were about to go on a general strike" for a variety of demands, primarily higher wages and shorter workdays. The manager of the mines in Jenny Lind told a reporter that Penna had recently spoken there too, and he added that Penna "was an agitator and his visit could do no good."[12] Penna did not convince the Arkansas miners to join the strike, but within six weeks the *Journal of the Knights of Labor* reported that "miners are requested to stay away from Coal Hill, Ark., as there is a lockout there at present."[13] In July, a letter in the *Alliance Patriot*, which was published in Mansfield near the state's mining communities, reported that the miners of Jenny Lind were "well organized"—a Knights of Labor local assembly of miners remained active there—but "not working full time."[14]

Such problems persisted in the state's mines throughout 1891. In December, a notice in the *Journal of the Knights of Labor* warned miners to stay away from Huntington, Arkansas, reporting that while the Kansas and Texas Coal Company there was advertising for miners, "For the past four months they have not furnished employment for the men at this place. Many of the miners are in debt to the company and are unable to get anything out of the company's store."[15] Railroad workers, too, were mobilizing again. In Little Rock, members of the various railroad trade unions met in July and resolved, among other goals, to create a "general federation of all employes [*sic*] in the train service" and to give "more attention" to state legislation.[16]

Assaulting Black Civil Rights: The Cotton Pickers' Strike of 1891 and Disfranchisement

African Americans in Arkansas, meanwhile, suddenly faced segregation not only on railroad cars in 1891 but also (once again) in the farmers' movement after the Arkansas State Wheel completed its merger with the Arkansas

6. Arkansas cotton pickers. United States Resettlement Administration, Shahn, Ben, photographer. Arkansas, United States, 1935 Oct. Photograph. Retrieved from the Library of Congress, accessed March 20, 2018, https://www.loc.gov/item/2017729969/.

Farmers' Alliance in February, which meant that the Wheel no longer existed. By then, the Colored Farmers' Alliance had already made significant inroads into the state. In December 1890 Richard M. Humphrey, the white General Superintendent of the Colored Alliance, claimed the organization had twenty thousand members in the state.[17] The Colored Farmers' Alliance sometimes worked in cooperation with the National Farmers' Alliance and Industrial Union, but tensions existed between the two organizations, especially since many members of the former worked as farmhands for members of the latter. This conflict of economic interests came to a brutal head in September 1891. During that month, Humphrey issued a call for a strike of African American cotton pickers after planters in some parts of the South, including Memphis and Charleston, South Carolina, held conventions at which they decided to pay pickers no more than fifty cents per hundred pounds. When Humphrey encountered significant opposition to this proposal within the ranks of the Colored Alliance, largely on the well-founded grounds that such a strike would be dangerous, he formed a splinter group called the Cotton Pickers League to facilitate the strike. He then declared that more than one million pickers would go on strike on September 12. Historian William F. Holmes suggested, however, that in all likelihood "the majority of cotton pickers—most of whom were illiterate—never knew of the proposed strike."[18]

In most parts of the South, the strike never materialized, but in a few isolated instances it did, most notably (and tragically) in Lee County, Arkansas. The Knights of Labor had been active in Lee County from 1885 until at least as late as 1890, and while no evidence establishes that organization's involvement in the strike, it may have laid a foundation for black labor protest. An African American labor organizer from Memphis named Ben Patterson apparently started organizing efforts in Lee County in early September 1891, but local blacks soon assumed control of the movement. The results, however, proved disastrous. The Lee County strike began on September 20, and five days later strikers killed two pickers on a plantation where the pickers refused to join the strike. Three days later, strikers killed a white plantation manager. By this point, the county sheriff already had formed a posse and launched a manhunt for Patterson and other strike leaders. By the beginning of October, the strike came to a dismal conclusion, after the posse had killed fourteen strikers and Patterson. The strike also essentially destroyed the Colored Alliance, which fell into a rapid and irreversible decline.[19]

The cotton pickers' strike and its horrendous outcome could not have helped the prospects of the People's Party in Arkansas. Insofar as white Alliancemen had condemned the strike before it even began, many black voters may well have developed doubts about supporting Populist candidates.[20] Moreover, while the Colored Alliance had played a role in launching the People's Party, its rapid demise after the strike further hindered the Populists' ability to mobilize black voters. On the other hand, the ability of many African American men in Arkansas to vote at all would be restricted sharply by the state legislature in 1891—truly a calamitous year for the state's black population—along with that of many poor whites. This would become the biggest obstacle for the People's Party in Arkansas.[21]

As early as 1889, Democrats in the Arkansas state legislature had tried to pass laws that would disfranchise poor, illiterate voters. They succeeded for the first (but not the last) time in these efforts with the Election Law of 1891, which created a centralized election bureaucracy that took control of the election machinery away from local authorities and gave it to state authorities (meaning, at this time and for decades to come, Democrats). Through its imposition of a standardized, secret ballot, the law also essentially disfranchised illiterate voters, which would mean a great deal in a state where, according to the Census of 1890, 13.4 percent of white men and 55.8 percent of black men age twenty or over had not learned to read and write.[22] "Quite clearly," as one historian has noted, "the [Arkansas] General Assembly of 1891 spent its efforts in erecting the bulwarks of the political status quo rather than in tending to the problems of the rural economy."[23]

The Arkansas People's Party

After the Cincinnati conference of May 1891, leaders of the Arkansas Farmers' Alliance, which had a membership in the range of seventy-five to one hundred thousand at the time, got behind the new People's Party. Just weeks after that conference, Arkansas State Alliance President Paul T. Davidson of Hollywood (Clark County) told the press, "We are for the People's Party. There is no use trying either of the old parties any further." Davidson explained that neither the Democrats nor the Republicans would grant the joint Alliance–Knights of Labor demands put forth at St. Louis in 1889, and he boldly added, "Enough of our members will support the new party to carry the state in 1892."[24] In July 1891, however, William Fishback, who would be the Democratic candidate for governor the next year, declared, "Every demand of the Alliance except two is Democratic to the core and it should not be difficult to convince sensible, honorable men that these two are . . . inconsistent with their fundamental doctrine . . . [of] 'equal justice to all, special privileges to none.'" The two Farmers' Alliance demands that Fishback criticized were the railroad plank, which called for either "government control and supervision" or "the government ownership" of the "means of communication and transportation," which meant the telegraph and fairly new telephone industries as well as the railroad industry, and the subtreasury plan. This proposal called for the federal government to build warehouses in heavily agricultural counties in which farmers could store excess nonperishable crops, allowing them to sell the crops later at higher prices rather than glutting the market at harvesttime. The subtreasury plan also called for the federal government to loan farmers 80 percent of the local market price for their crops upon storage at an annual interest rate of 1 percent.[25]

Many Alliancemen clearly did not agree with Fishback's pronouncements about the Democratic Party's affinity for the demands of their organization. Not only did Davidson openly support the People's Party, but the secretary of the State Alliance was Jasper W. Dollison, the former Union Labor state legislator who by this point had been appointed by President Benjamin Harrison as a federal revenue collector. By the time that the presidential campaign of 1892 got underway, Dollison was serving as the Arkansas member of the

People's Party national committee.[26] During a three-day meeting in August 1891, the State Alliance chose three delegates to the next meeting of the Supreme Council of the National Farmers' Alliance and Industrial Union, which would meet in Indianapolis four months later: former Union Labor Congressman L. P. Featherston of St. Francis County, State Alliance Vice President P. L. Montgomery of Washington County, and W. B. W. Heartsill of Sebastian County. In 1892 Montgomery would run for the state senate and Heartsill for the US House of Representatives as Populists.[27]

Just as some Arkansas Wheelers had opposed independent or third-party political activity during the period from the mid-1880s through 1890, however, so too did some Arkansas Alliancemen oppose supporting the People's Party. The increasing ties between the State Alliance and the third party contributed to the decline of the former's membership to about fifty-five thousand by the spring of 1892. Nevertheless, the Farmers' Alliance supplied all six Arkansas delegates to the St. Louis conference that met on Washington's Birthday (a favorite date for conferences among Gilded Age reformers) in 1892 where the People's Party was officially launched: Davidson, Featherston, Homer Prince, J. B. Suttler, D. E. Barker, and the ubiquitous Charles E. Cunningham, whose third-party activism in Arkansas stretched back to his involvement in the Grange and the Greenback-Labor Party. All of these delegates were white men, but the Arkansas delegation to the Populist nominating convention in Omaha in July 1892 included a woman and a black man.[28]

The Arkansas People's Party held its first state convention in Little Rock on June 21, 1892. Fifty-two of the state's seventy-five counties sent delegates. Most of the counties that did not send a delegate were located in the east Arkansas Delta or south Arkansas lowlands, regions where African Americans were prevalent, or in the interior counties of the Ozarks Mountains, where African Americans were not as common but Republicans nevertheless were. Virtually all of the state's Farmers' Alliance leaders came to the convention, and known members of the Knights of Labor in attendance included Isaac McCracken, Jasper W. Dollison, J. B. Suttler, Thomas Fletcher, and the Knights' State Secretary-Treasurer, John H. Robertson. Former Union Labor Congressman L. P. Featherston called the convention to order. Another old political Wheeler, Reuben CarlLee, was there, as was the ULP's gubernatorial candidate of 1890, Napoleon Bonaparte Fizer. Not surprisingly, then, the convention produced a platform much like that of the ULP, but with some additions. In keeping with demands made by the most recent session of the Arkansas Knights of Labor, the Populists called for the "the replacement of the 'barbarous' convict lease system by a penitentiary farm, and the employment of surplus prison labor in maintaining the public roads." The platform also contained an antilynching plank introduced by an African American delegate, I. N. Glasby. The Democratic *Arkadelphia Herald* would soon denounce this plank as "that celebrated nigger plank, offering him protection from the wrath of indignant white communities whose wives and daughters he may choose to outrage." The Populist platform also denounced the Election Law of 1891 as "but a servile imitation of the Lodge Force Bill." In addition, the Populists condemned a poll tax that voters would be deciding on that fall, another effort on the part of Arkansas Democrats to disfranchise the state's most impoverished men.[29]

About two weeks after the state Populist convention, and as the national Populist convention was beginning in Omaha, the Knights of Labor and the Farmers' Alliance held a joint picnic in Cushman (Independence County), which, according to Arkansas Knights stalwart M. S. Richey, "was attended by a large concourse of people." Featured speakers at the picnic included John H. Robertson, who extolled upon "the origin, progress and principles of the Knights of Labor," and D. B. Mayfield, who explained "the principles of the Farmers' Alliance." Two Populist political candidates also spoke: the Rev. T. M. C. Birmingham, who ran for Congress in the state's Fourth District that year, and A. A. Steele of Sharp County, who ran for state auditor.[30]

The joint picnic was more than just symbolic; clearly, Arkansas People's Party leaders hoped for and even expected support from laborers as well as struggling farmers. Before returning to Arkansas from the St. Louis conference in February 1892, the state's delegates began planning for the congressional races that fall. Reapportionment following the Census of 1890 gave Arkansas another district—six instead of five—which of course necessitated redrawing the districts. For the contest in the Second District, now farther to the west than when John Clayton had been robbed both of victory and his life during 1888–1889, the Arkansas Populists at St. Louis chose W. B. W. Heartsill from the mining and farming community of Greenwood as their candidate. One month later, J. B. Suttler, one of the state's Populist leaders, advised Heartsill to "see that the workingmen of the towns (like Ft Smith) have representation on your county ticket. We must unify all of the laboring element and the day is our own."[31] A veteran of the Brothers of Freedom, the Agricultural Wheel, and the Farmers' Alliance, Heartsill had joined a new Knights of Labor local assembly in Greenwood about two weeks before Suttler urged him to cultivate labor support, and he already had ties with labor groups. In 1890, a Little Rock printer (and Republican) named Horace

Addis, claiming to be speaking on behalf of not only himself but also other trade unionists in the city, wrote a letter to Heartsill urging him to run as an independent Democratic or Alliance congressional candidate.[32]

Labor, Populism, and the Elections of 1892

While the Knights of Labor had clearly passed its peak in Arkansas (as in the nation) by 1892, the Arkansas labor movement nevertheless showed more signs of activity, as well as discontent, in any year since the Great Upheaval of six years earlier. On June 7, 1892, about seventy-five delegates met in Little Rock for a state labor convention. The object of the convention, according to a report in the *Arkansas Gazette*, was "to locate a place to celebrate Labor Day and to influence legislation by the drafting of bills to be presented to the State Legislature in January next." Apparently all of the delegates came from Pulaski County or Hot Springs or Pine Bluff. Only one Knights of Labor local assembly, from Argenta (just north of Little Rock), sent any delegates. From the Farmers' Alliance came delegates from a local chapter in Pulaski County, Mount Pleasant Farmers' Alliance No. 401, and from the County Alliance of Pulaski. Most of the other delegates came from trade unions of the type affiliated with the American Federation of Labor, the organization that was challenging (and, in cities at least, surpassing) the Knights for leadership of the American labor movement. For example, two Carpenters' Union locals from Little Rock sent delegates, as did a Tailors' Union local and a Stone Masons' Union local. Other unions represented, from Hot Springs and Pine Bluff, included the Painters' Union, the Sheet Iron and Cornice Workers' Trades and Labor Council, the International Order of Machinists, and the Boiler Makers' Union.[33]

The State Labor Convention met for two days and reiterated the demands of the Knights of Labor regarding the abolition of the convict-lease system and of the Farmers' Alliance regarding the repeal of the crop-lien law. The convention chose Hot Springs as the site of its planned Labor Day celebration, and its committee on legislation resolved that labor unions should "support as candidates for the Legislature only such men as pledge themselves to aid in securing the legislation asked for by this convention." The committee on legislation also "denounce[d] all mob law [lynchings] as a disgrace to the State and the age." Just before the convention adjourned, Chairman E. M. Ford of the Carpenters' Council of Little Rock appointed a committee of delegates from that city to "take steps to form a Ladies' Council among the various unions of the city." On the first day of the convention, Governor James P. Eagle, "being present by invitation, made a short and appropriate address." On the second day, following the report of the committee on legislation, J. B. Suttler and Thomas Fletcher, both of whom were Alliancemen, Knights of Labor, and leaders of the People's Party, addressed the convention by invitation.[34]

Throughout the spring and summer of 1892, the *Journal of the Knights of Labor* published reports and letters from Arkansas that provided compelling evidence of the mounting problems and militancy of many of the state's laborers. Even though railroad workers and miners did not send representatives to the State Labor Convention, they had been the most militant workers in the state since the mid-1880s, and their absence at the convention certainly did not indicate a diminishment of union activity among either group. During the summer, five hundred shopmen of the Cotton Belt Railroad at Pine Bluff went on strike over the firing of one of their coworkers, and they succeeded in getting him reinstated.[35] At the end of September, the *Journal* reported that "the striking switchmen on the Texas and Arkansas Branch of the Iron Mountain Railway at Van Buren, Ark., have returned to work, their demands having been granted." The same issue also reported that the brakemen on the Arkansas Valley Branch of the Iron Mountain had gone on strike in response to the company's decree that freight trains run with two brakemen, instead of three. "The engineers, firemen and conductors have promised to stand by them," the *Journal* added.[36] Within weeks, according to the *Arkansas Gazette*, a "temporary settlement . . . granted the [brakemen] all their demands."[37]

At the same time, Arkansas miners bemoaned "scarce" work and "low" wages. Miners played a dominant role at the eighth annual session of the State Assembly of the Arkansas Knights of Labor at Little Rock in September 1892: Ed Harn and Henry Flowerseed of Jenny Lind were both elected to the State Executive Board—the former as State Master Workman—along with a Knight from Cushman, where one of the local assemblies consisted of manganese miners. The State Assembly chose another Knight from Cushman, Arkansas Knights of Labor stalwart M. S. Richey, as its delegate to that year's General Assembly session in St. Louis. Railroad workers did not go unrepresented at the Arkansas Knights of Labor State Assembly session; after the session closed on its second day, the Knights held an open meeting featuring three speakers: Harn, J. B. Suttler, and the leader of the Southwest railroad strike of 1886, Martin Irons.[38]

Yet if Arkansas Populists had reason to feel optimistic about support from organized labor, they also faced formidable obstacles. First, unlike the ULP in the previous two state elections, the Populists would not receive the endorsement of the Republican Party. The GOP nominated its own state candidates in 1892, including former Little Rock mayor William G. Whipple for governor. The *Faulkner County Wheel*, a newspaper whose name was by now an anachronism, sardonically commented that "the [state] Democratic committee will doubtlessly pay them well for the privilege of using their names as Republican candidates," predicting that "when [President Benjamin] Harrison is reelected he will appoint these martyrs to fill the post offices in this state." The Populists also faced competition from another new party, the Prohibition Party, which nominated William J. Nelson for governor.[39] Furthermore, the Populists proved unable to provide significant campaign funds for their candidates. J. B. Suttler admitted that W. B. W. Heartsill's congressional campaign was a "pauper campaign" and apologized that the party could not provide him with more money. When Suttler managed to come through with $8.50 in campaign funds, he tried to rally Hearstill: "Now, old man, you must hump yourself and make a stiff fight."[40]

The biggest problem facing both the Populists and Republicans in Arkansas in 1892, however, can be summarized in one word: disfranchisement. Democrat William M. Fishback won the governorship with 57.7 percent of the votes, a higher percentage than the victorious Democratic candidate officially received in the three previous elections, and after the results were in, the state People's Party chairman told Populist presidential candidate James B. Weaver that fifty thousand voters had been disfranchised by the Election Law of 1891. In fact, thirty-six thousand fewer voters cast ballots in the state elections of 1892 than two years earlier, but even that level of disfranchisement undermined opposition to the Democratic Party.[41]

The Populist candidate in the gubernatorial election of 1892, J. P. Carnahan, hailed from Washington County, one of the state's Farmers' Alliance strongholds. Carnahan failed to carry even that county, however; statewide he finished third with 19.9 percent of the vote, winning in only three counties in southwestern Arkansas: Polk, Clark, and Nevada, a center of third-party strength throughout the Greenback-to-Populist era.[42] Populist candidates won only nine of the 100 seats in the state house of representatives (including at least one Knight of Labor in Crawford County) and no state senate seats, although two of the 32 state senators were men who had been elected in 1890 as Union Laborites whose seats were not on the ballot in 1892.[43] In the congressional elections of 1892, the Arkansas Republican and Populist parties agreed (as had the Republicans and Union Laborites in the two previous elections) not to compete with each other. The Republicans only ran a candidate in the First District while Populists ran in the rest of the state's six districts. The best that any challenger to Democrats did was the 42.8 percent of the vote received by Populist J. E. Bryan, state Farmers' Alliance lecturer, in the Fifth, which consisted of counties in the north-central and northwestern parts of the state. No other non-Democratic candidate managed even to reach 40 percent.[44]

As bad as the Arkansas elections of 1892 were for the People's Party, they were even worse for African Americans. In Calhoun County, where racial tensions had been simmering for weeks before the state election day, four black men who could not vote under the new law showed up armed at the polling place in Hampton determined to do so. Officials responded with force, killing at least four. The results of the elections across the state clearly revealed the decimation of black political power. "By 1893," according to Carl H. Moneyhon, "all blacks had disappeared from the legislature, and they virtually vanished from local offices as well."[45] (Five black state legislators finished their terms in 1893, but not until eight decades later would any more be elected.) Furthermore, men who were able to participate in the state elections of 1892 voted on the ratification of a poll tax that the legislature had passed as a state constitutional amendment. According to the official results, 75,847 Arkansans voted to approve the poll tax while 56,589 voted against it. Consequently, the state elections of 1894 would tally the lowest voter turnout in fourteen years, to the detriment of African Americans and the People's Party.[46]

The Panic of 1893 and Another Great Upheaval

By 1893 the Knights of Labor, the Farmers' Alliance, and the People's Party all appeared to be on the wane in Arkansas, although the Knights and the Alliance were in decline just about everywhere else, too.[47] Then during the spring and summer of 1893, disaster struck and, paradoxically, gave renewed hope to the leaders of these reform organizations—who, to some extent, were the same group of men—while causing significant hardship in Arkansas and the rest of the nation. The calamity that became known as the Panic of 1893 began in May; on the fourth of that month one of the nation's largest corporations, the National Cordage Company, announced its fall into receivership. The next day the stock market crashed. As banks collapsed and several major railroads went bankrupt, the stock market fell sharply again in late July. Before 1893 ended, as many as sixteen thousand businesses went under, along with more than five hundred banks. Unemployment reached a rate of about

20 percent. As banks and industries collapsed, agricultural prices continued what by then was an ongoing decline.[48]

In Arkansas, where unemployment and falling crop prices already had been problems before the national depression began, the Panic of 1893 hit particularly hard. Cotton prices had risen slightly in late 1892, but they began falling again in 1893, down to 7.0 cents per pound by December 1893 and 4.6 cents by December 1894, below the break-even point and at their lowest level since the Civil War.[49] During the spring of 1893, miners struck at Spadra and took to posting notices "warning new men against accepting employment in the mines." When someone persisted in tearing down these notices, assassins killed the suspected culprit, a pit boss by the surname of Ingle. Police subsequently arrested two miners for the crime after using bloodhounds. By then, the strike had spread to Coal Hill.[50] Meanwhile, former Populist congressional candidate W. B. W. Heartsill became involved in a protracted dispute between the Knights of Labor and a succession of mine owners after a mine in Greenwood closed just before Christmas in 1892 without paying the miners. In this case the Knights resorted to a blacklist against the mine, posting notices not just locally but in the *Journal of the Knights of Labor* as well.[51] In July 1893 a state convention of miners met at Fort Smith, where those present resolved to strike in support of striking Kansas miners if called upon to do so.[52] Miners, of course, were not the only workers in Arkansas contending with hard times; in October, Knight of Labor William Murray of Hot Springs informed Heartsill (who by then was the organization's State Master Workman) that while the state's oldest local assembly, Hot Springs Assembly 2419, was still alive, "The prospect here is very gloomy. Work is in a maner [*sic*] played out and money is a thing of the past."[53] In February 1894 John H. Robertson told Heartsill that "there is near two thousand idle" in Little Rock, the population of which was just over twenty-five thousand in 1890, although he did report minor growth for the Knights of Labor there in the midst of this crisis.[54]

As the depression worsened in 1894, a third Great Upheaval of the Gilded Age would strike Arkansas and the nation. Leading the working-class revolt would be two groups of workers who already had been involved in labor turmoil in Arkansas in recent years: coal miners and railroad employees. In early April 1894, miners struck in Coal Hill and the Franklin County community of Denning in response to a 10 percent wage cut, as did their cohorts in several communities in Indian Territory (present-day Oklahoma).[55] As many other American miners faced larger wage cuts, the UMWA declared a strike—called a "suspension" by the union—on April 21. Some 125,000 miners in the United States and Canada heeded the call, including many in areas where, according to historian Jeremy Brecher, the UMWA "had no organization whatever." The union's membership did not exceed 20,000, but more than 125,000 miners stopped working. By the summer the strike had ended in failure, in part because, as Brecher notes, "The militia was called out in at least five states."[56] Arkansas, where the number of strikers grew to about 1,400, was not one of those states, but the strike still ended after thirty days in defeat for the miners, who, according to the Arkansas Bureau of Mines, Manufactures, and Agriculture, incurred "a direct loss of $100,000 in wages."[57] Miners at Jenny Lind remained on strike longer than elsewhere in the state, but they went back to work in June.[58]

On the heels of the miners' strike, however, came another even larger strike. The Pullman Strike of 1894 began in May when members of the American Railway Union (ARU) walked off the job at the Pullman Palace Car Company in response to severe wage cuts that were not accompanied by reductions in dividends and rental rates in the company-owned worker housing just outside of Chicago. To the consternation of ARU leader Eugene V. Debs, the executive committee of the union, which happened to be holding its first national convention in Chicago less than a month after the strike began, called upon ARU members across the nation to refuse to service trains carrying Pullman cars. This "boycott" began on June 26 and spread rapidly, soon encompassing 260,000 workers, nearly half of whom did not belong to the ARU, across twenty-seven states and territories. In Little Rock, strikers rioted when railroad officials began employing strikebreakers and, according to Missouri Pacific Railway attorneys, the strike interfered with mail delivery. Interference with mail delivery throughout much of the nation facilitated the use of federal force by President Grover Cleveland and Attorney General Richard Olney, a longtime railroad attorney who still served as a director of several railroad companies. On the Fourth of July, twelve thousand troops entered Chicago. The mayhem and warfare that followed claimed thirteen lives and left fifty-three people seriously wounded. In Arkansas, many railroad workers were members of the ARU, and the usually conservative *Arkansas Gazette* seemed to absolve them of blame for the strike in declaring, "There is no patriotism in Mr. Pullman nor any justice in his method of treating his men." As the strike dragged on, the newspaper said that merchants in Little Rock were losing money "because Pullman refuses to listen to a demand for arbitration with his employes [*sic*]."[59]

The sympathetic pronouncements of the *Gazette* notwithstanding, the Pullman strike would be crushed in Arkansas by the same method, albeit with much less bloodshed, as in Chicago. Governor Fishback sent state militiamen to Little Rock and Fort Smith. The Cleveland administration also sent federal marshals to the state, and in Little Rock Special Deputy Marshal R. L. Pate of Plumerville, Arkansas, "was accidentally [and fatally] shot in the head by a pistol dropped from the scabbard of another deputy." Not surprisingly, the strike collapsed—and with it, for all intents and purposes, the ARU—in the face of such governmental force.[60]

In terms of immediate results, the Great Upheaval of 1894 seemed to be an exercise in futility. The dismal conclusions of the miners' and railroad strikes certainly support such an appraisal, and the Coxey's Army march of unemployed laborers to Washington, DC, that spring in search of relief failed to bring any. Yet these efforts left a significant legacy for workers. In the case of Coxey's Army, the public works program for road building that Jacob Coxey and his followers advocated would be implemented along with many others four decades later during the New Deal.[61] The railroad labor battles converted Debs (who spent six months in jail following the Pullman strike for conspiring to obstruct interstate commerce) into a Socialist, and in 1897 the ARU would morph into the Social Democracy of America. Although short-lived, this organization helped launch the Socialist Party, which in Arkansas and other states would attract support from some leaders, as well as rank-and-file members, of the farmer and labor organizations of the Gilded Age.[62] In Arkansas, the miners' struggles had a similar effect. George E. Mikel, a miner and member of Knights of Labor LA 239 in Greenwood, later became a leader of the Arkansas UMWA and a Socialist candidate for governor. Journalist, lawyer, and Allianceman Dan Hogan, also of Sebastian County, had urged miners not to strike but nevertheless was sympathetic; in the years that followed, he would provide legal defense to miners on numerous occasions and would also run for governor (three times) as a Socialist. Sebastian County would be one of the state's Socialist strongholds in the early twentieth century.[63]

In the meantime, however, in 1894 Arkansas People's Party leaders hoped to capitalize on the depression and labor strife. After the state legislature passed a law in 1893 that was intended to abolish the convict-lease system but in fact, according to one careful analysis, "merely substituted a contract leasing system which continued most of the undesirable features of pure leasing," the Arkansas Populist platform of 1894 called upon the state to make further reforms. The platform also called for a state board of arbitration that would settle disputes between corporations and their employees and for vagrancy laws to be "amended so as to prevent the prosecution of industrious laboring men while in a condition of enforced idleness."[64]

In some parts of the state, the strikes and hard times seemed, indeed, to be strengthening alliances between the Populists and the Knights of Labor. In Sebastian County, a Knights local assembly of miners and farmers in Huntington passed a resolution in January 1894 condemning Democratic congressman Clifton R. Breckenridge for his opposition to two Populist demands, the graduated income tax and the free coinage of silver.[65] In April, just after the miners in that county went on strike, members of the Knights of Labor attended the People's Party county convention. One of the Knights at the convention, the recording secretary of a local assembly of miners in Jenny Lind, reported that "every intelligent farmer and miner is strictly in line and means business." About two weeks later, as the strike continued, the Knights held an open meeting at Jenny Lind, at which Populists W. B. W. Heartsill and John H. Robertson (the Knights' State Master Workman and State Secretary-Treasurer, respectively) spoke. Heartsill denounced antilabor judges and the financial policies of the Cleveland administration.[66] At the beginning of May, the Knights' State Worthy Foreman, Charles T. Foster of Eureka Springs, told Heartsill, "Taxes are paid and it has absolutely drained the county of money. . . . Deep and bitter are the curses of the men who voted for (hush, whisper it) Cleveland." Foster added, "We are organizing P.P. [People's Party] Clubs all over [Carroll] county." Here, it will be recalled, an independent ticket jointly nominated by the Agricultural Wheel and the Knights of Labor won control of the county offices eight years earlier. Nevertheless, Foster sounded a note of pessimism in his letter to Heartsill, musing, "I have tried to believe that we could bring about this revolution at the ballot box—do you think I will have to abandon this position and hunt for a cartridge box?"[67]

Foster's doubts proved well-founded. The Knights of Labor no longer possessed the clout that it had during its heyday, with only thirty-three local assemblies still in existence in the state (of which fourteen had been suspended for being in arrears on money owed to the Knights' State Assembly), about one-third of the number that existed during the latter half of the 1880s.[68] Even more significantly, the disfranchisement measures put in place by the Election Law of 1891 and the first application of the poll tax that voters approved in 1892 kept many black men and poor white men from voting in the state elections in September 1894. According to historian J. Morgan Kousser, white voter turnout in gubernatorial elections in the state dropped from 75 percent in 1890 to 68 percent in 1892 and then to 56 percent in 1894. Black voter turnout fell much more sharply during those same contests, from 71 to 39 to 24 percent.[69] In the governor's race in 1894, Democrat James P. Clarke won with 59.1 percent of the ballots, the highest percentage received by any candidate since former State Grange Worthy Master Simon P. Hughes a decade earlier. Populist D. E. Barker, the former State Wheel Vice President who had served on the Arkansas Democrats' platform committee in 1890, finished third with 19.1 percent of the vote. The Populists won nine seats in the state house of representatives, as they had two years earlier, but the party lost its two seats in the state senate.[70]

The Populists fared poorly in the congressional races as well. The party nominated candidates in four of the state's six congressional districts, but one of them—J. A. Norris from (ironically) the Populist stronghold of Polk County—withdrew before Election Day. None of the three Populist candidates who stayed in the race received more than 17.6 percent of the vote. As one historian has noted, "The People's Party showing in Arkansas was one of the least impressive of the region."[71] Unlike in other southern states, the true "Populist moment" in Arkansas, to borrow a phrase from historian Lawrence Goodwyn, was the era of the ULP (1888–1890).[72] Democrats' violent and fraudulent defeat of the ULP, followed by the Election Law of 1891, ended that moment in Arkansas, and the ratification of the poll tax in 1892 put the last nail in the third-party movement's coffin.

The Demise of the Knights of Labor and Populism

The Farmers' Alliance and the Knights of Labor proceeded along the same downward trajectory as did the third party. In the summer of 1894, John H. Robertson informed W. B. W. Heartsill that "the Alliance is losing ground in many places."[73] During the first half of 1895, the Knights of Labor appeared to be actually gaining some ground in Arkansas: Robertson reported that the lone remaining local assembly in Little Rock "is on the increase," and the Knights chartered new locals at Springdale and Newport while also reorganizing a lapsed local at Cushman.[74] By late August, however, Robertson told State Master Workman Heartsill that "we are holding our S.A. [State Assembly] charter under dispensation, having only eight locals in actual good standing with the G.A. [General Assembly]." The local assembly chartered in Springdale in January had apparently already ceased to exist by then, and

7. James R. Sovereign, General Master Workman of the Knights of Labor. 1894. From John Swinton, *A Momentous Question: The Respective Attitudes of Labor and Capital* (Philadelphia: Keller Publishing, 1895), 87.

while Heartsill's Greenwood Assembly No. 239 still existed, it was behind on its dues to the State Assembly and therefore not in good standing.[75] By mid-October, the Greenwood Assembly had disbanded.[76] On the other hand, when the Arkansas State Assembly of the Knights of Labor held its annual session in Little Rock in September 1895, "forty or more delegates" attended, according to the *Arkansas Gazette*, more than double the total of sixteen that met there for that meeting three years earlier during a campaign season. With Heartsill's local assembly disintegrating, the delegates chose Charles T. Foster of Eureka Springs as the new State Master Workman. Robertson retained the position of State Secretary-Treasurer.[77]

Ironically, as the farmer and labor reform movements in Arkansas stood at a low ebb, a reform leader of national prominence came to the state. In late 1895 James R. Sovereign, who had replaced Terence V. Powderly as the General Master Workman of the Knights of Labor two years earlier, moved from Iowa to Benton County. Despite the fact that he had drawn upon the support of eastern Socialists, such as Daniel DeLeon of New York, in replacing Powderly, Sovereign was, in the words of historian Bruce Laurie, a "Populist stalwart," and he would serve as an important Populist leader in Arkansas and nationally in 1896.[78] Sovereign had visited Arkansas in late July 1895 "looking," according to a newspaper report, "for desirable locations for such laboring men as want to abandon the trades and take up fruit and farm lands." The report added that Sovereign "has an idea that Arkansas offers superior advantages to agriculturalists."[79] He apparently liked what he saw; while his visit did not herald an influx of Knights of Labor into the state to take up fruit farming, the General Master Workman himself established an apple farm at Sulphur Springs and built a natural cold storage cave, although the continuation of his duties at the helm of the Order meant that the amount of time that he spent on his farm was limited.[80]

Sovereign became active in the Arkansas People's Party by the summer of 1896 and served on the Populist national executive committee that year as well. He also established a Bryan Free Silver Campaign Labor Bureau in Chicago.[81] In a campaign in which economic concerns were particularly paramount—the depression that began in 1893 was still ongoing—the Republicans nominated former Congressman William McKinley of Ohio, while the Democrats and subsequently the Populists nominated former Congressman William Jennings Bryan of Nebraska. (The Democrats and Populists differed in their nominees for vice president, with the former choosing Maine shipbuilder and banker Arthur Sewall and the latter choosing Tom

Watson, a former congressman and leader of the Georgia Populists.) The election of 1896 would become known as "the battle of the standards," with Republicans favoring the gold standard and Democrats and Populists supporting bimetallism or, in the parlance of the Populists, "free silver," which many hard-pressed farmers saw as an economic panacea that would make credit easier and cheaper and the prices of agricultural products higher. Bryan, notes historian Gretchen Ritter, "was a candidate on whom many pinned their hopes for the final success of a producers' alliance in America." McKinley smashed these hopes, however, even as Bryan carried every state in the former Confederacy as well as most states west of the Mississippi River. McKinley's campaign raised more than ten times the $300,000 raised by Bryan's, and the election could be seen as representing the triumph of big business, banking, and industry over farmers, producerism, and antimonopolism.[82]

In Arkansas and elsewhere in the South, many Populists viewed fusion with the Democrats, the party that many of them had turned their backs upon in the first place, as a betrayal and an outrage. African American Populists in particular protested their party's endorsement of Bryan. Leading Arkansas Populists could be found, however, in both camps: fusionists and "middle-of-the-roaders" who preferred a straight Populist ticket. Arkansas Populists who favored the endorsement of Bryan at the Populists' national convention in St. Louis included Sovereign and the veteran third-party men Reuben CarlLee and Charles M. Norwood. Among those who argued against the endorsement of the Democratic Party's candidate were W. Scott Morgan, former ULP legislator and Knights of Labor District Master Workman Jasper W. Dollison, and former Populist congressional candidate and State Farmers' Alliance Lecturer J. E. Bryan. Morgan, according to one account, "argued that a Populist endorsement of Bryan would surrender Populist identity and hinder local fights, which could not be made on such inconsistent ground." Some of the Arkansas Populists who favored the endorsement of Bryan, however, also insisted that the party should nominate, as Norwood put it, a "true Populist" for vice president.[83] Sovereign, in fact, delivered a speech at St. Louis that seconded the nomination of Watson for vice president. In doing so, Sovereign outraged Arkansas Democrats who had expected him to support the Populists' endorsement of Sewall as well as Bryan, and he also drew the ire of W. Scott Morgan, who in the months following the presidential election denounced the Knights of Labor leader as "the greatest political fakir in this country just now" and as a "Jumping Jack for the Democratic Party."[84]

Bryan received all eight of Arkansas's electoral votes in the election of 1896, while the fusion arrangement between the state's Democratic and Populist parties resulted in five electoral votes for Sewall and three for Watson. Sovereign occupied one of the Populist slots on the fusion electoral ticket, even though press reports revealed shortly before the election that he had failed to pay the state poll tax and it was "now too late to rectify the matter before election day."[85] Nevertheless, Sovereign cast his electoral votes for Bryan and Watson in January 1897, although in a letter to national People's Party chairman Marion Butler, he expressed as low an opinion of middle-of-the-road Populists as Morgan would of Sovereign: "I have conclusive evidence [which he did not provide in the letter] which convinces me that many of the so-called 'middle-of-the-road' leaders were simply 'middle-of-the-road' supporters of McKinley and the money power."[86] Neither Morgan's past nor future career, however, would support such an assessment of him. On the other hand, according to John H. Robertson, who was one of eight Arkansas Knights of Labor members at the Populists' St. Louis convention of 1896 (along with Sovereign and, among others, Dollison and McCracken), "Had it not been for the K. of L. in the St. Louis convention, Tom Watson would never have been nominated, had it not been for the K. of L. (and Louisiana was the only delegation that did not have K. of L. in it), Sewall would have been endorsed."[87]

Held two months before national Election Day, the Arkansas state elections of 1896 proved to be anticlimactic as far as the Populists were concerned. The party's fusion with Democrats at the national level could not have been helpful in mobilizing the Populist vote for these contests. Moreover, the Arkansas Democratic Party, like its counterparts in many other southern and western states, had adopted the "free silver" doctrine. Democratic gubernatorial nominee Daniel Webster Jones, an attorney, had lobbied before the state legislature in 1895 for the Iron Mountain Railroad in opposition to a proposed railroad commission bill, but in 1896 he proclaimed himself a champion of free silver and a state railroad commission. The Populists nominated former Democratic state legislator A. W. Files of Little Rock, but he was not their first choice. W. Scott Morgan, among others, had declined the nomination. A Texas newspaper reported "strong sentiment" among Arkansas Populists in favor of endorsing Jones, and the election was only one month away by the time Files accepted the nomination. He made little effort at campaigning, and he finished a distant third place (last) in the election with only 9.9 percent of the vote. The party's only nominee for state office, Files carried only one county, the third-party stronghold of Polk. There the Knights of Labor remained active and closely involved with the People's Party, which controlled the county offices. The Populists managed to elect a state senator from Nevada County, a bastion of third-party strength since the Greenback-Labor era, and eleven state representatives from nine counties, but for the first time in more than a decade there would be no third-party candidates in the Arkansas elections for the US House of Representatives, which Democrats easily swept.[88]

The elections of 1896 essentially marked the end of the Arkansas People's Party. (The same could be said for the national party as well.) The Populists nominated Morgan for governor in 1898 and Files again in 1900, but they did not even fare as well as Files had in 1896. Economic recovery from the depression in 1897 did not help the party's prospects, but its fate was probably already sealed. The Farmers' Alliance deteriorated too. By the end of 1900, Arkansas newspapers referred to the Alliance in the past tense.[89]

The Knights of Labor managed to hang on in Arkansas into the dawn of the twentieth century, but barely. In 1900, General Secretary-Treasurer John W. Hayes reported the reorganization of District Assembly 22, "very largely composed of the lumber industry, covering a portion of Alabama, Mississippi and Arkansas."[90] The Arkansas Knights of Labor State Assembly met at least as late as 1906, but it had become a mere shell of its former self.[91] The Arkansas Knights never sent a delegate to a national General Assembly meeting after 1896, even though those meetings continued until at least 1913.[92] Even the return of Dan Fraser Tomson, who had organized some three hundred local assemblies in the region, to Arkansas in 1895 could not stop the Order's decline. Nor for that matter did General Master Workman Sovereign's arrival in the state during that year. In 1898 the Arkansas Knights of Labor named the legendary Southwestern strike leader Martin Irons as State Master Workman, but despite the brief flurry of press coverage that his appointment drew, he too failed to reverse the downward trend. Even though Sovereign and Irons received more publicity, the person who did the most to keep the Knights alive and at least somewhat viable in Arkansas during much of the 1890s was John H. Robertson, who around 1898 left first for Missouri and then Kansas, where he campaigned for Bryan's second bid for the presidency. In Little Rock, once a Knights stronghold of the state and region, the last local assembly had disbanded by 1899. By then Sovereign was gone too; his reign as General Master Workman ended in November 1897, and in 1898 the Arkansas Populist state convention ended his tenure as a member of the party's national committee. By the summer of 1899 he was in Idaho, editing and publishing a newspaper and investigating the labor troubles in the Coeur d'Alene mining district.[93]

As the nineteenth century closed, then, so too did an era of farmer and labor protest in Arkansas. The organizations that had led those protest movements since 1882—the Brothers of Freedom, the Agricultural Wheel, the Knights of Labor, the Farmers' Alliance, the Colored Farmers' Alliance, the ULP, and the People's Party—were either gone or on the verge of disintegrating. Other organizations of farmers and laborers would follow in Arkansas; some, such as the UMWA, were already making inroads in the state before 1900.[94] With some exceptions, though, these organizations would generally display less radicalism and egalitarianism than had the Wheel and the Knights. Moreover, with the demise of the People's Party came the end of two decades of third-party protest and the last best chance to break one-party dominance in the state until the 1960s. Yet the legacy of Arkansas's Gilded Age farmer and labor protest movements would endure well into the twentieth century, not always in ways that involved electoral political activity or large organizations, but nevertheless in meaningful ways that could be clearly traced back to those efforts of farmers and laborers in the nineteenth century.

VI. TWENTIETH-CENTURY LEGACIES

JUDGED SOLELY ON THE RISE and fall of farmer and labor organizations and third parties, the story of populist and working-class protest and activism in Arkansas during the Gilded Age may seem to be one of frustration and failure. The legacy of these efforts, however, eventually would become apparent in many positive ways as the twentieth century progressed. For example, some of the demands for reform made by the Knights of Labor, its contemporary farmers' groups, and the third parties of the late nineteenth century would be granted by the state and federal governments. In addition, some radical organizations emerged in Arkansas that revitalized the biracialism of some of their Gilded Age predecessors in mobilizing poor whites and blacks alike. Black Arkansans, sometimes on their own and sometimes with white allies, carried forward their legacy of resistance from the last third of the nineteenth century into the twentieth.

In the wake of the demise of the Populist Party, its erstwhile leaders and small core of loyal followers found themselves in a quandary. Should they join (or, for many of them, rejoin) the ranks of the Democratic Party, which after all had pledged itself in 1896 to the free coinage of silver and, in Arkansas, the regulation of railroads? (The free silver issue, it should be noted, became a moot point after the Currency Act of 1900 put the nation on the gold standard.[1]) Should they support the Republican Party, which remained as hopelessly out of power in the state as it had been since the end of Reconstruction? Should they try to revive the Populist Party? Or did the emerging Socialist Party offer an outlet for their reformist agendas?

Some prominent ex-Populists chose to return to the Democratic fold, including former gubernatorial candidates Charles M. Norwood and D. E. Barker and former congressional candidates W. B. W. Heartsill and J. O. A. Bush. Norwood ran unsuccessfully in a Democratic primary for a state senate seat in 1906. Barker, Heartsill, and Bush, however, all won election to the Arkansas General Assembly as Democrats during the twentieth century.

Heartsill, the former Knights of Labor State Master Workman who had led coal miners in a dispute with a mining company in Greenwood, served three terms in the state house of representatives until his death in 1913. Arkansas United Mine Workers leaders, including Heartsill's former fellow Greenwood Knight George E. Mikel, relied on Representative Heartsill to look out for miners' interests. While the disfranchisement measures of the early 1890s meant that many former third-party voters could no longer vote at all, many of those who could—"undoubtedly a majority of them," according to one study—returned to the Democratic Party along with these leaders.[2]

That the third-party movement made the Arkansas Democratic Party more reform oriented became apparent shortly after the People's Party had been vanquished. In 1899, the Democratic-controlled state legislature created a railroad commission. During the early twentieth century, the commission would be moderately successful in reducing railroad rates and increasing competition within the industry. In 1897, partly due to the efforts of the only Populist in the state senate, Thomas Hayes, the state enacted what one scholar has described as a "mild" antitrust law.[3] Two years later the legislature passed another bill, the Rector Antitrust Law, which caused a furor among the state's business community when new state attorney general Jeff Davis filed over one hundred lawsuits against fire insurance companies doing business in Arkansas. Subsequently, the companies canceled policies and stopped doing business in Arkansas. The state supreme court restored order by ruling against Davis's sweeping interpretation of the law, which he insisted meant that the insurers should withdraw from industry-wide pricing agreements.

Davis, who was born in 1862 in Little River County, had succeeded in making a name for himself as a reformer, however, and in 1900 he won the governor's race, serving in that office from 1901 until he became a US senator in 1907. Davis spoke some of the Populist language in his eagerness to take on trusts, but he also engaged in race baiting that sharply distinguished him from Arkansas Populists, whom historian Lawrence Goodwyn contended "demonstrated the clearest record of racial liberalism of any of the southern third parties."[4] One of Davis's supporters, Democratic state senator (and, later, congressman) Otis Wingo of Sevier County would also be described as having Populist tendencies, as he tried to curb the power of corporations and what he called "too much government." In the US House of Representatives from 1913 until his death in 1930, he championed currency and banking reform and farm relief programs. Upon his arrival in the Arkansas state senate in 1907, however, he presented a resolution to request that Arkansas's members of Congress "urge the repeal of Amendments Fourteen [and] Fifteen to the Constitution of the United States." To the extent that Arkansas Democrats adopted the reformist ideology of the state's late nineteenth-century third parties, they did so in a manner that represented, as Arkansas native C. Vann Woodward later put it, "progressivism—for whites only."[5]

Some former third-party men in Arkansas, particularly in the Ozark hill country, became Republicans. Republican support probably contributed to Charles M. Norwood, the Union Labor gubernatorial candidate in 1888, carrying the counties of Carroll, Independence, Madison, Newton, Searcy, and Van Buren, none of which were carried by Populist J. P. Carnahan in 1892 when the Republicans nominated a candidate of their own. Some Arkansas Populists, however, stubbornly refused to give up the ghost even in the early twentieth century. A single Populist won election to the state house of representatives in 1900 and again four years later. In 1900 the Populists nominated a county ticket in the long-time third-party stronghold of Nevada County. The Populists held a state convention at Arkadelphia in July 1902, and A. W. Files continued to be the chairman of a Populist state central committee as late as 1904. In 1907 Reuben CarlLee wrote to Tom Watson, who ran as the Populist candidate for president in 1904 and 1908, asking whether the party's remaining followers should continue to "hold up the skeleton of the People's party," and Morgan wrote to Watson during the spring of 1908 promising to write articles in behalf of the latter's campaign.[6]

The United Mine Workers of America and the Arkansas State Federation of Labor

At least some former members of the Knights of Labor had an easier time finding a new affiliation. By 1898, a declining local assembly of miners and farmers in Huntington was probably the last remnant of Knights miners in the state, but the United Mine Workers of America (UMWA) had organized locals in western Arkansas, which became part of UMWA District 21. During February and early March 1899, a miners' strike broke out in Indian Territory (present-day Oklahoma) and western Arkansas. Over six thousand miners walked out. The *Arkansas Democrat* called the strike "the most important ever declared in that district." The strike encompassed Russellville, Dardanelle, Ouita, Spadra, Coal Hill, Denning, Altus, Jenny Lind, Huntington, and Bonanza in Arkansas, and Hartshorne, Krebs, Cherryvale, and Alderson in the Indian Territory. James Boston of the national executive board of the UMWA blamed the strike on the discharge of sixty union men by the Choctaw Coal Company in Hartshorne as well as the strikers' demand for higher wages. "While the price asked for may be higher than for other labor," Boston explained, "the high prices paid at company stores, high rents, long periods between pay days and the scrip system now in use leaves them but little to live upon."[7] The strike, described by one historian as "crippling" to the Arkansas coal industry, lasted as long as one to two years in some of the state's mines. Some mine operators employed black miners as strikebreakers, which in May 1899 led strikers to dynamite a "negro boarding house" in Huntington. Finally, by 1903, the UMWA had won its demands (including an eight-hour day) and secured a closed shop in the western Arkansas mines, which would remain unchallenged for eleven years.[8]

Subsequently, white miners apparently played a role in the Bonanza Race War of 1904, in which riotous whites expelled African Americans from that Sebastian County town, although, miraculously, no one was killed or wounded, according to all available reports. The African American laborers who left town included some forty miners who, according to some reports, were members of the UMWA. Although the white UMWA local in Bonanza unanimously passed a resolution denying any part in issuing the warnings to African Americans that preceded the riot, the historian who has most closely examined the episode concludes that "it is likely that the union had a hand in the expulsion of the black miners from Bonanza." This episode, which followed similar attacks by white mobs against black workers in Lawrence County in 1894, Polk County in 1896, Nevada County in 1897, and Paragould (Greene County) in 1899, must have had a significant, lasting impact. By 1910, "only a handful" of black miners remained in Arkansas. Bonanza became a "sundown town" after the riot—a euphemism for a town where African Americans are not welcome. Such towns became increasingly common in Arkansas between 1890 and 1930. At the beginning of that period, no county in the state had no African American residents, and only one had less than ten. Four decades later, three counties were totally devoid of African American residents, and eight other counties had fewer than ten. The legacy of the Bonanza Race War seems particularly potent and enduring in Bonanza itself: according to the Census of 2010, not one of the town's 575 residents was "black or African American."[9]

During the same year as the Bonanza Race War, Arkansas UMWA leaders played a key role in organizing a State Federation of Labor. UMWA District 21 Secretary-Treasurer S. F. Brackney of Sebastian County chaired the committee that issued the call for the convention, not surprisingly since he also served as an organizer for the American Federation of Labor. Brackney subsequently served as the chairman of the convention that formed the state federation. Newspaper reports stated that "every branch of organized labor in Arkansas" was represented at that convention, which was held in Little Rock in March. Delegates from the UMWA played the largest role, though, and Brackney was chosen as the state federation's first president. That the UMWA figured so prominently in the convention is not surprising, given its success in its "long strike" against the state's mining companies and the size of its Arkansas membership, which the *Arkansas Gazette* reported to be five thousand. (This figure nearly matched the peak membership achieved by the Knights of Labor in the state seventeen years earlier, which had included farmers, miners, railroad workers, and working men and women of many other occupations.) Cities and towns represented at the state federation's founding convention included Little Rock, Hartford, Fort Smith, Bonanza, Pine Bluff, Jenny Lind, and Coaldale. In addition to the UMWA, delegates came from a wide variety of trade unions, including bartenders, carpenters and joiners, retail clerks, cigar makers, decorators and painters, stationary firemen, tailors, and typographers, as well as representatives from central trades councils.[10]

In keeping with what Bruce Laurie has called the "prudential unionism" of the American Federation of Labor in this era, the founding convention of the Arkansas State Federation of Labor "eschewed" the discussion of "political topics" on its first day. When a delegate later introduced a "socialistic resolution" at the convention, Brackney "stated that it was out of the question for anyone to attempt to drag politics into the American Federation of Labor, of which the Arkansas Federation is a branch, and that once [and] for all this must be settled."[11] While the Arkansas State Federation of Labor would not emulate the involvement of the Knights of Labor in electoral politics, the federation would nevertheless pursue reform goals in the years ahead, such as the law passed in 1907 that prohibited the payment of wages in scrip. The federation would also be more limited in its diversity than the Knights of Labor; while women never served as officers in the Arkansas Knights State Assembly, an African American woman represented the Arkansas Knights at the Order's national General Assembly meeting in 1887. Press reports on the founding convention of the Arkansas State Federation of Labor made no mention of women. Since the federation consisted of trade unions, in contrast to the Knights of Labor, which had included many unskilled laborers and farmers and farm workers, African Americans would not be as heavily represented in the new body. The initial slate of officers in the federation included one African American, H. M. Thomas. A carpenter from Pine Bluff, Thomas held the lowest rank of any officer, seventh vice president. In December 1904, he rose to the rank of fourth vice president. At that same convention delegates chose a new president, George H. Jones of Sebastian County, a miner who had become involved in the labor movement when he joined the Knights of Labor twenty years earlier.[12]

Also in December 1904, the State Federation of Labor decided to reach out to the farmers' organizations in the state and to endeavor to bring them into the fold of not only the State Federation but also the American Federation of Labor. State Federation Secretary-Treasurer L. H. Moore introduced this motion at the conference. Some fifteen years earlier he had helped merge Arkansas's two competing State Farmers' Alliance organizations, and he subsequently served as a state organizer for the Alliance.[13]

The Farmers' Union

By this time, a significant new farmers' organization had entered Arkansas. From Texas—birthplace of the Southern Farmers' Alliance—came the Farmers' Educational and Cooperative Union. Newt Gresham, a former Farmers' Alliance organizer and Populist turned Bryan Democrat, started the Farmers' Union, as it came to be commonly called, in 1902 in Rains County, Texas, about seventy miles east of Dallas. Rains County, described by Elizabeth Sanders as "a hardscrabble county of small farmers and high tenancy," had been a center of Populist strength in Texas as well as a place where the Knights of Labor had been active. Like the Farmers' Alliance, the Farmers' Union did not admit African Americans to membership, and it tried to alleviate its members' economic hardship through cooperative enterprises and lobbying efforts. The organization built some 1,600 cotton warehouses across the cotton states by about 1910, and it tried to limit the supply and control the marketing of cotton. It established cooperative cotton gins, stores, fertilizer factories, flour mills, oil mills, and banks. The Farmers' Union eventually established itself in thirty-three states, primarily those where famers produced cotton, wheat, or tobacco, and its membership may have reached about nine hundred thousand during the first decade of the century.[14]

The Farmers' Union entered Arkansas when J. K. Huffman organized the state's first local chapter in the Hempstead County community of Spring Hill on September 30, 1903. J. S. Turner of Hope, also in Hempstead County, soon became Arkansas's first Farmers' Union state organizer. Turner called for a meeting at Hot Springs on April 27–28, 1905, at which delegates organized the Arkansas State Farmers' Union. The convention elected J. T. Batton of Tuckerman as the state organization's first president and former Union Labor gubernatorial candidate Charles M. Norwood, by then a resident of Stamps, as vice president. By the summer of 1907, the Arkansas State Farmers' Union reported 2,540 locals and 78,085 members.[15]

As a counterpart of sorts to the all-white Farmers' Union, in June 1905, an organization based in Houston, Texas—the National Colored Farmers' Progressive Union of America—filed articles of incorporation. The *Washington Post* reported the stated purpose of the organization to be "to organize the colored farmers of the United States for their mutual benefit and protection in the growing and sale of farm products."[16] This organization soon reached Arkansas, resulting in the formation of the Grand State Colored Farmers' Progressive Union of Arkansas at Pine Bluff in May 1906. A black speaker at the state organization's founding convention proclaimed that "his people were not looking for social equality. What they wanted was that the white Farmers' Union should blaze the way and his people would follow." Within three months of its founding, the Grand State Colored Farmers' Progressive Union of Arkansas reported a membership of about eight thousand.[17] When the Arkansas State Farmers' Union held a convention in Little Rock in August 1906, the question of organizing African Americans posed "a grave problem" for the delegates. Some of the State Farmers' Union organizers had been recruiting black farmers and forming locals of the Colored Farmers' Progressive Union. "This was," according to a contemporary account, "deemed a reflection upon the good name of the [Arkansas State Farmers'] Union and the commission of organizers, who had thus organized negro Unions, was revoked."[18] In 1908 the National Farmers' Union considered the possibility of admitting African Americans to membership, but the debate grew so contentious that the matter was dropped.[19]

The Farmers' Union, according to one historical account, approached politics with the knowledge of "what had happened to the Grange and [Farmers'] Alliance when they entered the political field," and therefore tried to avoid involvement in partisan politics. Yet like its predecessors, the Farmers' Union represented the political interests of farmers, advocated legislation, and kept a keen eye on state and national politics. Therefore staying out of politics was not really possible, even though the Farmers' Union "never created or endorsed a given political party."[20] Nevertheless, in the campaign for the Arkansas Democratic gubernatorial nomination in 1908, State Farmers' Union secretary Ben Griffin led the organization's support of "business progressive"

George W. Donaghey against the preferred candidate of US senator and former governor Jeff Davis, state attorney general William F. Kirby.[21]

Progressivism and Socialism

Leaders of the Arkansas State Federation of Labor also supported Donaghey, who would go on to serve as governor from 1909 to 1913. The Farmers' Union and the State Federation of Labor made common cause in other instances as well. In 1906 the two organizations agreed to "respect one another's labels and assist one another in other ways."[22] Their efforts, sometimes aided by women's groups led by the Arkansas Federation of Women's Clubs, helped bring about some significant reforms that the Knights of Labor, farmers' organizations, and third parties had called for during the Gilded Age. For example, after Donaghey took strong measures against convict leasing, even pardoning 360 convicts in December 1912 as a way of underscoring his opposition to the abuse-ridden system, Governor Joseph T. Robinson and the state legislature abolished the convict-lease system during the following year. In 1915, what one historian deemed "the state's first significant child labor law" took effect, although the law proved difficult to enforce. The Knights of Labor had called for equal pay for equal work for both sexes in the Reading platform of 1878. Well over a decade after the Knights had essentially faded into oblivion, the Arkansas Federation of Women's Clubs picked up the cause, campaigning not only for equal pay for equal work but also for legislation that would mandate minimum wages and maximum hours for women and seating accommodations for women in venues of public employment. The state legislature partially met these demands by enacting a wages and hours law in 1915, although it, too, proved to be of limited effectiveness.[23]

The Progressive movement of this era was national in scope, of course, and the federal government also delivered some of the demands of the Knights of Labor and the Populists. Both groups had called for the enactment of a graduated income tax and the direct election of US senators. The Sixteenth Amendment allowed for, and the Underwood-Simmons Tariff of 1913 imposed, a graduated income tax, and the Seventeenth Amendment assured that all senators would be elected by voters (rather than by state legislatures) after its ratification during that same year.[24] The Southern Farmers' Alliance's subtreasury plan, which had been opposed by Democrats in Arkansas and elsewhere in the South, came to partial fruition with the passage of the Warehouse Act of 1916 as well as various federal farm loan plans. The Warehouse Act "permitted Federal Reserve member banks to give loans to farmers on the security of their staple crops which were kept in Federal storage units as collateral."[25]

Some old Knights of Labor, Wheelers, Alliancemen, and Populists, however, continued along the third-party path during the early twentieth century. In 1901 Dan Hogan, who a decade earlier had published the *Alliance Patriot* in Mansfield, began publishing the first Socialist newspaper in Arkansas, the *Southern Worker*, in Huntington. Former Knight of Labor George E. Mikel, who became an officer in both UMWA District 21 and the Arkansas State Federation of Labor, soon joined Hogan as one of the state's leading Socialist activists.[26] W. Scott Morgan, a loyal Populist even after the party scarcely existed on paper, let alone in reality, scoffed at the notion of Democrats delivering any assistance to the state's working classes, declaring in *Morgan's Buzz-Saw* in 1905 that "the Democratic party is never a reform party when in power."[27] When even Morgan finally had to concede that the Populist Party was no more, he "moved leftward to Socialism," as one historian has noted. From 1911 until 1918, he contributed regularly to the St. Louis *National Rip-Saw*, a Socialist organ, where he wielded his pen not just against capitalists as in the past but also against capitalism itself.[28]

With the assistance of two Socialists from outside the state—C. C. Ross of Virginia and John C. Chase, the "shoemaker mayor" of Haverhill, Massachusetts—Arkansas Socialists held their first state convention at Little Rock on May 23, 1903, forming a state organization and choosing officers. Delegates also adopted a platform. In addition to endorsing the national Socialist Party's demands of cooperative government and public ownership of utilities and industries, the state platform called for demands that in some cases echoed those of the Knights of Labor and the Populists but in other cases went further. Arkansas Socialists called for "the collective ownership of all means of transportation and communication, as well as all industries controlled by trusts and combines," the reduction of hours of labor along with increased wages, equal civil and political rights for men and women (in sharp contrast to the Populists, who had refused to endorse women's suffrage), and some demands that were far ahead of their time—namely, "state or national insurance of working people in case of accident, lack of employment, sickness and want in old age" and a public works program to provide employment for the unemployed, which was reminiscent of Jacob Coxey's "good roads" proposal of the previous decade.[29]

Although the Socialist Party never elected any state officers in Arkansas, it did make significant inroads with certain segments of the population in certain parts of the state. Its supporters included trade unionists in Pulaski County, not only in Little Rock but also in Argenta, a center of strike activity in the Southwestern strike of 1886. In 1905 Arkansas Socialists helped organize locals of the Industrial Workers of the World (IWW), which combined the "one big union" approach of the Knights of Labor with a more radical critique of capitalism. The IWW recruited timber workers in southern Arkansas, who had been some of the state's last Knights, and during the mid-1910s, the union endeavored to organize black tenant farmers and farm laborers in the Arkansas Delta.[30]

The Socialist Party also found followers among farmers in some of the agricultural counties in the central and northeastern parts of the state, including the old Knights of Labor and Union Labor Party stronghold of Independence County, as well as Jefferson County (another former bastion of Knights and ULP support) farther south and, in the western part of the state, Scott and Polk Counties, the latter a late-in-the-day center of Knights and Populist strength. Sebastian County, where the Knights of Labor had organized coal miners and farmers in the 1890s, became a hotbed of Socialist activism and support. From Sebastian came two of the party's gubernatorial candidates: Dan Hogan, who ran in 1906, 1910, and 1914, and George E. Mikel, who ran in 1912. Hogan became a close friend of Eugene V. Debs, who visited Arkansas in both 1904 and 1908, drawing enthusiastic crowds in Little Rock, Fort Smith (Sebastian County), and in Pine Bluff (Jefferson County), where in 1908 he addressed a "farmer audience." In the Sebastian County coal mining town of Hartford, the Socialist Pete Stewart, president of UMWA District 21, won the mayoral race in 1912. Also during that year, Mikel made the best showing ever by a Socialist candidate for governor in Arkansas with 7.9 percent of the vote. Historian John Wheeler suggested that "disoriented" ex-Populists contributed to Mikel's relatively strong showing.[31]

In 1914 Dr. Wells LeFevre, who had helped form the Arkansas Socialist Party eleven years earlier, revived an offshoot of the party called the Working Class Union (WCU) at "Hobo's Hollow" near Van Buren, where the Knights of Labor had been active from 1886 until at least 1893. The WCU got started in Louisiana in 1913 but did not establish itself effectively; it soon petered out, but not before sending an organizer into southeastern Oklahoma and western Arkansas, which led to LeFevre resurrecting the union after its initial lapse. The WCU then formed locals not only in Arkansas but also in Kansas, Nebraska, Texas, and most successfully in Oklahoma, reportedly home to twenty thousand of the total membership of thirty-five thousand.

Like the Knights of Labor, the WCU allowed "all members of the working class, regardless of race, sex, color or occupation" to join. The similar inclusiveness of the two organizations may have resulted from the fact that the author of the WCU charter had been a member of the Knights as well as a Populist. Farmers constituted the bulk of the WCU's membership, though, and most of them were tenants, sharecroppers, or farmhands. True to its word, the WCU organized blacks in addition to whites, and it proved far more radical than the Farmers' Union. On May Day (May 1) in 1916, the WCU led a strike of farmhands in the vicinity of Moffatt, Oklahoma, just across the state line from Fort Smith, Arkansas, in an attempt to raise their daily wages from $1.00 to $1.25. The strike failed, and the WCU also became "hampered by its terrorist reputation" after some of its members resorted to night riding and even robbing banks.[32] Nevertheless, the WCU kept alive the legacy of the Knights of Labor and the Agricultural Wheel in organizing poor white and black farmers, which in turn would be repeated later by the Southern Tenant Farmers' Union (STFU).

The Socialist Party, the IWW, and the WCU would all meet their demise in Arkansas (and elsewhere), however, due to their opposition to American involvement in World War I, in particular the Conscription Act of 1917. (Eugene V. Debs infamously spent three years in jail after an antidraft speech in Canton, Ohio, resulted in his conviction for violating the Espionage Act.)[33] Federal repression did not entirely destroy the Socialist movement, however, and in 1925 Missouri Socialists Frank and Kate O'Hare established Commonwealth College at Mena (Polk County), Arkansas—which like the WCU, had begun in Louisiana (in 1923)—as a training school for radical organizers. Trainees of Commonwealth College would help establish the STFU in 1934.[34]

The Persistence of Radicalism and Activism

In the meantime, radicalism persisted in Arkansas even as the WCU disappeared and Socialism waned. In 1919, African Americans in Drew County formed a union for sharecroppers and tenant farmers called the Progressive Farmers and Household Union of America (or, according to some sources, the Farmers' and Laborers' Household Union of America). The limited available evidence suggests that some of the men involved in this union may have been supporters or descendants of men involved in the cotton pickers' strike of 1891. Tragically, white opposition to the Progressive Farmers and Household Union resulted in even more bloodshed than that strike had.

After white men exchanged gunfire with black guards at a church in Phillips County where the union was holding a meeting, the result was the Elaine Race Massacre of 1919, in which armed white citizens and state troops killed an unknown number of African Americans that may have reached into the hundreds. (Five white men also died in the incident.) Yet some of the surviving union activists reemerged in the STFU, which was formed in 1934 in Poinsett County. Isaac Shaw personified this connection; the black sharecropper had belonged to the Progressive Farmers and Household Union and became one of the founding members of the STFU. Formed largely because the Agricultural Adjustment Act of 1933 led to many tenants and sharecroppers being evicted, the union's membership exceeded thirty-five thousand by 1938. Most of those members lived in eastern Arkansas.[35]

The Socialist Party, revitalized by the Great Depression, figured prominently in the creation of the STFU and thereby further linked the union to past working-class protest movements. Like its predecessors in Arkansas and elsewhere in the South, the STFU had its limits when it came to crossing the color line. One recent study suggests that historians have exaggerated the STFU's "commitment to biracial cooperation and equality." Most of its locals were segregated, many of its leaders were white even though blacks constituted most of the membership, and the white leaders downplayed the union's potential racial radicalism.[36] Nevertheless, not only did the STFU revive Greenback-to-Socialist era efforts at interracial activism in Arkansas and elsewhere—although it too met with violent repression that contributed to its demise—but in some significant ways it provided a useful legacy for the civil rights movement that followed some two decades later, even to the extent that "many younger members of the STFU went on to become leaders in the local civil rights movement in Arkansas." For example, STFU secretary Carrie Dilworth of Lincoln County later became the first person in the state to invite Student Nonviolent Coordinating Committee (SNCC) activists into her home, and she subsequently became involved in SNCC efforts against continued resistance to the desegregation of schools in the state years after the Little Rock Central High School crisis of 1957. The STFU also benefited southern tenant farmers and sharecroppers of both races by bringing national publicity—including attention from the federal government—to their problems. For example, the Bankhead-Jones Farm Tenant Act of 1937 created the Farm Security Administration, which fought rural poverty in a variety of ways, including a program that helped tenants, including the displaced, become landowners.[37]

8. Loading cotton in Lehi, Arkansas. Lee, Russell, photographer. Lehi, Arkansas, United States, Sept. 1938. Photograph. Retrieved from the Library of Congress, accessed March 20, 2018, https://www.loc.gov/item/2017737316/.

In other ways, too, the legacy of Gilded Age labor activism in Arkansas lived on far into the twentieth century. The UMWA survived a serious challenge by Arkansas mine operators who tried to destroy the union in 1914 by breaking the closed shop in the mines. The resultant strike proved violent, and the two sides battled each other in courts as well.[38] By 1918 the union had recovered sufficiently to negotiate raises for miners throughout the Southwestern Competitive Field (Missouri, Kansas, Arkansas, Oklahoma, and Texas).[39] In 1925, however, Arkansas mine operators tried again to break the closed shop and this time they succeeded. The National Industrial Recovery Act of 1933 subsequently helped the UMWA reimpose the closed shop. But in 1944 Arkansas adopted a right-to-work (open-shop) law, as would most other southern states. Nevertheless, as late as the 1960s Arkansas had one of the strongest labor movements of any state in the South: in 1964, 26.2 percent of the state's nonagricultural workers were organized.[40] The UMWA still endures in the state; Arkansas members are affiliated with District 12, which stretches northward from Louisiana with headquarters in Springfield, Illinois, representing over fourteen thousand miners as of 2016.[41]

Measured by what transpired during the Gilded Age, the story of farmer and labor protest in Arkansas during that era may seem like one of defeat and despair, marked by reform organizations and third parties that did not last, stolen elections, the disfranchisement of blacks and poor whites, and, all too often, murderous violence committed by men who were never brought to justice. Moreover, in light of the "second Gilded Age" that began in the early twenty-first century, one might say that many of the problems of economic, social, and racial injustice that plagued the post-Reconstruction South have returned to blight the entire nation.[42] On the other hand, the protest movements of the Gilded Age, in Arkansas and elsewhere, also left a more positive legacy. They played a pioneering role in substantially changing the state, the South, and the nation in positive ways that cannot be denied. Their efforts helped to abolish the convict-lease system, child labor (and the resultant lack of schooling of working-class children), and payment of wages in scrip rather than cash; helped to establish workplace safety laws, minimum wage laws, and the eight-hour day; and in some cases even helped to end Jim Crow. That some of these gains are now under attack in the United States does not diminish their significance but rather underscores the need for continued working-class activism. Working-class Arkansans—rural and urban, male and female, black and white—ultimately demonstrated that if enough citizens display enough courage and commitment to a movement with just causes, then meaningful progress can be achieved, even if not always in one's own lifetime.

APPENDIX 1

Statistical Report of Membership, Farmers' State Alliance, Quarter Ending December 31, 1890

County Alliance	Present Membership	
	Male	Female
Benton	187	153
Boone	113	38
Carroll	331	207
Clark	285	18
Conway	124	34
Crawford	55	71
Franklin	274	117
Hot Springs		
Howard	50	5
Johnson		
Logan	360	101
Madison	360	350
Miller	157	198
Montgomery	52	32
Newton		
Perry	90 (or 40?)	0 (?)
Phillips	106	--
Pike		
Polk	552	209
Pope	116	53
Sebastian	580	212
Scott		
Sevier		
Washington	1,236	515
Yell	240	--

A dash (--) appears in the table wherever it appears in the original document.

Source: W. B. W. Heartsill Papers, 1864–1945, Center for Arkansas History and Culture, University of Arkansas at Little Rock Library, Box 7, Item 4.

APPENDIX 2

Knights of Labor District Assemblies in Arkansas

District Assembly No.	Location or description	Year of formation
22	Lumber workers in Alabama, Mississippi, and Arkansas–headquarters in Mobile, Ala.	1895
101	Employees of the Gould Southwestern system of railroads, midwestern and southwestern states, including Arkansas–headquarters in Sedalia, MO	1885
171	Texarkana, Ark.	1886
221	Hot Springs	1887
223	Paragould	1887
233	Brinkley	1887 or 1888
234	Little Rock	1887 or 1888
238	Brinkley	1887 or 1888
239	Pine Bluff	1887 or 1888
242	Little Rock	1887 or 1888
244	Fort Smith	1887 or 1888

Sources: T. V. Powderly, *Thirty Years of Labor, 1859 to 1889* (Columbus, Ohio: Excelsior Publishing House, 1889); *Journal of the Knights of Labor* (Washington, DC), April 11, 1895; *Proceedings of the General Assembly of the Knights of Labor, Special Session Held at Washington, District of Columbia, June 18–21, 1900*, microfilm (Madison: State Historical Society of Wisconsin, 1950).

APPENDIX 3

Arkansas Union Labor Party Platform, 1888

We, the Union Labor Party of the state of Arkansas, in convention assembled at Little Rock, April 30, 1888, endorse the planks of the nation[al] platform adopted at Cincinnati, February 22, 1887, on land, transportation, money, income tax, and Chinese labor.

We favor such legislation as will secure the reforms demanded by the Agricultural Wheel, the National Farmers' Alliance, and the Knights of Labor.

We pledge ourselves to do our utmost to enforce:

1. Taxation of all lands held for speculative purposes at their full value.
2. A strict execution of the election laws and such legislation as will secure a free ballot and a fair count.
3. The consolidation of the elections, state and national.
4. A change in the convict system, the abolition of the contract system, and the working of the convicts within the walls of the penitentiary at Little Rock.
5. A road tax and a reduction of days for road working.
6. A public school system that will educate all the people and we favor national aid to education.
7. A law regulating mining and proper ventilation for same.
8. Laws subjecting trusts, railroads, and other corporations to state control.

We favor the establishment of a labor and agricultural bureau.

Source: Little Rock *Daily Arkansas Gazette*, May 1, 1888.

APPENDIX 4

Platform Demands of the Arkansas Socialist Party, 1912

1. Woman's suffrage
2. Proposal to limit rent to 10 percent of the assessed value of the property
3. Compulsory education to the age of 18 years
4. Absolute prohibition of child labor
5. State to own and operate cotton mills, the net proceeds of which are to be turned over to the farmer[s] producing the cotton

The party's convention endorsed the proposed state constitutional amendments for the recall, for the textbook commission, for a state printing plant, and for the placing of the members of the state legislature on a salary.

The convention declared against proposed state constitutional amendments for the grandfather clause, the exemption from taxation of all capital invested in the manufacture of cotton goods for ten years, and the issue of bonds for cities of the first and second class, on the grounds that it would give four men the right to declare the results of elections.

Source: Little Rock *Arkansas Gazette*, April 4, 1912.

NOTES

Introduction

1. Jeremy Brecher, *Strike!*, rev. 3rd ed. (Oakland, Calif.: PM Press, 2014), 369–75; Gil Troy, *The Age of Clinton: America in the 1990s* (New York: Thomas Dunne Books, 2015), 124, 126, 135, 136–38, 149–50, 167–71, 177, 179–81.

2. Mark Twain and Charles Dudley Warner, *The Gilded Age: A Tale of To-day* (Hartford, Conn.: American Publishing Company, 1873). The hyphenated spelling of "to-day" in the subtitle was common at the time of the book's publication.

3. Claire Goldstene, *The Struggle for America's Promise: Equal Opportunity at the Dawn of Corporate Capital* (Jackson: University Press of Mississippi, 2014), 11–15; William A. Link, *Southern Crucible: The Making of an American Region* (New York: Oxford University Press, 2015), 289, 293; Eric Foner, *A Short History of Reconstruction, 1863–1877*, updated ed. (New York: Harper Perennial, 2015), 46–47.

4. Robert C. McMath Jr., *American Populism: A Social History, 1877–1898* (New York: Hill and Wang, 1993), 50–53.

5. Recent studies that examine producerism include Goldstene, *Struggle for America's Promise*, and Benjamin F. Alexander, *Coxey's Army: Popular Protest in the Gilded Age* (Baltimore: Johns Hopkins University Press, 2015).

6. McMath, *American Populism*, 52, 170–71; T. V. Powderly, *Thirty Years of Labor, 1859 to 1889* (Columbus, Ohio: Excelsior Publishing House, 1889), 245.

I. The Roots of Discontent

1. Thomas A. DeBlack, *With Fire and Sword: Arkansas, 1861–1874* (Fayetteville: University of Arkansas Press, 2003), 201.

2. Ibid., 216–24 (quotation on 224).

3. C. Vann Woodward, *Origins of the New South, 1877–1913* (Baton Rouge: Louisiana State University Press, 1951), 69.

4. Conservative southern Democrats used the term "redemption" to describe their takeover of state governments from Republicans between 1869 and 1877, implying that they had "saved" the South from Republicans and "black rule." Edward L. Ayers, *The Promise of the New South: Life after Reconstruction* (New York: Oxford University Press, 1992), 8; David Emory Shi and George Brown Tindall, *America: A Narrative History*, brief 10th ed. (New York: W. W. Norton, 2016), 607.

5. Carl H. Moneyhon, *Arkansas and the New South, 1874–1929* (Fayetteville: University of Arkansas Press, 1997), 5, 21 (quotation); Stanford University, "Per Capita Income in the United States: 1880–1910," *Railroaded*, accessed October 20, 2016, http://web.stanford.edu/group/spatialhistory/cgi-bin/railroaded/gallery/interactive-visualizations/capita-income-united-states-1880-1910.

6. Moneyhon, *Arkansas and the New South*, 25–26; Foner, *Short History of Reconstruction*, 168, 169.

7. *Proceedings of the Fifth Annual Session of the Arkansas State Grange, Patrons of Husbandry, Held at Little Rock, January 22, 23, 24, 25 and 26, 1877* (Little Rock: Webb and Burrows, 1877), 6.

8. Moneyhon, *Arkansas and the New South*, 6–7; Foner, *Short History of Reconstruction*, 169–70; *The National Economist Almanac 1890: National Farmers Alliance and Industrial Union Hand-Book* (Washington, DC: National Economist Print, 1890), 71; Matthew Hild, *Greenbackers, Knights of Labor, and Populists: Farmer-Labor Insurgency in the Late-Nineteenth-Century South* (Athens: University of Georgia Press, 2007), 210; W. Scott Morgan, *History of the Wheel and Alliance, and the Impending Revolution*, 3rd ed. (Hardy, Ark.: s.p., 1891; repr., New York: Burt Franklin, 1968), 56–57.

9. John M. Wheeler, "The People's Party in Arkansas, 1891–1896" (PhD diss., Tulane University, 1975), 35–36.

10. *Department of Agriculture. Miscellaneous. Special Report No. 2. Proceedings of a Convention of Agriculturalists Held at the Department of Agriculture, January 23, 24, 25, 26, 27, and 29, 1883. (Second Convention.)* (Washington, DC: Government Printing Office, 1883), 56–57.

11. Gilbert C. Fite, *Cotton Fields No More: Southern Agriculture, 1865–1980* (Lexington: University Press of Kentucky, 1984), 51.

12. Granville D. Davis, "The Granger Movement in Arkansas," *Arkansas Historical Quarterly* 4 (Winter 1945): 340–41 (quotation on 341); O. H. Kelley, *Origins and Progress of the Order of the Patrons of Husbandry in the United States; A History from 1866 to 1873* (Philadelphia: A. Wagenseller, 1875), 389, 396.

13. Davis, "Granger Movement," 342–43; Fite, *Cotton Fields No More*, 51.

14. Moneyhon, *Arkansas and the New South*, 14; Theodore Saloutos, "The Grange in the South, 1870–1877," *Journal of Southern History* 19 (Nov. 1953): 476–77 (quotation on 477); Story L. Matkin-Rawn, "'We Fight for the Rights of Our Race': Black Arkansans in the Era of Jim Crow" (PhD diss., University of Wisconsin—Madison, 2009), 39.

15. Davis, "Granger Movement," 347.

16. Ibid., 349–50.

17. Moneyhon, *Arkansas and the New South*, 78.

18. *Proceedings of the Fifth Annual Session of the Arkansas State Grange*, 24.

19. Ayers, *Promise of the New South*, 214.

20. Davis, "Granger Movement," 347, 349; Wheeler, "People's Party in Arkansas," 83 (quotation).

21. *Proceedings of the Fifth Annual Session of the Arkansas State Grange*, 4.

22. *New York Times*, February 12, 1874.

23. C. Fred Williams et al., eds., *A Documentary History of Arkansas* (Fayetteville: University of Arkansas Press, 1984), 132–34 (includes a reprint of an article from the *Crawford* [Ark.] *Bulletin*, June 25, 1874).

24. Utica (N.Y.) *Herald*, n.d., quoted in the *Marietta* (Ga.) *Journal*, June 20, 1873.

25. Davis, "Granger Movement," 351.

26. Ibid., 349, 351–52; Moneyhon, *Arkansas and the New South*, 18; Jeannie M. Whayne et al., *Arkansas: A Narrative History*, 2nd ed. (Fayetteville: University of Arkansas Press, 2013), 261.

27. On the decline of the Grange in Arkansas and elsewhere during the mid- to late 1870s, see Davis, "Granger Movement," 347–51; Whayne et al., *Arkansas*, 277; *Proceedings of the Fifth Annual Session of the Arkansas State Grange*, 4, 9–11; Saloutos, "Grange in the South," 486–87; D. Sven Nordin, *Rich Harvest: A History of the Grange, 1867–1900* (Jackson: University Press of Mississippi, 1974), 35–40. For an example of corruption in the cooperative enterprises of the Arkansas Grange, see Clark Grange #232, Pope County, Arkansas, Records, Organizational Materials, Committee Reports, August 21, 1875, microfilm, Arkansas State Archives, Little Rock.

28. Hild, *Greenbackers*, 20–21, 30; *Biographical and Historical Memoirs of Pulaski, Jefferson, Lonoke, Faulkner, Grant, Saline, Perry, Garland, and Hot Springs Counties, Arkansas* (Chicago: Goodspeed Publishing, 1889), 438–39.

29. Charles Postel, *The Populist Vision* (New York: Oxford University Press, 2007), 32.

30. Judith Barjenbruch, "The Greenback Political Movement: An Arkansas View," *Arkansas Historical Quarterly* 36 (Summer 1977): 108.

31. Little Rock *Daily Arkansas Gazette*, September 13, 1876.

32. Barjenbruch, "Greenback Political Movement," 108; Wheeler, "People's Party in Arkansas," 98.

33. On the Grange and currency reform, see Hild, *Greenbackers*, 21–22.

34. M. Langley Biegert, "Legacy of Resistance: Uncovering the History of Collective Action by Black Agricultural Workers in Central East Arkansas from the 1860s to the 1930s," *Journal of Social History* 32 (Fall 1998): 78–79 (quotation on 76); Grif Stockley, *Ruled By Race: Black/White Relations in Arkansas from Slavery to the Present* (Fayetteville: University of Arkansas Press, 2009), 49–50 (second quotation on 49).

35. Whayne et al., *Arkansas*, 237, 241–46; Foner, *Short History of Reconstruction*, 125–26; Randy Finley, "Arkansas," in *Encyclopedia of the Reconstruction Era*, ed. Richard Zuczek (Westport, Conn.: Greenwood Publishing Group, 2006), 51.

36. Michael J. Dubin, comp., *United States Congressional Elections, 1788–1997: The Official Results of the Elections of the 1st through 105th Congresses* (Jefferson, N.C.: McFarland, 1998), 236; Gretchen Ritter, *Goldbugs and Greenbacks: The Antimonopoly*

Tradition and the Politics of Finance in America, 1865–1896 (Cambridge: Cambridge University Press, 1997), 52.

37. John R. Commons et al., *History of Labour in the United States* (New York: Macmillan, 1926), 2:244 (quotation); *New York Times*, February 23, 1878.

38. Barjenbruch, "Greenback Political Movement," 110–11 (first two quotations on 110); Little Rock *Daily Arkansas Gazette*, July 14, 1878 (third and fourth quotations).

39. Moneyhon, *Arkansas and the New South*, 78–79; Barjenbruch, "Greenback Political Movement," 108–9, 112; Whayne et al., *Arkansas*, 269–71; *New York Times*, September 2, 1878.

40. Barjenbruch, "Greenback Political Movement," 110; Little Rock *Daily Arkansas Gazette*, August 22, 1878.

41. John L. Moore, Jon P. Preimesberger, and David R. Tarr, eds., *Congressional Quarterly's Guide to U.S. Elections*, 4th ed. (Washington, DC: CQ Press, 2001), 922; Little Rock *Daily Arkansas Gazette*, July 6, 1873, September 19, 27, 1878; Wheeler, "People's Party in Arkansas," 99, 100; Barjenbruch, "Greenback Political Movement," 112; Tom W. Dillard, "Gillam, Isaac T.," in *Arkansas Biography: A Collection of Notable Lives*, ed. Nancy A. Williams (Fayetteville: University of Arkansas Press, 2000), 122–23. Milton Rice was the lone Greenback congressional candidate in Arkansas in 1876, receiving 681 votes. Dubin, *United States Congressional Elections*, 236.

42. Moneyhon, *Arkansas and the New South*, 79 (quotation), 83; *Compendium of the Ninth Census (June 1, 1870)* (Washington, DC: Government Printing Office, 1872), 118–24.

43. Barjenbruch, "Greenback Political Movement," 112–13 (quoting the Little Rock *Daily Arkansas Gazette*, August 5, 1879).

44. Ibid., 113–15 (quotation on 113); Mark A. Lause, *The Civil War's Last Campaign: James B. Weaver, the Greenback-Labor Party & the Politics of Race & Section* (Lanham, Md.: University Press of America, 2001), 154.

45. Lause, *Civil War's Last Campaign*, 112–16 (quotation on 115), 234; Wheeler, "People's Party in Arkansas," 107; Moore, Preimesberger, and Tarr, *Congressional Quarterly's Guide to U.S. Elections*, 926.

46. Little Rock *Daily Arkansas Gazette*, June 21, 1882 (quotations); *New York Times*, June 21, 1882. The opponents of "Redeemer" Democrats used the term "Bourbon" derisively, comparing the Redeemers to the French Bourbons who, upon being restored to power in 1814, seemed to have "learned nothing and . . . forgotten nothing from the French Revolution." The Bourbon Democrats, their critics charged, reacted similarly to the Civil War. See Leonard Schlup and James G. Ryan, eds., *Historical Dictionary of the Gilded Age* (Armonk, N.Y.: M. E. Sharpe, 2003), 56. Regarding the integrity of elections, Democratic election officials in Pulaski County voided election returns from some of the county's black-majority precincts in every state election from 1876 to 1888, claiming that the returns in

these precincts had been marred by fraudulent votes. See Wheeler, "People's Party in Arkansas," 76.

47. Little Rock *Daily Arkansas Gazette*, July 8, 1882.

48. Moneyhon, *Arkansas and the New South*, 79; Moore, Preimesberger, and Tarr, *Congressional Quarterly's Guide to U.S. Elections*, 1419.

49. Moore, Preimesberger, and Tarr, *Congressional Quarterly's Guide to U.S. Elections*, 930. Barjenbruch, "Greenback Political Movement," 118, says that Cunningham "withdrew from the Greenback slate and joined the Republicans," but this is contradicted by both Moore et al. and the Little Rock *Daily Arkansas Gazette*, November 3, 1882.

50. Barjenbruch, "Greenback Political Movement," 118–19; Wheeler, "People's Party in Arkansas," 110–11 (quotation on 111), 114, 281, 381. On the racial composition of Arkansas counties, see the *Compendium of the Tenth Census (June 1, 1880)*, Part 1 (Washington, DC: Government Printing Office, 1883), 336–37.

51. Wheeler, "People's Party in Arkansas," 114.

52. David A. Epstein, *Left, Right, Out: The History of Third Parties in America* (New York: Arts and Letters Imperium Publishing, 2012), 86–87.

53. Barjenbruch, "Greenback Political Movement," 109.

54. Charles Hillman Brough, "The Industrial History of Arkansas," *Publications of the Arkansas Historical Association* 1 (1906): 224. On the reorganization of the Arkansas State Grange in 1887, see the Magnolia (Ark.) *Columbia Banner*, July 21, 1887. Brough later served as the governor of Arkansas from 1917 until 1921.

55. Whayne et al., *Arkansas*, 144, 171.

56. Moneyhon, *Arkansas and the New South*, 25–26.

57. Whayne et al., *Arkansas*, 268; Brough, "Industrial History," 196 (quotation).

58. Moneyhon, *Arkansas and the New South*, 33.

59. Goldstene, *Struggle for America's Promise*, 4–5 (quotations on 5; emphasis in Hayes quotation is in source); Brecher, *Strike!*, 11–30; Kevin C. Brown, "1877 Great Railroad Strike," in *Disasters, Accidents, and Crises in American History: A Reference Guide to the Nation's Most Catastrophic Events*, ed. Ballard C. Campbell (New York: Infobase Publishing, 2008), 147–49; Foner, *Short History of Reconstruction*, 238–47.

60. Little Rock *Daily Arkansas Gazette*, June 14, 1881 (quotations); Little Rock *Arkansas Democrat*, June 14, 1881; Richard Reinhardt, ed., *Workin' on the Railroad: Reminiscences from the Age of Steam* (Norman: University of Oklahoma Press, 1970), 89. For background information on the Iron Mountain Railroad, which was part of the St. Louis, Iron Mountain, and Southern Railroad, see Moneyhon, *Arkansas and the New South*, 26.

61. Little Rock *Daily Arkansas Gazette*, August 18, 1881.

62. *Third Annual Report of the Commissioner of Labor, 1887. Strikes and Lockouts* (Washington, DC: Government Printing Office, 1888), 40; Jonathan Garlock, comp., *Guide to the Local Assemblies of the Knights of Labor* (Westport, Conn.: Greenwood Press, 1982), 14.

63. *Third Biennial Report from the Bureau of Mines, Manufactures and Agriculture of the State of Arkansas for the Years 1893 and 1894* (Morrilton, Ark.: Pilot Printing, 1894), 150; Whayne et al., *Arkansas*, 268.

64. Theresa A. Case, *The Great Southwest Railroad Strike and Free Labor* (College Station: Texas A&M University Press, 2010).

II. Building the Foundations of Rebellion

1. *Fayetteville* (Ark.) *Democrat*, December 14, 1882.

2. Morgan, *History of the Wheel and Alliance*, 3rd ed., 60.

3. Ibid., 55–58 (quotation on 55, emphasis in original).

4. F. Clark Elkins, "Arkansas Farmers Organize for Action: 1882–1884," *Arkansas Historical Quarterly* 13 (Autumn 1954): 231, including n. 2.

5. Morgan, *History of the Wheel and Alliance*, 3rd ed., 60–62 (quotations on 61); Meridian Agricultural Wheel, Minutes and Proceedings Book, 1887–1889, September 29, 1887, Arkansas State Archives, Little Rock. On the tenets of secrecy within the Grange, see Nordin, *Rich Harvest*, 23, 26. On secret rituals in farmer and labor organizations in this era, see also Robert C. McMath Jr., *Populist Vanguard: A History of the Southern Farmers' Alliance* (Chapel Hill: University of North Carolina Press, 1975), 73; Robert E. Weir, *Beyond Labor's Veil: The Culture of the Knights of Labor* (University Park: Pennsylvania State University Press, 1996), esp. chap. 1.

6. Morgan, *History of the Wheel and Alliance*, 3rd ed., 62.

7. Wheeler, "People's Party in Arkansas," 117.

8. Morgan, *History of the Wheel and Alliance*, 3rd ed., 62.

9. Ibid., 63.

10. Ibid., 63–64 (quotations); Whayne et al., *Arkansas*, 275; Davis, "Granger Movement," 345; Nordin, *Rich Harvest*, 90.

11. Morgan, *History of the Wheel and Alliance*, 3rd ed., 64.

12. Magnolia (Ark.) *Columbia Banner*, September 2, 1886; Morgan, *History of the Wheel and Alliance*, 3rd ed., 72–73; Meridian Agricultural Wheel, Minutes and Proceedings Book, October 13, 1887.

13. N. A. Dunning, ed., *The Farmers' Alliance History and Agricultural Digest* (Washington, DC: Alliance Publishing, 1891; repr., New York: Arno Press, 1975), 206, 209 (quotation).

14. Morgan, *History of the Wheel and Alliance*, 3rd ed., 64 (first quotation), 69 (second quotation); *Biographical and Historical Memoirs of Eastern Arkansas* (Chicago: Goodspeed Publishing, 1890), 678.

15. Dunning, *Farmers' Alliance History*, 216.

16. Nashville (Tenn.) *Weekly Toiler*, September 5, 1888 (quotation); Berton E. Henningson Jr., "Northwest Arkansas and the Brothers of Freedom: The Roots of a Farmer Movement," *Arkansas Historical Quarterly* 34 (Winter 1975): 312; *National Economist Almanac 1890*, 75; F. Clark Elkins, "State Politics and the Agricultural Wheel," *Arkansas Historical Quarterly* 38 (Autumn 1979): 252–53; John H. Robertson to W. B. W. Heartsill, August 31, 1896, W. B. W. Heartsill Papers, 1864–1945,

Center for Arkansas History and Culture, University of Arkansas at Little Rock Library (hereafter cited as Heartsill Papers), Box 4, File 11.

17. See the preamble of the Brothers of Freedom's Declaration of Principles in Dunning, *Farmers' Alliance History*, 217, and the Wheel's preamble in Morgan, *History of the Wheel and Alliance*, 3rd ed., 63–65.

18. *Russellville* (Ark.) *Democrat*, February 14, 1884, quoted in Henningson, "Northwest Arkansas and the Brothers of Freedom," 320–21; Morgan, *History of the Wheel and Alliance*, 3d. ed., 68.

19. *Russellville* (Ark.) *Democrat*, February 14, 1884, quoted in Henningson, "Northwest Arkansas and the Brothers of Freedom," 316.

20. Henningson, "Northwest Arkansas and the Brothers of Freedom," 318; Lead Hill (Ark.) *Bugle*, September 25, 1884, quoted in Berton E. Henningson Jr., "Root Hog or Die: The Brothers of Freedom and the 1884 Arkansas Election," *Arkansas Historical Quarterly* 45 (Autumn 1986): 213.

21. Fort Smith (Ark.) *Elevator*, July 17, 1885, quoted in Henningson, "Root Hog or Die," 213.

22. Morgan, *History of the Wheel and Alliance*, 3rd ed., 71–72.

23. Carl C. Taylor, *The Farmers' Movement, 1620–1920* (New York: American Book, 1953; repr., Westport, Conn.: Greenwood Press, 1971), 206; Henningson, "Northwest Arkansas and the Brothers of Freedom," 313 (quotation).

24. Henningson, "Root Hog or Die," 200–201 (quotation on 201, citing the Russellville [Ark.] *Democrat*, August 21, 1884).

25. Henningson, "Northwest Arkansas and the Brothers of Freedom," 307–8. On cotton culture in the Ozark Mountains during this era, see Brooks Blevins, *Hill Folks: A History of Arkansas Ozarkers and Their Image* (Chapel Hill: University of North Carolina Press, 2002), 32–38.

26. The sixteen Brothers of Freedom counties examined here are Boone, Conway, Crawford, Faulkner, Franklin, Johnson, Logan, Marion, Newton, Perry, Pope, Scott, Searcy, Sebastian, Van Buren, and Yell. The fourteen Agricultural Wheel counties are Conway, Faulkner, Garland, Jackson, Lonoke, Pope, Prairie, Pulaski, St. Francis, Sebastian, Van Buren, White, Woodruff, and Yell. These lists of counties in which the Brothers or the Wheel (or both) are known to have been active were compiled from the following sources: Elkins, "Arkansas Farmers Organize for Action"; F. Clark Elkins, "The Agricultural Wheel: County Politics and Consolidation, 1884–1885," *Arkansas Historical Quarterly* 29 (Summer 1970): 152–75; Henningson, "Northwest Arkansas and the Brothers of Freedom"; Henningson, "Root Hog or Die." The statistical data used in this analysis are drawn from the *Compendium of the Tenth Census*, 687–88, 744–47; and the *Report on the Productions of Agriculture as Returned at the Tenth Census (June 1, 1880)* (Washington, DC: Government Printing Office, 1883), 32–33. For a map showing the geographical regions of Arkansas, see Wheeler, "People's Party in Arkansas," 5. For a list of the counties in the Arkansas Delta, see John Solomon Otto, *The Final Frontiers, 1880–1930: Settling the Southern Bottomlands* (Westport, Conn.: Greenwood Press, 1999), 16.

27. Little Rock *Arkansas Gazette*, September 22, 1907. Some sources spell A. A. Talmage's surname "Tallmage" or "Talmadge."

28. Powderly, *Thirty Years of Labor*, 136–38; Bruce Laurie, *Artisans into Workers: Labor in Nineteenth-Century America* (New York: Hill and Wang, 1989), 142; Weir, *Beyond Labor's Veil*, 21–22, 26–30, including 30n27.

29. Laurie, *Artisans into Workers*, 142; Leon Fink, *Workingmen's Democracy: The Knights of Labor and American Politics* (Urbana: University of Illinois Press, 1983), xii; Jonathan E. Garlock, "A Structural Analysis of the Knights of Labor: A Prolegomenon to the History of the Producing Classes" (PhD diss., University of Rochester, 1974), 235–36.

30. Powderly, *Thirty Years of Labor*, 238–43 (quotations on 243).

31. McMath, *American Populism*, 79.

32. Powderly, *Thirty Years of Labor*, 243–45.

33. Ibid., 136–38, 242; Melton Alonza McLaurin, *The Knights of Labor in the South* (Westport, Conn.: Greenwood Press, 1978), 43; Garlock, *Guide to the Local Assemblies*, 54; Garlock, "Structural Analysis," 235.

34. *Journal of United Labor*, June 25, 1884 (first quotation), April 10, 1886 (other quotations); University of Arkansas at Little Rock, "Census State Data Center, Population by City and Town, 1840–1900," Arkansas Economic Development Institute, accessed December 18, 2016, http://iea.ualr.edu/arkansas-census-data.html?id=168:population-by-city-1840-1900&catid=1&tmpl=component. The *Journal of United Labor* was the national newspaper of the Knights of Labor. It was published from 1880 until 1917; in December 1889 its name was changed to the *Journal of the Knights of Labor*. It was originally published in Marblehead, Mass., and later in Pittsburgh, then Philadelphia, and finally Washington, DC.

35. "Constitution of the General Assembly, District Assemblies, and Local Assemblies of the Order of the Knights of Labor of America" (1885), 59, in the Terence Vincent Powderly Papers, microfilm edition (Glen Rock, N.J.: Microfilming Corporation of America, 1974; hereafter cited as Powderly Papers), reel 64 (quotations); Terence V. Powderly, *The Path I Trod: The Autobiography of Terence V. Powderly*, ed. Harry J. Carman, Henry David, and Paul N. Guthrie (New York: Columbia University Press, 1940; repr., New York: AMS Press, 1968), 47n1.

36. Paul D. Moreno, *Black Americans and Organized Labor: A New History* (Baton Rouge: Louisiana State University Press, 2008), 46; *Compendium of the Tenth Census*, 336.

37. *Journal of United Labor*, June 25, 1884, April 10, 1886.

38. Matthew Hild, "Dan Fraser Tomson (1850–1924)," *Encyclopedia of Arkansas History & Culture*, accessed December 18, 2016, http://www.encyclopediaofarkansas.net/encyclopedia/entry-detail.aspx?entryID=8652.

39. Dan Fraser Tomson to Terence V. Powderly, January 12, 1884, Powderly Papers, reel 6.

40. Powderly, *The Path I Trod*, 103; T. V. Powderly to William Wright, September 19, 1880, Powderly Papers, reel 44.

41. McLaurin, *Knights of Labor in the South*, 134.

42. *Journal of United Labor*, June 25, 1884 (quotations), April 10, 1886.

43. Tomson to Powderly, January 12, 1884, Powderly Papers, reel 6.

44. Garlock, *Guide to the Local Assemblies*, 12.

45. LeeAnn Whites, "Paternalism and Protest in Augusta's Cotton Mills: What's Gender Got to Do with It?," in *Paternalism in a Southern City: Race, Religion, and Gender in Augusta, Georgia*, ed. Edward J. Cashin and Glenn T. Eskew (Athens: University of Georgia Press, 2001), 78 (italics in original quote).

46. Susan Levine, *Labor's True Woman: Carpet Weavers, Industrialization, and Labor Reform in the Gilded Age* (Philadelphia: Temple University Press, 1984), 106.

47. *Journal of United Labor*, January 21, 1888.

48. Garlock, *Guide to the Local Assemblies*, 11–21; *Journal of United Labor*, April 10, 1886; Knights of Labor, Van Buren Assembly, No. 6307, Records, 1886–1892, minute book, April 15, August 5, October 21, 1886, Special Collections Division, University of Arkansas Libraries, Fayetteville. The number of African American local assemblies in the state is based on Garlock, who identifies nineteen of them, the *Journal of United Labor*, October 10–25, 1886, which identifies another (LA 4225 of Argenta, for which Garlock provides no racial designation), and the Van Buren Assembly No. 6307 minute book, which identifies another (Crawford Assembly No. 7558, also in the town of Van Buren, for which Garlock provides no racial designation). Due to incomplete data, the numbers of assemblies including women and including African Americans were probably higher than indicated here.

49. On black female domestic labor in the postbellum South, see Jacqueline Jones, *Labor of Love, Labor of Sorrow: Black Women, Work, and the Family from Slavery to the Present* (New York: Basic Books, 1985); Tera W. Hunter, *To 'Joy My Freedom: Southern Black Women's Lives and Labors after the Civil War* (Cambridge, Mass.: Harvard University Press, 1997). On the Knights of Labor's organizing activities among black domestic workers across the South, see Hild, *Greenbackers*, 82; McLaurin, *Knights of Labor in the South*, 138.

50. *Charlotte* (N.C.) *Home-Democrat*, June 25, 1886.

51. Hunter, *To 'Joy My Freedom*, 108–11.

52. *Journal of United Labor*, June 25, 1884.

53. Ibid., April 10, 1886 (quotations); Garlock, "Structural Analysis," 235. Pine Bluff Assembly No. 2677, founded in 1883, must have experienced a revival after lapsing, for Garlock, *Guide to the Local Assemblies*, 14, lists it being active as late as 1887.

54. Little Rock *Daily Arkansas Gazette*, April 10–11, 1883; Moneyhon, *Arkansas and the New South*, 84.

55. *Third Annual Report of the Commissioner of Labor*, 40. Unlike the Spadra coal miners' strike of 1881, the strikes of 1884 and 1885 were ignored by the Little Rock *Daily Arkansas Gazette* and the Little Rock *Arkansas Democrat*.

56. Arkansas Records Catalog, "International Typographical Union, Local 92, 1884–1978," accessed December 20, 2016, http://www.ark-cat.com/browse

/fulldetail.aspx?id=1882; Little Rock *Daily Arkansas Gazette*, February 2, 1884 (quotations).

57. *Biographical and Historical Memoirs of Eastern Arkansas*, 678; Henningson, "Root Hog or Die," 213.

58. Morgan, *History of the Wheel and Alliance*, 3rd ed., 68; Henningson, "Root Hog or Die," 198.

59. *Journal of United Labor*, May 15, 1880 (quotation); Craig Phelan, *Grand Master Workman: Terence Powderly and the Knights of Labor* (Westport, Conn.: Greenwood Press, 2000), 28–30; Edward T. James, "T.V. Powderly, A Political Profile," *Pennsylvania Magazine of History and Biography* 99 (October 1975): 445–46.

60. Little Rock *Arkansas Democrat*, May 23, 1884.

61. Little Rock *Daily Arkansas Gazette*, May 21, 1884.

62. Henningson, "Root Hog or Die," 199 (quotation, citing the Russellville [Ark.] *Democrat*, June 5, 1884), 200–201, 210.

63. J. D. Yant to Secretary of Center Common Council No. 5 (of the Brothers of Freedom), May 17, 1884, Heartsill Papers, Box 4, File 12.

64. Henningson, "Root Hog or Die," 204; Elkins, "Agricultural Wheel: County Politics," 156–58 (quotations on 158, citing the Conway [Ark.] *Ledger-Democrat*, n.d., as quoted in the Little Rock *Arkansas Daily Democrat*, August 8, 1884).

65. Tomson to Powderly, September 26, 1884, Powderly Papers, reel 8.

66. Tomson to Powderly, January 12, 1884, Powderly Papers, reel 6 (quotations); Tomson to Powderly, September 26, 1884, Powderly Papers, reel 8. On Butler, see Hugh Tulloch, *The Routledge Companion to the American Civil War Era* (London and New York: Routledge, 2006), 114, 145; United States Congress, *Biographical Directory of the United States Congress, 1774–2005* (Washington, DC: Government Printing Office, 2005), 756.

67. Little Rock *Arkansas Daily Democrat*, July 25, 1884, quoted in Elkins, "Agricultural Wheel: County Politics," 162.

68. Henningson, "Root Hog or Die," 209.

69. Kenneth C. Barnes, *Who Killed John Clayton? Political Violence and the Emergence of the New South, 1861–1893* (Durham, N.C.: Duke University Press, 1998), 52–53; Henningson, "Root Hog or Die," 209 including n. 41.

70. *Journal of United Labor*, March 25, 1885.

71. Barjenbruch, "Greenback Political Movement," 112.

72. *Journal of United Labor*, January 10, 1885.

73. Little Rock *Daily Arkansas Gazette*, September 9, 1884.

74. Barnes, *Who Killed John Clayton?*, 53–55; Louise Spears McCants Barry, "Answers in an Autobiography," *Ancestry* 20, no. 5 (2002): 59–63; Guy Lancaster, *Racial Cleansing in Arkansas, 1883–1924: Politics, Land, Labor, and Criminality* (Lanham, Md.: Lexington Books, 2014): 28–30; *Compendium of the Tenth Census*, 336.

75. Morgan, *History of the Wheel and Alliance*, 3rd ed., 69 (last quotation), 85 (other quotations).

76. Henningson, "Root Hog or Die," 213.

77. Tomson to Powderly, September 26, 1884, Powderly Papers, reel 8. Powderly's instructions about contacting McCracken and Walter are handwritten on this letter.

78. Norman J. Ware, *The Labor Movement in the United States, 1860–1895: A Study in Democracy* (New York: D. Appleton, 1929; repr., Gloucester, Mass.: Peter Smith, 1959), 66.

79. Tomson to Powderly, September 26, 1884, Powderly Papers, reel 8. For similar complaints from Knights of Labor leaders in other southern states, see McLaurin, *Knights of Labor in the South*, 160–61.

80. Phelan, *Grand Master Workman*, 152; *Journal of United Labor*, March 25, 1885.

81. Moneyhon, *Arkansas and the New South*, 84; Hild, *Greenbackers*, 66–67.

82. Kenneth D. Ackerman, *The Gold Ring: Jim Fisk, Jay Gould, and Black Friday, 1869* (New York: Dodd, Mead, 1988).

83. *Proceedings of the Thirteenth Regular Session of the General Assembly* [of the Knights of Labor], *Held at Atlanta, Ga., 1889*, in *Record of the Proceedings of the General Assembly of the Knights of Labor, 1878-1913*, microfilm (Madison: State Historical Society of Wisconsin, 1950), 107. On Garrett, see Henry Davenport Northrup, *Life and Achievements of Jay Gould, the Wizard of Wall Street: Being a Complete and Graphic Account of the Greatest Financier of Modern Times* (Philadelphia: National Publishing, 1892), 163.

84. Theodore Saloutos, "The Agricultural Wheel in Arkansas," *Arkansas Historical Quarterly* 2 (March 1943): 133, 138–39.

85. On contact between Powderly and McCracken, see Morgan, *History of the Wheel and Alliance*, 3rd ed., 72–73; Hild, *Greenbackers*, 123.

III. The Great Upheaval

1. Brecher, *Strike!*, chap. 1; Laurie, *Artisans into Workers*, 160–66, 173, 194, 217; Fink, *Workingmen's Democracy*, 26–29, 32–33; Phelan, *Grand Master Workman*, chap. 5.

2. For a table showing the known number of strikes occurring in the United States each year from 1881 through 1905, the number of workers involved, and other statistical data, see David Montgomery, *Workers' Control in America: Studies in the History of Work, Technology, and Labor Struggles* (Cambridge: Cambridge University Press, 1979), 20.

3. On the dominance of railroads in American industry and commerce during the Gilded Age, see, among others, Vincent P. De Santis, *The Shaping of Modern America: 1877–1920*, 3rd ed. (Wheeling, Ill.: Harlan Davidson, 2000), 6–7; Glenn Porter, *The Rise of Big Business, 1860–1920*, 3rd ed. (Wheeling, Ill.: Harlan Davidson, 2006), 34–43.

4. Jerry W. Chandler, "The Knights of Labor and the Southwestern Strikes" (MA thesis, Florida State University, 1970), 17–18 (quotation on 17); Ware, *Labor Movement*, 66, 134–36.

5. Moneyhon, *Arkansas and the New South*, 84.

6. Tomson to Powderly, March 24, 1885, Powderly Papers, reel 9 (quotation); Garlock, *Guide to the Local Assemblies*, 13, 16, 18, 668, 676. Garlock provides a membership figure from 1886 of 200 for LA 3646. For a higher estimate (250 to 300),

see Ralph V. Turner and William Warren Rogers, "Arkansas Labor in Revolt: Little Rock and the Great Southwestern Strike," *Arkansas Historical Quarterly* 24 (Spring 1965): 31.

7. Tomson to Powderly, March 24, 1885, Powderly Papers, reel 9. On district assemblies, see "Constitution of the General Assembly, District Assemblies, and Local Assemblies of the Order of the Knights of Labor of America" (1885), Powderly Papers, reel 64. In addition to district assemblies, the Knights of Labor would soon allow the creation of state assemblies, which served the same function as district assemblies and were more practical in predominantly rural states like Arkansas, although ultimately the Arkansas Knights of Labor would create district assemblies as well as a state assembly. See the *Journal of United Labor*, February 25, 1886; *Proceedings of the General Assembly of the Knights of Labor of America, Eleventh Regular Session, Held at Minneapolis, Minnesota, October 4 to 19, 1887*, 1677–78, in *Record of the Proceedings of the General Assembly of the Knights of Labor*; Phelan, *Grand Master Workman*, 120, 201, 208, 275. The Knights of Labor changed the title "Grand Master Workman" to "General Master Workman" in 1883, but the original title remained in common use, as it has by historians. (Note the title of Phelan's biography of Powderly cited above.) On the title change, see US Congress, House of Representatives, 49th Cong., 2d sess., H.R. 4174, *Investigation of Labor Troubles in Missouri, Arkansas, Kansas, Texas, and Illinois*, Part 1 (Washington, DC: Government Printing Office, 1887), 27 (testimony of Terence V. Powderly).

8. Tomson to Powderly, March 24, 1885, Powderly Papers, reel 9.

9. Phelan, *Grand Master Workman*, 152.

10. Tomson to Powderly, March 24, 1885, Powderly Papers, reel 9.

11. Chandler, "Knights of Labor and the Southwestern Strikes," chap. 2 (quotations on 32 and 38).

12. Garlock, *Guide to the Local Assemblies*, 18, lists "Little Rock/Argenta" as the location of LA 3646. Argenta, now part of North Little Rock, included railroad shops at this time.

13. Ware, *Labor Movement*, 140–41 (quotation on 141); Chandler, "Knights of Labor and the Southwestern Strikes," 43.

14. Chandler, "Knights of Labor and the Southwestern Strikes," 48.

15. Ibid., 52–54.

16. Ware, *Labor Movement*, 144 (quoting the *St. Louis Chronicle*, n.d., quoted in *John Swinton's Paper* [New York], September 30, 1885).

17. Garlock, "Structural Analysis," 235; Garlock, *Guide to the Local Assemblies*, 11–21, 644; Guy Lancaster, "Marianna (Lee County)," *Encyclopedia of Arkansas History & Culture*, accessed February 25, 2018, http://www.encyclopediaofarkansas.net/encyclopedia/entry-detail.aspx?search=1&entryID=918.

18. Tomson to Powderly, December 12, 1885, Powderly Papers, reel 12; Little Rock *Daily Arkansas Gazette*, November 26–27, 1885, January 10, 1886; *Journal of United Labor*, April 10, 1886 (quotations).

19. Tomson to Powderly, December 12, 1885, Powderly Papers, reel 12.

20. Elkins, "Agricultural Wheel: County Politics," 168; Taylor, *Farmers' Movement*, 206; Henningson, "Root Hog or Die," 213–14; Morgan, *History of the Wheel and Alliance*, 3rd ed., 86 (quotations).

21. Morgan, *History of the Wheel and Alliance*, 3rd ed., 85–86; Little Rock *Daily Arkansas Gazette*, August 15, 1885 (quotation).

22. Little Rock *Daily Arkansas Gazette*, September 30, 1885.

23. Ibid., October 15, 1885.

24. John Cameron Simonds and John T. McEnnis, *The Story of Manual Labor in All Lands and Ages: Its Past Condition, Present Progress, and Hope for the Future* (Chicago: R. S. Peale, 1887), 451; Ruth A. Allen, *The Great Southwest Strike*, University of Texas Publication No. 4214 (Austin: University of Texas, 1942), 47.

25. Phelan, *Grand Master Workman*, 179.

26. Case, *Great Southwest Railroad Strike*, 151.

27. Simonds and McEnnis, *Story of Manual Labor*, 451–52; Allen, *Great Southwest Strike*, 50; Garlock, *Guide to the Local Assemblies*, 499. Hall's foreman, J. A. Crosbie, later claimed that he had only granted Hall "leave of absence for a couple of hours" and that Hall "had been discharged for absence without leave and incompetency." Little Rock *Daily Arkansas Gazette*, April 7, 1886.

28. Powderly, *Path I Trod*, 121; Ruth A. Allen, "Irons, Martin," *Handbook of Texas Online*, accessed January 6, 2017, https://tshaonline.org/handbook/online/articles/fir07; *Sedalia* (Mo.) *Sunday Democrat*, November 25, 1900.

29. Powderly, *Path I Trod*, 121–22; Allen, *Great Southwest Strike*, chap. 5 (first quote on 56, second quote on 62); Phelan, *Grand Master Workman*, 179.

30. Case, *Great Southwest Railroad Strike*, 174.

31. *Proceedings of the First Annual Session of District Assembly No. 78, Knights of Labor, Held at Galveston, Texas, Jan. 4–9, 1886* (Fort Worth: Labor Siftings Cooperative Publishing, 1886), 52–53; *Record of the Proceedings of the Tenth Regular Session of the General Assembly* [of the Knights of Labor], *Held at Richmond, Va., Oct. 4–20, 1886*, 170; Garlock, *Guide to the Local Assemblies*, 492; Allen, *Great Southwest Strike*, 45–46; Case, *Great Southwest Railroad Strike*, 90.

32. Turner and Rogers, "Arkansas Labor in Revolt," 29, 31–32 (first quotation on 32); Little Rock *Daily Arkansas Gazette*, March 12, 1886 (second quotation).

33. Turner and Rogers, "Arkansas Labor in Revolt," 29–46 (quotation on 40); Little Rock *Daily Arkansas Gazette*, March 7, 12, 1886; Chandler, "Knights of Labor and the Southwestern Strikes," 87.

34. Phelan, *Grand Master Workman*, 180–83, 189; Turner and Rogers, "Arkansas Labor in Revolt," 44–45; Bureau of Labor Statistics and Inspection of Missouri, *The Official History of the Great Strike of 1886 on the Southwestern Railway System* (Jefferson City, Mo.: Tribune Printing, State Printers and Binders, 1887), 109; Thekla Ellen Joiner, *Sin in the City: Chicago and Revivalism, 1880–1920* (Columbia: University of Missouri Press, 2007), 47–48; Knights of Labor, Van Buren Assembly, No. 6307, Records, minute book, April 29, 1886; US Congress, House of Representatives, 49th Cong., 2d sess., H.R. 4174, *Investigation of Labor Troubles in Missouri, Arkansas,*

Kansas, Texas, and Illinois, Part 2 (Washington, DC: Government Printing Office, 1887), 406 (testimony of James Yates); *Record of the Proceedings of the Tenth Regular Session of the General Assembly*, 126. For a full account of the Haymarket Riot, see James Green, *Death in the Haymarket: A Story of Chicago, the First Labor Movement, and the Bombing That Divided Gilded Age America* (New York: Pantheon, 2006).

35. Chandler, "Knights of Labor and the Southwestern Strikes," iii, 85, 89; Turner and Rogers, "Arkansas Labor in Revolt," 44–45; Laurie, *Artisans into* Workers, 169–74; Ware, *Labor Movement*, 66, 148–49. Weir, *Beyond Labor's Veil*, 12, suggests that the Knights of Labor's self-reported membership figure of 729,677 in 1886 was an undercount, and that actual membership that year probably exceeded one million.

36. Hild, *Greenbackers*, 74–75, 225.

37. Little Rock *Daily Arkansas Gazette*, December 2, 1884, April 6, 1886 (quotations).

38. Magnolia (Ark.) *Columbia Banner*, April 22, 1886. McCracken's letter undoubtedly appeared in other Agricultural Wheel newspapers that are no longer extant. The Columbia County Wheel endorsed the *Columbia Banner* as its official organ about two months later, as reported in the July 8, 1886 issue.

39. Little Rock *Daily Arkansas Gazette*, May 16, 1886; Steven Teske, "Mabelvale (Pulaski County)," *Encyclopedia of Arkansas History & Culture*, accessed January 16, 2017, http://www.encyclopediaofarkansas.net/encyclopedia/entry-detail.aspx?entryID=6341; Garlock, *Guide to the Local Assemblies*, 18. Mabelvale was annexed into Little Rock in the 1970s and is now a neighborhood in the southern part of that city.

40. Little Rock *Daily Arkansas Gazette*, June 9, 1886 (all quotations except Langley); Elkins, "State Politics and the Agricultural Wheel," 252, 255 (Langley quotation). Jack Abramowitz, "The Negro in the Populist Movement," *Journal of Negro History* 38 (July 1953): 266–67, claims that Isom P. Langley was black, but a biographical sketch (with illustration) of him in Morgan, *History of the Wheel and Alliance*, 3rd ed., 335–36, clearly shows that he was white.

41. Elkins, "State Politics and the Agricultural Wheel," 252–55 (quotations); Magnolia (Ark.) *Columbia Banner*, June 17, 1886.

42. Little Rock *Daily Arkansas Gazette*, June 10, 1886. For more examples of opposition among Arkansas Wheelers to the nomination of a State Wheel political ticket, see the Magnolia (Ark.) *Columbia Banner*, July 15, 1886; W. B. W. Heartsill to T. W. Newton, June 11, 1886, Heartsill Papers, Box 4, File 13.

43. Little Rock *State Wheel-Enterprise*, n.d., quoted in the Yellville (Ark.) *Mountain Echo*, June 11, 1886.

44. Little Rock *Daily Arkansas Gazette*, June 11, 1886. The Knights of Labor Reading platform of 1878 did not address the graduated income tax or the regulation of railroads, but in 1884 the platform was revised, and that platform included both a demand for a graduated income tax and another calling for government ownership of telegraphs, telephones, and railroads. See Ware, *Labor Movement*, 377–80, for the platforms of the Knights of Labor, and the *New York Times*, February 23, 1878, for the National (Greenback-Labor) Party platform.

45. Matthew J. Mancini, *One Dies, Get Another: Convict Leasing in the American South, 1866–1928* (Columbia: University of South Carolina Press, 1996), 117–20; Jane Zimmerman, "The Convict Lease System in Arkansas and the Fight for Abolition," *Arkansas Historical Quarterly* 8 (Autumn 1949): 174–75. The convict-lease law that the state enacted in 1883 required the state to pay only one expense associated with the care of the prisoners: the salary of a physician who would be responsible for their medical care.

46. Elkins, "State Politics and the Agricultural Wheel," 256–57; Moneyhon, *Arkansas and the New South*, 29.

47. *Journal of United Labor*, October 10–25, 1886.

48. Ibid. (all quotations except the "until the [cotton crop] was out of the grass" quotation); Little Rock *Daily Arkansas Gazette*, July 6, 1886 ("until the [cotton crop] was out of the grass" quotation); *New York Times*, July 7, 1886; William Warren Rogers, "Negro Knights of Labor in Arkansas: A Case Study of the 'Miscellaneous' Strike," *Labor History* 10 (Summer 1969): 498–505; Case, *Great Southwest Railroad Strike*, 214–15. Rogers says that the strike began on July 2, 1886, but the Little Rock *Daily Arkansas Gazette*, July 6, 1886, and the *New York Times*, July 7, 1886, both reported that it began on July 1.

49. *Journal of United Labor*, October 10–25, 1886.

50. Garlock, *Guide to the Local Assemblies*, 11–21.

51. Little Rock *Daily Arkansas Gazette*, July 10, 1886; Little Rock *Arkansas Democrat*, July 9, 1886.

52. Little Rock *Arkansas Democrat*, July 10, 1886.

53. *Proceedings of the General Assembly of the Knights of Labor, 1887*, 1396 (quotation), 1631, 1832, 1842.

54. Little Rock *Daily Arkansas Gazette*, July 8, 1886.

55. Case, *Great Southwest Railroad Strike*, 215–16.

56. Ibid., 216–17; Rogers, "Negro Knights of Labor in Arkansas," 499, 505; Little Rock *Arkansas Democrat*, August 30, September 16, 1886.

57. Edward T. James, "American Labor and Political Action, 1865–1896: The Knights of Labor and Its Predecessors" (PhD diss., Harvard University, 1954), 315n87.

58. Magnolia (Ark.) *Columbia Banner*, September 16, 1886.

59. Little Rock *Daily Arkansas Gazette*, September 8 (first quotation), 18, 1886; Magnolia (Ark.) *Columbia Banner*, October 21, 1886; F. Clark Elkins, "The Agricultural Wheel in Arkansas, 1887," *Arkansas Historical Quarterly* 40 (Autumn 1981): 249n2 (second quotation).

60. *New York Times*, August 6, 1886; Little Rock *Daily Arkansas Gazette*, August 6, 1886.

61. Little Rock *Daily Arkansas Gazette*, August 14, 1886.

62. Elkins, "State Politics and the Agricultural Wheel," 257.

63. Magnolia (Ark.) *Columbia Banner*, August 26, 1886.

64. *New York Times*, August 16, 1886.

65. Moore, Preimesberger, and Tarr, *Congressional Quarterly's Guide to U.S. Elections*, 1419; *New York Times*, September 26, 1886; Elkins, "State Politics and the Agricultural Wheel," 256; Little Rock *Daily Arkansas Gazette*, October 1, 1886.

66. Moore, Preimesberger, and Tarr, *Congressional Quarterly's Guide to U.S. Elections*, 938; United States Congress, *Biographical Directory*, 215, including n. 8; Prescott (Ark.) *Times-Picayune*, April 12, 1900.

67. Elkins, "State Politics and the Agricultural Wheel," 254; Little Rock *Daily Arkansas Gazette*, November 27, 1886; Henningson, "Root Hog or Die," 209. Elkins claims that CarlLee ran as a Union Labor candidate for Congress in 1884 but bases this erroneous statement on a misprint or mistake in *Biographical and Historical Memoirs of Eastern Arkansas* that says 1884 where it should say 1886 (237). That CarlLee did not run for Congress in 1884 is confirmed by Moore, Preimesberger, and Tarr, *Congressional Quarterly's Guide to U.S. Elections*, 934. As for the claim that CarlLee ran for Congress as a Union Labor candidate, the Union Labor Party was not formed until February 1887; see Hild, *Greenbackers*, 105–6.

68. Prescott (Ark.) *Times-Picayune*, April 12, 1900; Little Rock *Daily Arkansas Gazette*, September 21 (first quotation), 24 (second and third quotations), October 20, 1886. Moore, Preimesberger, and Tarr, *Congressional Quarterly's Guide to U.S. Elections*, 938, refers to Hitt as a Greenback candidate.

69. Little Rock *Arkansas Democrat*, October 27, 1886. On Williams as a Knight of Labor, see the Little Rock *Daily Arkansas Gazette*, July 31, 1888.

70. Little Rock *Daily Arkansas Gazette*, November 27, 1886; Garlock, *Guide to the Local Assemblies*, 16.

71. Little Rock *Daily Arkansas Gazette*, November 27, 1886; Garlock, *Guide to the Local Assemblies*, 17–19; Elizabeth Sanders, *Roots of Reform: Farmers, Workers, and the American State, 1877–1917* (Chicago: University of Chicago Press, 1999), 46; Morgan, *History of the Wheel and Alliance*, 3rd ed., 335–36; *Biographical and Historical Memoirs of Eastern Arkansas*, 189–90 (quotation on 190); Dubin, *United States Congressional Elections*, 271; Moore, Preimesberger, and Tarr, *Congressional Quarterly's Guide to U.S. Elections*, 938. No copies of the *Industrial Liberator* are known to be extant.

72. Jasper *Arkansas Wheel*, September 30, 1886.

73. *Biographical and Historical Memoirs of Eastern Arkansas*, 190.

74. Knights of Labor, Van Buren Assembly, No. 6307, Records, minute book, September 16, October 28, December 13, 1886, June 21, July 19, 1887, February 8, 1890; Little Rock *Daily Arkansas Gazette*, November 27, 1886; Garlock, *Guide to the Local Assemblies*, 12–14, 19; *Third Annual Report of the Commissioner of Labor*, 40. On the Knights of Labor's ban upon "electioneering for any candidate," see the *Journal of United Labor*, May 15, 1880; for the ban on discussing "the merit of the candidates" during local assembly meetings, see T. V. Powderly to B. H. Webster, July 30, 1886, Powderly Papers, reel 47.

75. Tomson to Powderly, January 24, 1887, Powderly Papers, reel 20.

76. Powderly, *Thirty Years of Labor*, 645–48.

77. Tomson to Powderly, January 24, 1887, Powderly Papers, reel 20 (emphasis is in the letter); Garlock, "Structural Analysis," 235; *Record of the Proceedings of the Tenth*

Regular Session of the General Assembly, 328; *Record of the Proceedings of the Eleventh Regular Session of the General Assembly*, 1850.

78. *Journal of United Labor*, August 13, 1887 (quotations); Garlock, *Guide to the Local Assemblies*, 20. For additional examples of opposition faced by the Knights of Labor in Arkansas in 1887, see the *Journal of United Labor*, September 24, October 29, 1887.

79. Garlock, *Guide to the Local Assemblies*, 11–21; *Compendium of the Eleventh Census: 1890* (Washington, DC: Government Printing Office, 1892), 477.

80. *Journal of United Labor*, October 22, 1887 (all quotations except "cooperative institutions"); Ware, *Labor Movement*, 378.

81. *Journal of United Labor*, December 3, 1887.

82. Saloutos, "Agricultural Wheel," 135; Morgan, *History of the Wheel and Alliance*, 3rd ed., 73.

83. Elkins, "Agricultural Wheel in Arkansas," 254, 259.

84. Little Rock *Daily Arkansas Gazette*, February 3, 1887.

85. Elkins, "Agricultural Wheel in Arkansas," 250–51.

86. *Fordyce* (Ark.) *Enterprise*, n.d., quoted in the Little Rock *Arkansas Democrat*, July 30, 1887. On the Knights of Labor in Dallas County, see Garlock, *Guide to the Local Assemblies*, 12. On the Agricultural Wheel in Dallas County, see *Biographical and Historical Memoirs of Southern Arkansas* (Chicago: Goodspeed Publishing, 1890), 726, 734.

87. Isbell *Alabama State Wheel*, n.d., quoted in the *Journal of United Labor*, July 2, 1887.

88. Elkins, "Agricultural Wheel in Arkansas," 253–56 (quotation on 256).

89. Dunning, *Farmers' Alliance History*, 206–8.

90. The *Arkansas Gazette* only reported on one strike in 1887, a strike by workers on a courthouse project in Pulaski County in July. While this may not have been the only strike that occurred in the state that year, the newspaper's index for 1886 lists strikes under four subheadings. Shannon J. Henderson, comp., *Arkansas Gazette Index: An Arkansas Index, 1886* (Russellville: Arkansas Tech University Library, 1985), 107; Shannon J. Henderson, comp., *Arkansas Gazette Index: An Arkansas Index, 1887* (Russellville: Arkansas Tech University Library, 1985), 88, 136. Nationally, the number of recorded strikes rose from 1,432 in 1886 to 1,436 in 1887, but the number of workers involved in those strikes dropped from 407,000 in 1886 to 273,000 in 1887. Montgomery, *Workers' Control in America*, 20.

91. Fink, *Workingmen's Democracy*, 26 (quotation), 28–29.

IV. The Union Labor Party

1. John William Graves, *Town and Country: Race Relations in an Urban-Rural Context, Arkansas, 1865–1905* (Fayetteville: University of Arkansas Press, 1990), 107.

2. William L. Shea, "Isaac Murphy, 1864–1868," in *The Governors of Arkansas: Essays in Political Biography*, ed. Timothy P. Donovan and Willard B. Gatewood Jr. (Fayetteville: University of Arkansas Press, 1981), 39–40; Barnes, *Who Killed John Clayton?*, 21 (quotation).

3. Staff of the Encyclopedia of Arkansas History & Culture, "Office of the Governor," *Encyclopedia of Arkansas History & Culture*, accessed March 28, 2017, http://www.encyclopediaofarkansas.net/encyclopedia/entry-detail.aspx?search=1&entryID=5676.

4. Nathan Fine, *Labor and Farmer Parties in the United States, 1828–1928* (New York: Rand School of Social Science, 1928; repr., New York: Russell and Russell, 1961), 71–72; *New York Times*, February 23, 1887; Birmingham *Alabama Sentinel*, September 3, 1887 (quotations, from reprinted platform adopted by the ULP at Cincinnati); McMath, *American Populism*, 167–68, 170–71.

5. *Cincinnati Enquirer*, February 24, 1887; Little Rock *Arkansas Gazette*, June 12, 1890.

6. On the negligible strength of the ULP nationally, see Fine, *Labor and Farmer Parties*, 69–72; Fink, *Workingmen's Democracy*, 27, 32.

7. According to Henderson, *Arkansas Gazette Index 1887*, 165, that newspaper only mentioned the Union Labor Party twice that year, once on February 23 and again two days later, both times reporting on the formation of the national party in Cincinnati.

8. Little Rock *Daily Arkansas Gazette*, February 26, 1888; Forrest City *East Arkansian*, March 10, 1888, reprinted in ibid., March 14, 1888 (quotation).

9. *Journal of United Labor*, March 31, 1888.

10. Little Rock *Arkansas Democrat*, March 14, 1888.

11. Ibid., March 22, 1888.

12. Little Rock *Daily Arkansas Gazette*, March 22, 1888.

13. Little Rock *Arkansas Democrat*, March 26, 1888.

14. *Fayetteville* (Ark.) *Democrat*, April 6, 1888.

15. Little Rock *Daily Arkansas Gazette*, April 8, 1888.

16. *Marianna* (Ark.) *Index*, n.d., quoted in ibid., April 11, 1888. The spelling of Featherston's name with an *e* added to the end is not uncommon in primary and secondary sources. This study uses the spelling without the added *e* because it seems more common in most sources and because that is the spelling used in the Wheel history that later became the official Farmers' Alliance history: Morgan, *History of the Wheel and Alliance*, 3rd ed., 73, 74, 113, 318–19.

17. Little Rock *Arkansas Democrat*, April 16, 1888.

18. Barnes, *Who Killed John Clayton?*, 70; Dubin, *United States Congressional Elections*, 279; Bradley S. Jordan, "A Path Less Traveled: The Life and Times of Louis Porter Featherston" (MA thesis, University of Arkansas at Little Rock, 2016), 14–17.

19. Wheeler, "People's Party in Arkansas," 143; Clifton Paisley, "The Political Wheelers and Arkansas's Election of 1888," *Arkansas Historical Quarterly* 25 (Spring 1966): 4 (first quotation); Little Rock *Daily Arkansas Gazette*, May 1, 1888 (second quotation).

20. Wheeler, "People's Party in Arkansas," 144.

21. *St. Louis Post-Dispatch*, May 1, 1888; Little Rock *Daily Arkansas Gazette*, August 14, 1888.

22. Little Rock *Daily Arkansas Gazette*, April 5, May 1, 1888; *St. Louis Post-Dispatch*, May 1, 1888; Graves, *Town and Country*, 205–6.

23. Graves, *Town and Country*, 140; Hild, *Greenbackers*, 116.

24. Moneyhon, *Arkansas and the New South*, 86.

25. Little Rock *Daily Arkansas Gazette*, March 24, April 3 (first quotation), May 1 (other quotations), May 3, September 2, 1888; Mancini, *One Dies, Get Another*, 121–22. On contract labor in the United States during this era, see De Santis, *Shaping of Modern America*, 4; Melvyn Dubofsky and Foster Rhea Dulles, *Labor in America: A History*, 8th ed. (Wheeling, Ill.: Harlan Davidson, 2010), 86–87.

26. *Journal of United Labor*, April 28, 1888 (quotation); Garlock, *Guide to the Local Assemblies*, 13.

27. *Journal of United Labor*, March 17, 1888.

28. Ibid., June 30, 1888.

29. Knights of Labor, Van Buren Assembly, No. 6307, Records, minute book, June 5, 1888. Despite the efforts of the Arkansas Knights of Labor State Executive Board, Tomson may have lost his farm at this time; the *Journal of United Labor*, July 5, 1888, reported that "the address of Dan Fraser Tomson, Master Workman of Arkansas State Assembly, is changed from Hot Springs to Washburn, Ark."

30. *Journal of United Labor*, December 20, 1888; Little Rock *Daily Arkansas Gazette*, July 31, 1888.

31. Garland E. Bayliss, "Public Affairs in Arkansas, 1874–1896" (PhD diss., University of Texas at Austin, 1972), 301. Ironically, the Knights of Labor State Assembly met in the same city where State Master Workman Dan Fraser Tomson had been hanged in effigy earlier in the year, but nevertheless he received a grand welcome; see the *Journal of United Labor*, August 23, 1888.

32. *Journal of United Labor*, August 16, 1888.

33. Ibid., June 30, 1888. For a list of district assemblies chartered between the Knights of Labor General Assembly meeting of October 1887 and that of November 1888, including seven in Arkansas, see Powderly, *Thirty Years of Labor*, 647–48.

34. Kenneth C. Martis, *The Historical Atlas of United States Congressional Districts, 1789–1983* (New York: Free Press, 1982), 123; Dubin, *United States Congressional Elections*, 279.

35. Knights of Labor, Van Buren Assembly, No. 6307, Records, minute book, February 14, 1888.

36. Martis, *Historical Atlas*, 123; Dubin, *United States Congressional Elections*, 279; Moore, Preimesberger, and Tarr, *Congressional Quarterly's Guide to U.S. Elections*, 942.

37. Little Rock *Daily Arkansas Gazette*, July 26, 1888 (all quotations except the last one); Bayliss, "Public Affairs in Arkansas," 301. McCracken himself offered the resolution thanking the ULP.

38. Little Rock *Arkansas Democrat*, April 6, 1888.

39. Meridian Agricultural Wheel, Minutes and Proceedings Book, July 21, 1888; Little Rock *Daily Arkansas Gazette*, June 7, 1888; Magnolia (Ark.) *Columbia Banner*, September 27, 1888.

40. *Osceola* (Ark.) *Times*, June 9, 1888.

41. Little Rock *Daily Arkansas Gazette*, June 16, 1888.

42. *Hot Springs* (Ark.) *Sentinel*, n.d., quoted in the Little Rock *Arkansas Democrat*, June 20, 1888.

43. Little Rock *Daily Arkansas Gazette*, June 16, 1888.

44. Paisley, "Political Wheelers," 14–15; Elkins, "State Politics and the Agricultural Wheel," 255 (Langley quotation); W. Scott Morgan, *History of the Wheel and Alliance, and the Impending Revolution* (Hardy, Ark.: s.p., 1889), 255–56, 258–59 (quotation on 258).

45. Little Rock *Daily Arkansas Gazette*, August 17, 1888.

46. Ibid., September 2, 1888.

47. Whayne et al., *Arkansas*, 235–36; Graves, *Town and Country*, 29; Matkin-Rawn, "We Fight for the Rights of Our Race," 28.

48. "Report of the General Secretary," 5, in *Record of the Proceedings of the Twelfth Regular Session of the General Assembly* [of the Knights of Labor], *Held at Indianapolis, Ind., Nov. 13–27, 1888.*

49. Paisley, "Political Wheelers," 3.

50. Garlock, *Guide to the Local Assemblies*, 15; Little Rock *Daily Arkansas Gazette*, May 22, 1888 (quotations).

51. Little Rock *Daily Arkansas Gazette*, May 19, 1888.

52. Ibid., July 19, 1888.

53. Ibid., July 20, 1888.

54. Yellville (Ark.) *Mountain Echo*, July 20, 1888; *Appleton's Annual Cyclopaedia and Register of Important Events of the Year 1891* (New York: D. Appleton, 1892), 29.

55. *Lonoke* (Ark.) *Democrat*, n.d., quoted in the Little Rock *Daily Arkansas Gazette*, July 20, 1888.

56. Whayne et al., *Arkansas*, 279; Krista M. Jones, "'It Was Awful, but It Was Politics': Crittenden County and the Demise of African American Political Participation" (MA thesis, University of Arkansas, 2012), 62–77; Matkin-Rawn, "We Fight for the Rights of Our Race," 47–48.

57. Randy Finley, *From Slavery to Uncertain Freedom: The Freedmen's Bureau in Arkansas, 1865–1869* (Fayetteville: University of Arkansas Press, 1996), 150.

58. Nancy E. Marion and Willard M. Oliver, *Killing Congress: Assassinations, Attempted Assassinations and Other Violence against Members of Congress* (Lanham, Md.: Lexington Books, 2014), 2, 8–12; William B. Darrow, "The Killing of Congressman James Hinds," *Arkansas Historical Quarterly* 74 (Spring 2015): 18–55.

59. Little Rock *Daily Arkansas Gazette*, May 19, July 21 (quotation), 1888; Little Rock *Arkansas Democrat*, July 20, 1888.

60. Little Rock *Arkansas Democrat*, July 20, 1888; *Osceola* (Ark.) *Times*, July 28, 1888.

61. *Chicago Mail*, n.d., quoted in the Little Rock *Daily Arkansas Gazette*, July 13, 1888.

62. Paisley, "Political Wheelers," quoting the Little Rock *Daily Arkansas Gazette*, August 3, 1888.

63. Little Rock *Daily Arkansas Gazette*, August 17, 1888; Little Rock *Arkansas Democrat*, August 17, 1888.

64. Little Rock *Daily Arkansas Gazette*, September 2, 1888.

65. *Journal of United Labor*, September 6, 1888.

66. *Appleton's Annual Cyclopaedia 1891*, 29.

67. Paisley, "Political Wheelers," 17 (first and last quotations); Little Rock *Arkansas Democrat*, October 2, 1888 (Streeter quotations).

68. Mark Wahlgren Summers, *Party Games: Getting, Keeping, and Using Power in Gilded Age Politics* (Chapel Hill: University of North Carolina Press, 2004), 12–13, 117–21; Barnes, *Who Killed John Clayton?*, 96 (quotation).

69. Chris M. Branam, "Another Look at Disfranchisement in Arkansas, 1888–1894," *Arkansas Historical Quarterly* 69 (Autumn 2010): 245–46. On election fraud elsewhere in the South during this era, see William Warren Rogers, *The One-Gallused Rebellion: Agrarianism in Alabama, 1865–1896* (Baton Rouge: Louisiana State University Press, 1970), 222, 224–26; Barton C. Shaw, *The Wool-Hat Boys: Georgia's Populist Party* (Baton Rouge: Louisiana State University Press, 1984), 75–76, 93–94, 115–18, 122; Matthew Hild, "The Knights of Labor and the Third-Party Movement in Texas, 1886–1896," *Southwestern Historical Quarterly* 119 (July 2015): 40–42.

70. Other newspapers that published this letter include the Little Rock *Daily Arkansas Gazette*, September 22, 1888, and the Fayetteville (N.C.) *Messenger*, October 12, 1888. The *Messenger* was the official organ of the North Carolina Knights of Labor State Assembly and a staunch supporter of the Union Labor Party. For a secondary source that corroborates and sheds additional light upon some of CarlLee's charges, see Kenneth C. Barnes, *Journey of Hope: The Back-to-Africa Movement in Arkansas in the Late 1800s* (Chapel Hill: University of North Carolina Press, 2004), 50–51.

71. Little Rock *Arkansas Democrat*, October 2, 1888 (quotation); Little Rock *Daily Arkansas Gazette*, September 22, 1888.

72. Little Rock *Daily Arkansas Gazette*, September 22, 1888. See also the Little Rock *Arkansas Democrat*, September 22, 1888; *Fayetteville* (Ark.) *Democrat*, September 28, 1888.

73. Little Rock *Daily Arkansas Gazette*, September 23, 1888.

74. Paisley, "Political Wheelers," 17; Hild, *Greenbackers*, x (map); Branam, "Another Look at Disfranchisement," 257–62 (appendix listing racial composition of each Arkansas county in 1890 and the results of the gubernatorial elections of 1888 through 1894 and the poll tax referendum of 1892 by county); Garlock, *Guide to the Local Assemblies*, 11–21; Michael Pierce, "Labor Movement," *Encyclopedia of Arkansas History & Culture*, accessed May 16, 2017, http://www.encyclopediaofarkansas.net/encyclopedia/entry-detail.aspx?search=1&entryID=4235.

75. Jason McCollom, "The Agricultural Wheel, the Union Labor Party, and the 1889 Arkansas Legislature," *Arkansas Historical Quarterly* 68 (Summer 2009): 157, 161; Magnolia (Ark.) *Columbia Banner*, October 21, 1886, September 27, 1888; *Journal of United Labor*, August 22, 1889 (quotation). The number of Republican and Union Labor candidates elected to the state house of representatives is taken from

McCollom; the *Columbia Banner*, September 27, 1888, a Wheel but also Democratic newspaper, claims that only nine Republicans and seven Union Laborites won election to the state house.

76. Dubin, *United States Congressional Elections*, 271, 279; Little Rock *Daily Arkansas Gazette*, September 12, October 3, November 4, 1888; *Eureka Springs* (Ark.) *Echo*, n.d., quoted in the Little Rock *Daily Arkansas Gazette*, October 17, 1888; Mountain Home (Ark.) *Baxter County Citizen*, n.d., quoted in the Little Rock *Daily Arkansas Gazette*, October 17, 1888; Barnes, *Who Killed John Clayton?*, 60; Conway (Ark.) *Faulkner County Wheel*, n.d., quoted in the Little Rock *Daily Arkansas Gazette*, November 4, 1888.

77. Shannon J. Henderson, comp., *Arkansas Gazette Index: An Arkansas Index, 1888* (Russellville: Arkansas Tech University Library, 1986), 48–51.

78. *Memphis Appeal*, n.d., quoted in the Little Rock *Daily Arkansas Gazette*, November 3, 1888; *New York Times*, April 11, 1888.

79. Little Rock *Daily Arkansas Gazette*, November 3, 1888.

80. *Lonoke* (Ark.) *Democrat*, n.d., quoted in the Little Rock *Daily Arkansas Gazette*, October 25, 1888.

81. Dubin, *United States Congressional Elections*, 279; Little Rock *Daily Arkansas Gazette*, November 16, 1888.

82. Little Rock *Daily Arkansas Gazette*, November 18, 1888; *Appleton's Annual Cyclopaedia 1891*, 29; Garlock, *Guide to the Local Assemblies*, 11–21; Jones, "It Was Awful, but It Was Politics," 69–70.

83. Fine, *Labor and Farmer Parties*, 70.

84. Jordan, "Path Less Traveled," 35; Barnes, *Who Killed John Clayton?*, 74; Chester H. Rowell, comp., *Digest of Contested-Election Cases in the Fifty-First Congress* (Washington, DC: Government Printing Office, 1891), 75 (quotation).

85. Barnes, *Who Killed John Clayton?*, 66–87 (quotation on 87); Larry Taylor, "Plumerville (Conway County)," *Encyclopedia of Arkansas History & Culture*, accessed May 19, 2017, http://www.encyclopediaofarkansas.net/encyclopedia/entry-detail.aspx?search=1&entryID=6166; *Savannah* (Ga.) *Tribune*, April 6, 1889. The newspaper account gives Joseph Smith's middle initial as P., whereas Barnes (85) says it was W.

86. Dubin, *United States Congressional Elections*, 271, 279, 285, 286nn2–3, 287.

87. Graves, *Town and Country*, 143–44 (quotation on 144); Matkin-Rawn, "We Fight for the Rights of Our Race," 45. Graves refers to the four Pulaski County representatives who were given their seats in February 1889 as Union Labor–Republican nominees, but both the Little Rock *Arkansas Democrat*, August 17, 1888, and the Little Rock *Daily Arkansas Gazette*, August 17, 1888, report that the Union Labor Party nominated these men while indicating that the county Republican convention was split about endorsing them.

88. Melanie K. Welch, "Violence and the Decline of Black Politics in St. Francis County," *Arkansas Historical Quarterly* 60 (Winter 2001): 360–93 (quotation on 368).

89. *Journal of United Labor*, November 1, 1888. See also ibid., December 20, 1888.

90. Ibid., November 22 (first quotation), December 20 (other quotations), 1888; John H. Robertson to T. V. Powderly, August 31, 1892, Powderly Papers, reel 39; Robertson to Heartsill, August 31, 1896, Heartsill Papers, Box 4, File 11.

91. Tomson, Wilson, McSlarrow, Dill, and Williams to Powderly, January 2, 1889, Powderly Papers, reel 28. Someone other than Tomson must have signed his name to this letter, since it is misspelled as "Thompson."

92. Phelan, *Grand Master Workman*, 250–51; Ware, *Labor Movement*, 66.

93. Paisley, "Political Wheelers," 3, 16, 19; Wheeler, "People's Party in Arkansas," 159.

94. Moneyhon, *Arkansas and the New South*, 86; Wheeler, "People's Party in Arkansas," 160, 162; McMath, *Populist Vanguard*, 33, 59.

95. McMath, *Populist Vanguard*, 44–45, 59; William F. Holmes, "The Arkansas Cotton Pickers Strike of 1891 and the Demise of the Colored Farmers' Alliance," *Arkansas Historical Quarterly* 32 (Summer 1973): 107–19; Wheeler, "People's Party in Arkansas," 162 (quotations); F. G. Blood, *Hand Book and History of the National Farmers' Alliance and Industrial Union* (Washington, DC: n.p., 1893), 45–46. The author has corrected Wheeler's use of the term "Colored National Farmers' Alliance" to "Colored Farmers' National Alliance." Adding to the confusion regarding first the consolidation of the two separate state Alliance organizations and then the approval of the Farmers' Alliance–Agricultural Wheel merger in Arkansas was the adoption by the Arkansas State Wheel—at some point after the Meridian, Miss., meeting—of the name State Farmers' and Laborers' Union. The merger agreement made between the Southern Farmers' Alliance and the National Agricultural Wheel at Meridian had named the new combined organization the Farmers' and Laborers' Union of America, although that name proved short-lived and was soon changed to the National Farmers' Alliance and Industrial Union of America. See Wheeler, "People's Party in Arkansas," 164; Blood, *Hand Book*, 45; McMath, *Populist Vanguard*, 59–60, 87. Exactly when the Arkansas State Wheel changed its name is unclear; the *Arkansas Gazette* continued to use the Wheel name throughout 1889. See Shannon J. Henderson, comp., *Arkansas Gazette Index: An Arkansas Index, 1889* (Russellville: Arkansas Tech University Library, 1986), 4–5.

96. *Journal of United Labor*, February 28, March 28, April 11, 18, 25, May 9, 16, June 6, 1889; Little Rock *Arkansas Gazette*, August 20, 1890.

97. *Journal of United Labor*, March 14, 1889.

98. Ibid., May 30, 1889.

99. Daniel Letwin, *The Challenge of Interracial Unionism: Alabama Coal Miners, 1878–1921* (Chapel Hill: University of North Carolina Press, 1998), 43; *Report of the Committee of the Senate upon the Relations between Labor and Capital, and Testimony Taken by the Committee* (Washington, DC: Government Printing Office, 1885), 33.

100. Little Rock *Arkansas Gazette*, March 15, 1889.

101. Ibid., May 14, 1889; Little Rock *Arkansas Democrat*, February 13, 1889.

102. *Journal of United Labor*, August 22, 1889.

103. Ibid., September 19, 1889.

104. McMath, *American Populism*, 165 (quotation); United States Congress, *Biographical Directory*, 1285.

105. Dewey W. Grantham, *The Life and Death of the Solid South: A Political History* (Lexington: University Press of Kentucky, 1988), 53.

106. McCollom, "Agricultural Wheel," 159 (first quotation), 172–74 (second quotation on 172).

107. Little Rock *Daily Arkansas Gazette*, August 15, 1885.

108. Powderly, *Thirty Years of Labor*, 244.

109. McCollom, "Agricultural Wheel," 173–44; *Biographical and Historical Memoirs of Eastern Arkansas*, 59 (quotation).

110. *Journal of United Labor*, August 22, 1889 (first quotation); Conway (Ark.) *Faulkner County Wheel*, February 5, 1890, quoted in the Little Rock *Arkansas Gazette*, February 8, 1890 (second and third quotations).

111. Little Rock *Arkansas Gazette*, February 8, 1890.

112. Little Rock *Arkansas Democrat*, June 11, 1890; Little Rock *Arkansas Gazette*, June 11, 1890; Graves, *Town and Country*, 141; Moneyhon, *Arkansas and the New South*, 89.

113. Little Rock *Arkansas Gazette*, August 22, 1890.

114. Ware, *Labor Movement*, 66; Little Rock *Arkansas Gazette*, August 20, 21, 1890; *Journal of the Knights of Labor*, January 30, February 6, April 17, May 15, June 26, July 24, September 4, 1890; Garlock, *Guide to the Local Assemblies*, 11–21. The *Journal*, February 6, 1890, misspells M. S. Richey's last name as "Rilhey," which most likely resulted from an editor or compositor misreading Richey's handwritten letter. The *Arkansas Gazette*, August 21, 1890, and other primary sources use the correct spelling. Unfortunately, copies of *The People's Vindicator* apparently do not exist. On Potts Station later becoming Pottsville, see Annielaura Jaggers, "Pottsville (Pope County)," *Encyclopedia of Arkansas History & Culture*, accessed June 1, 2017, http://www.encyclopediaofarkansas.net/encyclopedia/entry-detail.aspx?entryID=32.

115. Little Rock *Arkansas Democrat*, March 29, 1890.

116. Little Rock *Arkansas Gazette*, March 15, 1890.

117. *Journal of the Knights of Labor*, July 24, 1890.

118. Little Rock *Arkansas Gazette*, August 20, 1890.

119. *Journal of the Knights of Labor*, May 29, September 11, 1890.

120. Paisley, "Political Wheelers," 20; Wheeler, "People's Party in Arkansas," 166; Dubin, *United States Congressional Elections*, 285, 287.

121. *Journal of the Knights of Labor*, June 5, 1890.

122. Bayliss, "Public Affairs in Arkansas," 315–16.

123. *New York Times*, September 1, 1890.

124. Moneyhon, *Arkansas and the New South*, 89.

125. Barnes, *Who Killed John Clayton?*, 71–72, 76–79, 97 (quotation).

126. Moore, Preimesberger, and Tarr, *Congressional Quarterly's Guide to U.S. Elections*, 1419.

127. Dubin, *United States Congressional Elections*, 279, 285, 286nn2–3, 287; United States Congress, *Biographical Directory*, 1566; Little Rock *Arkansas Democrat*, December 26, 1889.

128. Wheeler, "People's Party in Arkansas," 168; *Congressional Record*, vol. 21 (Washington, DC: Government Printing Office, 1890), pt. 4, 3276, pt. 9, 8840–41, pt. 11, 10456; vol. 22 (1891), pt. 2, 1503, pt. 4, 3516 (quotation); Birmingham *Alabama Sentinel*, September 3, 1887; Nell Irvin Painter, *Standing at Armageddon: A Grassroots History of the Progressive Era*, 2nd ed. (New York: W. W. Norton, 2008), 69; Herman C. Nixon, "The Cleavage within the Farmers' Alliance Movement," *Mississippi Valley Historical Review* 15 (June 1928): 28–31.

129. Wheeler, "People's Party in Arkansas," 156; Arthur M. Schlesinger Jr., ed., *The Almanac of American History* (New York: G. P. Putnam's Sons, 1983), 370. The Lodge Election Bill, or Force Bill, passed in the House of Representatives but failed in the Senate.

130. Little Rock *Arkansas Gazette*, June 19, 1890 (first quotation); *Little Rock Republican*, n.d., quoted in the Arkadelphia (Ark.) *Southern Standard*, August 22, 1890 (other quotations). According to the Little Rock *Arkansas Gazette*, September 21, October 9, 1890, Langley later publicly equivocated on his support of the Lodge Election Bill.

131. Woodward, *Origins of the New South*, 211–12.

132. John William Graves, "The Arkansas Separate Coach Law of 1891," *Arkansas Historical Quarterly* 32 (Summer 1973): 148–65 (quotations on 153–54).

133. Mildred Diane Gleason, *Dardanelle and the Bottoms: Environment, Agriculture, and Economy in an Arkansas River Community, 1819–1970* (Fayetteville: University of Arkansas Press, 2017), 53.

134. *Chicago Daily Tribune*, September 30, 1890.

135. *San Francisco Chronicle*, October 2, 1890.

136. Dubin, *United States Congressional Elections*, 286n3.

137. *New York Times*, November 5, 1890.

138. *Journal of the Knights of Labor*, November 13 (first quotation), December 11 (second quotation), 1890. Enacted in 1890, the McKinley Tariff raised tariff rates on some goods and lowered rates on others, but overall it carried "a general increase in duties from 38 percent to 49.5 percent." Joanne Reitano, *The Tariff Question in the Gilded Age: The Great Debate of 1888* (University Park: Pennsylvania State University Press, 1994), 129–30.

139. *Journal of the Knights of Labor*, January 15, 1891.

140. Dubin, *United States Congressional Elections*, 279, 285, 287.

141. Barnes, *Who Killed John Clayton?*, 98–99; Graves, *Town and Country*, 275n48; Wheeler, "People's Party in Arkansas," 168. For a brief discussion of election contests during the Gilded Age that explains the unlikelihood of legislative bodies unseating a member of the majority party, see Summers, *Party Games*, 114–15.

142. *Biennial Report of the Secretary of State of the State of Arkansas, 1892* (Little Rock: Press Printing, 1893), 60; Garlock, *Guide to the Local Assemblies*, 11, 12, 14–16, 19; Jones, "It Was Awful, but It Was Politics," 69–70. The *Biennial Report* for 1892

provides abstracts of the returns for the congressional elections of 1890. The precise years when Knights of Labor local assemblies formed or lapsed after 1886 are often unclear due to less comprehensive record keeping by the organization after that year.

143. Jeffrey J. Crow and Robert F. Durden, *Maverick Republican in the Old North State: A Political Biography of Daniel L. Russell* (Baton Rouge: Louisiana State University Press, 1977), 50.

144. Ibid., 49–50; J. Morgan Kousser, *The Shaping of Southern Politics: Suffrage Restriction and the Establishment of the One-Party South, 1880–1910* (New Haven, Conn.: Yale University Press, 1974), 185–87 (quotation on 187); Ayers, *Promise of the New South*, 293.

145. Hild, *Greenbackers*, 202.

146. Graves, "Arkansas Separate Coach Law"; C. Vann Woodward, *The Strange Career of Jim Crow*, 3rd rev. ed. (New York: Oxford University Press, 1974), 97. An amendment was introduced in the state house of representatives to the "separate coach" law that would have segregated street cars, but it did not make it into the final bill.

V. Populism and the Depression of the 1890s

1. Magnolia (Ark.) *Columbia Banner*, October 7, 1886; *Fayetteville* (Ark.) *Democrat*, January 30, 1891.

2. Little Rock *Arkansas Gazette*, February 17, 1891; Graves, "Arkansas Separate Coach Law."

3. Little Rock *Arkansas Gazette*, February 1, 20, 21, April 5 (quotations), 1891.

4. Barnes, *Journey of Hope*, 49–73 (first two quotations on 49, others on 57).

5. Hild, *Greenbackers*, 122–29, 136–39; John D. Hicks, *The Populist Revolt: A History of the Farmers' Alliance and the People's Party* (Minneapolis: University of Minnesota Press, 1931; repr., Lincoln: University of Nebraska Press, 1961), 113–26, 205–18; Lawrence Goodwyn, *The Populist Moment: A Short History of the Agrarian Revolt in America* (New York: Oxford University Press, 1978), 151.

6. On the origins of the names People's Party and Populists, see McMath, *American Populism*, 135, 146.

7. Hicks, *Populist Revolt*, 213; Mansfield (Ark.) *Alliance Patriot*, May 28, 1891; Lawrence Goodwyn, *Democratic Promise: The Populist Moment in America* (New York: Oxford University Press, 1976), 245–46; McMath, *American Populism*, 157; Wheeler, "People's Party in Arkansas," 225–26; Arkadelphia (Ark.) *Southern Standard*, July 11, 1890; Charlie Daniels, *Historical Report of the Secretary of State, 2008* (Fayetteville: University of Arkansas Press, 2008), 501. The author was unable to find any source that identifies the sixth delegate to the Cincinnati conference from Arkansas.

8. *Cincinnati Enquirer*, May 21, 1891. The author was unable to find any source that reveals which Arkansas delegate denounced Polk's letter.

9. Little Rock *Arkansas Gazette*, May 23, 1891.

10. *Morrilton* (Ark.) *Pilot*, n.d., quoted in ibid., May 31, 1891.

11. Wheeler, "People's Party in Arkansas," 170, 173–74, 188–89, 189n47 (quotation on 173); Mansfield (Ark.) *Alliance Patriot*, July 23, 1891; Little Rock *Arkansas Democrat*, March 19, 1891.

12. *Fort Smith* (Ark.) *Call*, n.d., reprinted in the Little Rock *Arkansas Gazette*, May 1, 1891 (quotations); Clifton J. Phillips, *Indiana in Transition: The Emergence of an Industrial Commonwealth, 1880–1920* (1968; repr., Indianapolis: Indiana Historical Society Press, 2016), 345.

13. *Journal of the Knights of Labor*, June 11, 1891.

14. Mansfield (Ark.) *Alliance Patriot*, July 23, 1891 (quotations); Garlock, *Guide to the Local Assemblies*, 20.

15. *Journal of the Knights of Labor*, December 17, 1891.

16. Little Rock *Arkansas Gazette*, July 14, 1891.

17. Omar H. Ali, *In the Lion's Mouth: Black Populism in the New South, 1886–1900* (Jackson: University Press of Mississippi, 2010), 49.

18. Holmes, "Arkansas Cotton Pickers Strike," 107–19 (quotations on 113).

19. Ibid., 113–19; Gerald H. Gaither, *Blacks and the Populist Movement: Ballots and Bigotry in the New South*, rev. ed. (Tuscaloosa: University of Alabama Press, 2005), 27–30; Garlock, *Guide to the Local Assemblies*, 15; Biegert, "Legacy of Resistance," 81–83; William F. Holmes, "The Demise of the Colored Farmers' Alliance," *Journal of Southern History* 41 (May 1975): 200. Garlock does not specify that any of the Knights of Labor local assemblies in Lee County included African Americans, but as he notes, the data available "reveals relatively little about the actual racial, sex, or ethnic composition of the Knights of Labor . . . such information about the members of specific LAs [local assemblies] is limited to 5 percent of all assemblies" (*Guide to the Local Assemblies*, xxi–xxii).

20. Holmes, "Demise of the Colored Farmers' Alliance," 199.

21. Kousser, *Shaping of Southern Politics*, 43–44.

22. Ibid., 123–30; Graves, *Town and Country*, 164–74, 282n19; Michael Perman, *Struggle for Mastery: Disfranchisement in the South, 1888–1908* (Chapel Hill: University of North Carolina Press, 2001), 61–64; Branam, "Another Look at Disfranchisement," 245–46.

23. Wheeler, "People's Party in Arkansas," 192.

24. Ibid., 170, 207 (quotations, citing the *Chicago Tribune*, June 8, 1891); Edward McPherson, ed., *Tribune Almanac and Political Register for 1893* (New York: Tribune Association, 1893), 232.

25. Wheeler, "People's Party in Arkansas," 203 (first quotation, citing the Little Rock *Arkansas Gazette*, July 30, 1891); Hicks, *Populist Revolt*, 431 (remaining quotations); Morgan, *History of the Wheel and Alliance*, 3rd ed., 180–81. The Southern Farmers' Alliance's Ocala platform of December 1890 is reprinted in Hicks, *Populist Revolt*, 430–31.

26. Mansfield (Ark.) *Alliance Patriot*, August 6, 1891; *Osceola* (Ark.) *Times*, August 30, 1890; Little Rock *Arkansas Gazette*, July 6, 1892.

27. Wheeler, "People's Party in Arkansas," 213–14, including 214n114.

28. Ibid., 222–23, 227, 244–45; Little Rock *Arkansas Democrat*, August 21, 1891; Little Rock *Arkansas Gazette*, May 6, 1891. For accounts of the St. Louis conference of February 1892 and the Omaha nominating convention of July 1892, see Hicks, *Populist Revolt*, 223–37; McMath, *American Populism*, 160–63, 166–69.

29. Wheeler, "People's Party in Arkansas," 232, 233, 235 (first quotation, regarding convict lease), 236–37, including note 35 (third quotation, regarding Lodge Force Bill, on 236); Little Rock *Arkansas Gazette*, August 29, 1891, June 22, 1892; Matthew Hild, "Labor, Third-Party Politics, and New South Democracy in Arkansas, 1884–1896," *Arkansas Historical Quarterly* 63 (Spring 2004): 38–39, 40n59; *Arkadelphia* (Ark.) *Herald*, n.d., quoted in the Little Rock *Arkansas Gazette*, July 10, 1892 (second quotation, regarding antilynching plank).

30. *Journal of the Knights of Labor*, July 21, 1892 (quotations); Moore, Preimesberger, and Tarr, *Congressional Quarterly's Guide to U.S. Elections*, 951.

31. Martis, *Historical Atlas*, 123, 127; J. B. Suttler to W. B. W. Heartsill, February 29, March 29 (first of two letters of that date), 1892, Heartsill Papers, Box 4, File 4.

32. Thomas S. Baskett Jr., "*Miners Stay Away!*: W.B.W. Heartsill and the Last Years of the Arkansas Knights of Labor, 1892–1896," *Arkansas Historical Quarterly* 42 (Summer 1983): 107–33; Knights of Labor Minute Book, 1892–1895, Greenwood Local Assembly 239, minutes of March 12, 1892, Heartsill Papers, Box 4, File 17; Little Rock *Arkansas Gazette*, July 22, 1890; Horace Addis to W. B. W. Heartsill, August 10, 1890, Heartsill Papers, Box 4, File 1.

33. Little Rock *Arkansas Gazette*, June 8, 1892. On the rivalry between the Knights of Labor and the American Federation of Labor, and the shift of the declining Knights from urban America to small towns and rural areas, see, among others, Laurie, *Artisans into Workers*, 174–76, 182–83; Phelan, *Grand Master Workman*, 241–49.

34. Little Rock *Arkansas Gazette*, June 8–9, 1892.

35. *Journal of the Knights of Labor*, July 28, 1892.

36. Ibid., September 29, 1892.

37. Little Rock *Arkansas Gazette*, October 23, 1892.

38. *Journal of the Knights of Labor*, April 7, 28, May 12, 19, June 2, 9, 16, August 25, September 1 (quotations), 29, October 6, 13, November 3, 1892; Garlock, *Guide to the Local Assemblies*, 13, 20; *St. Louis Post-Dispatch*, November 15, 1892.

39. Graves, *Town and Country*, 108, 210–11, 214; Whayne et al., *Arkansas*, 280; Conway (Ark.) *Faulkner County Wheel*, n.d., quoted in the Atlanta (Ga.) *People's Party Paper*, August 5, 1892; Moneyhon, *Arkansas and the New South*, 90. Whipple later became a federal prosecutor in Arkansas.

40. Suttler to Heartsill, May 5 (first quotation), October 3, 6 (second quotation), 1892, Heartsill Papers, Box 4, File 4.

41. Moore, Preimesberger, and Tarr, *Congressional Quarterly's Guide to U.S. Elections*, 1419; J. B. Weaver to T. V. Powderly, September 9, 1892, Powderly Papers, reel 39; Wheeler, "People's Party in Arkansas," 280.

42. Brough, "Industrial History," 226; "Statistical Report of Membership FSA [Farmers' State Alliance], Quarter ending Dec. 31st, 1890," Heartsill Papers, Box 7, Item 4; Moore, Preimesberger, and Tarr, *Congressional Quarterly's Guide to U.S. Elections*, 1419; Wheeler, "People's Party in Arkansas," 281.

43. Wheeler, "People's Party in Arkansas," 375; Arkadelphia (Ark.) *Southern Standard*, September 23, 1892; Little Rock *Arkansas Gazette*, September 17, 1892; Robertson to Heartsill, October 4, 1893, Heartsill Papers, Box 4, File 6.

44. Moore, Preimesberger, and Tarr, *Congressional Quarterly's Guide to U.S. Elections*, 951; Wheeler, "People's Party in Arkansas," 200–201, 304; Martis, *Historical Atlas*, 127.

45. Moneyhon, *Arkansas and the New South*, 90–91 (quotation on 91); Barnes, *Journey of Hope*, 217n20.

46. Blake J. Wintory, "African-American Legislators in the Arkansas General Assembly, 1868–1893," *Arkansas Historical Quarterly* 65 (Winter 2006): 388; Graves, *Town and Country*, 185–94; Kousser, *Shaping of Southern Politics*, 125–30; Perman, *Struggle for Mastery*, 64–67; Branam, "Another Look at Disfranchisement," 245–46, 249, 253–56; Wheeler, "People's Party in Arkansas," 374; Moore, Preimesberger, and Tarr, *Congressional Quarterly's Guide to U.S. Elections*, 1419.

47. Baskett, "*Miners Stay Away!*," 121–22; Richard Oestreicher, "A Note on Knights of Labor Membership Statistics," *Labor History* 25 (Winter 1984): 102–8; McMath, *Populist Vanguard*, 142–44, 148; Robert L. Tontz, "Memberships of General Farmers' Organizations, United States, 1874–1960," *Agricultural History* 38 (July 1964): 147 (table 1).

48. Painter, *Standing at Armageddon*, 116; Douglas Steeples and David O. Whitten, *Democracy in Desperation: The Depression of 1893* (Westport, Conn.: Greenwood Press, 1998), 33–36, 50; De Santis, *Shaping of Modern America*, 68; Alexander, *Coxey's Army*, 33.

49. Wheeler, "People's Party in Arkansas," 318–19; Woodward, *Origins of the New South*, 185–86.

50. *Junction City* (Kan.) *Union*, April 29, 1893; Little Rock *Arkansas Gazette*, March 25, 1893.

51. Baskett, "*Miners Stay Away!*"; *Journal of the Knights of Labor*, March 23, 1893.

52. *Journal of the Knights of Labor*, August 3, 1893.

53. William Murray to W. B. W. Heartsill, October 1, 1893, Heartsill Papers, Box 4, File 6; Baskett, "*Miners Stay Away!*," 123, including n. 80. According to Garlock, *Guide to the Local Assemblies*, 12–13, two Knights of Labor local assemblies remained active in Hot Springs in 1893: 2419 and the newer 231. Months later Murray informed Heartsill that LA 231 "has lapsed and . . . the whole body has since joined the Farmers' Alliance." LA 2419 persisted, though. Murray to Heartsill, January 13, 1894, Heartsill Papers, Box 4, File 7.

54. Robertson to Heartsill, February 15, 1894, Heartsill Papers, Box 4, File 7; *Compendium of the Eleventh Census*, 66.

55. *Engineering and Mining Journal* (New York), April 7, 1894, reprinted in *Public Opinion* 17 (April 1894–January 1895): 43.

56. Brecher, *Strike!*, 77–84 (first two quotations on 77, last on 81).

57. *Third Biennial Report*, 198. See also Baskett, "*Miners Stay Away!*," 127–28; Dana M. Caldemeyer,"Unfaithful Followers: Rethinking Southern Nonunionism in the Late Nineteenth Century," in *Reconsidering Southern Labor History: Race, Class, and Power*, ed. Matthew Hild and Keri Leigh Merritt (Gainesville: University Press of Florida, 2018), 120–21.

58. *Pittsburg* (Kan.) *Daily Headlight*, June 28, 1894.

59. Laurie, *Artisans into Workers*, 205–8; Brecher, *Strike!*, 85–100; Moneyhon, *Arkansas and the New South*, 111; US Congress, House of Representatives, 54th Cong., 2d sess., Doc. 9, *Annual Report of the Attorney-General of the United States for the Year 1896* (Washington, DC: Government Printing Office, 1896), 9–16; Little Rock *Arkansas Gazette*, July 1, 12, 1894.

60. Moneyhon, *Arkansas and the New South*, 111; Little Rock *Arkansas Gazette*, July 12, 1894; U.S. Congress, House of Representatives, *Annual Report of the Attorney-General*, 13 (quotation); Laurie, *Artisans into Workers*, 209.

61. The Coxey march and movement of 1894 is the topic of two recent monographs: Alexander, *Coxey's Army*; and Jerry Prout, *Coxey's Crusade for Jobs: Unemployment in the Gilded Age* (DeKalb: Northern Illinois University Press, 2016).

62. Laurie, *Artisans into Workers*, 207–10; Ira Kipnis, *The American Socialist Movement, 1897–1912* (New York: Columbia University Press, 1952; repr., New York: Greenwood Press, 1968), 47–48, 51–61.

63. Baskett, "*Miners Stay Away!*," 114–15, 117, 127–28, 132; G. Gregory Kiser, "The Socialist Party in Arkansas, 1900–1912," *Arkansas Historical Quarterly* 40 (Summer 1981): 126, 138, 145, 148; Michael Pierce, "Great Women All, Serving a Glorious Cause: Freda Hogan Ameringer's Reminiscences of Socialism in Arkansas," *Arkansas Historical Quarterly* 69 (Winter 2010): 295, 297; William H. Pruden III, "Dan Hogan (1871–1935)," *Encyclopedia of Arkansas History & Culture*, accessed July 14, 2017, http://www.encyclopediaofarkansas.net/encyclopedia/entry-detail.aspx?search=1&entryID=6885.

64. Zimmerman, "Convict Lease System," 176–77 (first quotation on 177); Mancini, *One Dies, Get Another*, 126–27; Little Rock *Arkansas Gazette*, July 21, 1894 (second quotation).

65. *Journal of the Knights of Labor*, February 15, 1894; Garlock, *Guide to the Local Assemblies*, 20.

66. *Journal of the Knights of Labor*, May 3, 1894 (quotation); Garlock, *Guide to the Local Assemblies*, 20.

67. C. T. Foster to W. B. W. Heartsill, May 1, 1894, Heartsill Papers, Box 4, File 7.

68. "c. 1894" list of current and suspended LAs, Heartsill Papers, Box 5, File 2; Garlock, "Structural Analysis," 236.

69. Wheeler, "People's Party in Arkansas," 374; Kousser, *Shaping of Southern Politics*, 130 (table 5.6).

70. Moore, Preimesberger, and Tarr, *Congressional Quarterly's Guide to U.S. Elections*, 1419; Wheeler, "People's Party in Arkansas," 375.

71. Moore, Preimesberger, and Tarr, *Congressional Quarterly's Guide to U.S. Elections*, 956; Wheeler, "People's Party in Arkansas," 385, 391 (quotation).

72. Goodwyn, *Democratic Promise*; Goodwyn, *Populist Moment*.

73. Robertson to Heartsill, July 27, 1894, Heartsill Papers, Box 4, File 8.

74. Robertson to Heartsill, January 10 (quotation), 30, April 30, July 1, 1895, Heartsill Papers, Box 4, Files 9 and 10; J. Frank Cleveland to Heartsill, March 31, 1895, Heartsill Papers, Box 4, File 9.

75. Robertson to Heartsill, August 29, 1895, Heartsill Papers, Box 4, File 10.

76. John W. Hayes to L. D. Barnes, October 28, 1895, Heartsill Papers, Box 4, File 10.

77. Little Rock *Arkansas Gazette*, September 13, 1895; Baskett, "*Miners Stay Away!*," 115–16.

78. Ware, *Labor Movement*, 112, 369; *Journal of the Knights of Labor*, January 23, July 30, September 3, 1896; Wheeler, "People's Party in Arkansas," 420–23; Laurie, *Artisans into Workers*, 175; Robert F. Durden, *The Climax of Populism: The Election of 1896* (Lexington: University of Kentucky Press, 1965), 55, 63, 132; Richard L. Niswonger, *Arkansas Democratic Politics, 1896–1920* (Fayetteville: University of Arkansas Press, 1990), 57, 60, 69, 78–80.

79. Monticello (Ark.) *Monticellonian*, August 2, 1895.

80. Little Rock *Arkansas Gazette*, January 28, 1896.

81. Ibid., July 14, 1896; Niswonger, *Arkansas Democratic Politics*, 78; J. R. Sovereign to Marion Butler, September 24, 1896, Marion Butler Papers, microfilm, reel 2, Southern Historical Collection, University of North Carolina at Chapel Hill.

82. Painter, *Standing at Armageddon*, 135–40; McMath, *American Populism*, 137, 157, 173, 193, 196, 201–6; De Santis, *Shaping of Modern America*, 74–79; Ritter, *Goldbugs and Greenbacks*, 58–61 (quotation on 58); Postel, *Populist Vision*, 150–53.

83. Postel, *Populist Vision*, 273–74 (first quotation); McMath, *American Populism*, 203–4; Goodwyn, *Democratic Promise*, 497–503; Wheeler, "People's Party in Arkansas," 424 (second quotation), 422 (third quotation, citing the Little Rock *Arkansas Gazette*, July 16, 1896), 425n80.

84. Richard L. Niswonger, "Arkansas and the Election of 1896," *Arkansas Historical Quarterly* 34 (Spring 1975): 75; Niswonger, *Arkansas Democratic Politics*, 78 (quotations, citing the Hardy [Ark.] *Morgan's Buzz-Saw*, March 1, April 1, 1897).

85. Niswonger, "Arkansas and the Election of 1896," 77; *Savannah* (Ga.) *Tribune*, November 7, 1896 (quotation).

86. Sovereign to Butler, January 12, 1897, Butler Papers, reel 5.

87. Robertson to Heartsill, August 31, 1896, Heartsill Papers, Box 4, File 11.

88. Niswonger, "Arkansas and the Election of 1896," 43–52; Wheeler, "People's Party in Arkansas," 426–27, 438, 445, 448, 456; Little Rock *Arkansas Gazette*, July 16, September 16, 18, 1896; *Austin* (Tex.) *Weekly Statesman*, July 16, 1896 (quotation);

Moore, Preimesberger, and Tarr, *Congressional Quarterly's Guide to U.S. Elections*, 961, 1419; *Journal of the Knights of Labor*, July 23, August 13, 1896.

89. Wheeler, "People's Party in Arkansas," 471, 473, 482–85; McMath, *American Populism*, 205–6; Lewisville (Ark.) *Lafayette Recorder*, n.d., quoted in the Little Rock *Arkansas Democrat*, December 24, 1900. According to Little Rock city directories, the Farmers' Alliance had one local chapter there as late as 1899, but none by the following year. *Arkansas Democrat Co.'s Little Rock City Directory, 1899* (Little Rock: Press of Arkansas Democrat, 1899), 77–78; *Arkansas Democrat Co.'s Little Rock City Directory, 1900–1901* (Little Rock: Press of Arkansas Democrat, 1900), 72–73.

90. *Proceedings of the General Assembly of the Knights of Labor, Special Session Held at Washington, District of Columbia, June 18–21, 1900*, 11.

91. Gentry (Ark.) *Journal-Advance*, February 23, 1906.

92. Baskett, "*Miners Stay Away!*," 129n116, 132n131; *Proceedings of the General Assembly of the Knights of Labor, Thirtieth Regular Session, held at New York City, December 9, 10, 11, 1913*, in *Record of the Proceedings of the General Assembly of the Knights of Labor.*

93. *Journal of the Knights of Labor*, October 24, 1895; Little Rock *Arkansas Gazette*, March 26, 1898; Little Rock *Arkansas Democrat*, March 26, September 2, 1898, October 30, 1900; Hild, "Labor, Third-Party Politics, and New South Democracy," 42; *Report of the Industrial Commission on the Relations and Conditions of Capital and Labor Employed in the Mining Industry, Including Testimony, Review of Evidence, and Topical Digest*, vol. 12 (Washington, DC: Government Printing Office, 1901), 389; Niswonger, *Arkansas Democratic Politics*, 78; Martin Tuohy, "Sovereign, James R. (1854–1928)," in *Encyclopedia of U.S. Labor and Working-Class History*, edited by Eric Arnesen (New York: Routledge, 2007), 1308–10.

94. Harry S. Ashmore, *Arkansas: A Bicentennial History* (New York: W. W. Norton, 1978), 175.

VI. Twentieth-Century Legacies

1. T. Jason Soderstrum, "Currency Act of 1900," in *The American Economy: A Historical Encyclopedia*, rev. ed., edited by Cynthia Clark Northrup, vol. 1 (Santa Barbara, Calif., and other cities: ABC-CLIO, 2011), 117.

2. Wheeler, "People's Party in Arkansas," 485–91 (quotation on 490); Niswonger, *Arkansas Democratic Politics*, 74–79; Baskett, "*Miners Stay Away!*"

3. Niswonger, *Arkansas Democratic Politics*, 7–9, 84–85 (quotation on 85).

4. Ibid., 6-9, 85, 120–23; Raymond Arsenault, *The Wild Ass of the Ozarks: Jeff Davis and the Social Bases of Southern Politics* (Philadelphia: Temple University Press, 1984; repr., Knoxville: University of Tennessee Press, 1988), 3, 21, 63–72, 110–15, 145–46; Goodwyn, *Democratic Promise*, 298. Davis's birthplace, near Rocky Comfort, Arkansas, was in Sevier County at the time; its current county, Little River, was not created until 1867. The town of Rocky Comfort is now called Foreman. See Arsenault, *Wild Ass*, 22; Steven Teske, "Foreman (Little River County)," *Encyclopedia of Arkansas History & Culture*, accessed July 26, 2017, http://www

.encyclopediaofarkansas.net/encyclopedia/entry-detail.aspx?search=1&entry-ID=922; Martha P. Trusley "Little River County," *Encyclopedia of Arkansas History & Culture*, accessed July 26, 2017, http://www.encyclopediaofarkansas.net/encyclopedia/entry-detail.aspx?entryID=785.

5. Niswonger, *Arkansas Democratic Politics*, 222–23; Edgar E. Mountjoy, comp., *Official Congressional Directory*, 63rd Congress, 3rd Session (Washington, DC: Office of Congressional Directory, 1915), 8; Little Rock *Arkansas Democrat*, June 17, 1907; Lindley C. Shedd, "Effiegene Wingo: An Early Congresswoman from Arkansas," *Arkansas Historical Quarterly* 67 (Spring 2008): 29 (first quotation); *Osceola* (Ark.) *Times*, March 28, 1907 (second quotation); Robert C. McMath Jr., "C. Vann Woodward and the Burden of Southern Populism," *Journal of Southern History* 67 (November 2001): 742, 762–63; Woodward, *Origins of the New South*, 369 (third quotation).

6. Wheeler, "People's Party in Arkansas," 485–90 (quotation on 486, citing Reuben CarlLee to Tom Watson, September 13, 1907); Niswonger, *Arkansas Democratic Politics*, 74–75, 169; Hild, *Greenbackers*, x (map); Dallas (Tex.) *Southern Mercury*, July 26, 1900, July 31, 1902; McMath, *American Populism*, 206; W. S. Morgan to Thomas E. Watson, April 25, 1908, Thomas E. Watson Papers #755, Southern Historical Collection, Wilson Library, University of North Carolina at Chapel Hill.

7. John W. Hayes to the Officers and Members of LA 10,973, February 19, 1898; Thomas (?) Shaw to John W. Hayes, March 4, 1898, both in John William Hayes Papers, microfilm edition (Glen Rock, N.J.: Microfilming Corporation of America, 1974), reel 11; Garlock, *Guide to the Local Assemblies*, 11–21; Ashmore, *Arkansas*, 175; *Annual Report of the Mine Inspector for the Indian Territory to the Secretary of the Interior for the Fiscal Year Ended June 30, 1899* (Washington, DC: Government Printing Office, 1899), 57–61; Little Rock *Arkansas Democrat*, March 3, 1899 (quotations).

8. Arsenault, *Wild Ass*, 59 (first quotation), 292n42; Lancaster, *Racial Cleansing in Arkansas*, 66 (second quotation); *Bulletin of the Bureau of Labor* (Washington, DC), No. 50 (January 1904): 401; John H. Barnhill, "A History of District Twenty-One, United Mine Workers of America" (MA thesis, Oklahoma State University, 1978), 7. The United Mine Workers organized a local in Huntington in September 1894. See Baskett, "*Miners Stay Away!*," 130.

9. Guy Lancaster, "'Negroes Warned to Leave Town': The Bonanza Race War of 1904," *Journal of the Fort Smith Historical Society* 34 (April 2010): 24–29 (quotations on 27); Lancaster, *Racial Cleansing in Arkansas*, 50, 61–62; James W. Loewen, *Sundown Towns: A Hidden Dimension of American Racism* (New York: New Press, 2005), 71; United States Census Bureau, "Profile of General Population and Housing Characteristics: 2010. Bonanza City, Arkansas," United States Census Bureau American Fact Finder, accessed July 28, 2017, https://factfinder.census.gov/bkmk/table/1.0/en/DEC/10_DP/DPDP1/1600000US0507540. Loewen explains that "sundown towns" are called such "owing to the signs that many of them formerly sported at their corporate limits" that warned African Americans to leave town before the sun went down (p. 1).

10. Little Rock *Arkansas Democrat*, March 11, 15, 1904; Little Rock *Arkansas Gazette*, March 13, 16, 1904; *Fort Smith* (Ark.) *Times*, March 13, 16, 1904; *Pine Bluff* (Ark.) *Daily Graphic*, March 15, 1904 (quotation). For annual membership figures of the Arkansas Knights of Labor State Assembly from 1886 through 1888, see Hild, *Greenbackers*, 225. The phrase "long strike" is used, in reference to the coal miners' strike that began in 1899, by both Arsenault, *Wild Ass*, 292n42, and James R. Green, *Grass-Roots Socialism: Radical Movements in the Southwest, 1895–1943* (Baton Rouge: Louisiana State University Press, 1978), 32.

11. Laurie, *Artisans into Workers*, 13, 177, 219–20; Little Rock *Arkansas Gazette*, March 15, 1904 (first two quotations after Laurie's); *Fort Smith* (Ark.) *Times*, March 17, 1904.

12. John T. Castle, *Supplement to Kirby's Digest of the Statutes of Arkansas Embracing the General Statutes Enacted at the Legislative Sessions of 1905, 1907, 1909, and the Regular Session of 1911* (Indianapolis: Bobbs-Merrill, 1911), 58–60; *Record of the Proceedings of the Eleventh Regular Session of the General Assembly*, 1631, 1842; *Pine Bluff* (Ark.) *Daily Graphic*, December 9, 1904; Little Rock *Arkansas Democrat*, December 14, 16, 17, 1904. The state legislature passed a law in 1905 that outlawed the payment of wages in scrip, but it contained a provision "rendering it inapplicable to coal mines when not less than twenty men are employed under the ground." A court declared that provision to be unconstitutional, and therefore the provision was not included in the 1907 law. Castle, *Supplement*, 60.

13. Little Rock *Arkansas Gazette*, December 16, 1904; Brough, "Industrial History," 191, 225–26, 228.

14. Taylor, *Farmers' Movement*, 336–57; Theodore Saloutos, *Farmer Movements in the South, 1865–1933* (Berkeley: University of California Press, 1960; repr., Lincoln: University of Nebraska Press, 1964), chap. 12; Worth Robert Miller, "Building a Progressive Coalition in Texas: The Populist-Reform Democrat Rapprochement, 1900–1907," *Journal of Southern History* 52 (May 1986): 176; Sanders, *Roots of Reform*, 150–52 (quotation on 150); Woodward, *Origins of the New South*, 413–15; Hild, *Greenbackers*, xii (map).

15. Charles Simon Barrett, *The Mission, History and Times of the Farmers' Union: A Narrative of the Greatest Industrial-Agricultural Organization in History and Its Makers* (Nashville, Tenn.: Marshall & Bruce, 1909), 206, 208.

16. *Washington Post*, June 21, 1905.

17. Saloutos, *Farmer Movements*, 192 (quotation cites the Dallas [Tex.] *Southern Mercury United with Farmers' Union Password*, May 24, 1906).

18. Barrett, *Mission, History and Times of the Farmers' Union*, 207–8.

19. Saloutos, *Farmer Movements*, 192–93.

20. Taylor, *Farmers' Movement*, 357–58.

21. Arsenault, *Wild Ass*, 224–25, 233–35; Calvin R. Ledbetter Jr., *Carpenter from Conway: George Washington Donaghey as Governor of Arkansas, 1909–1913* (Fayetteville: University of Arkansas Press, 1993), 54–55.

22. Ledbetter, *Carpenter from Conway*, 55; Moneyhon, *Arkansas and the New South*, 122; Little Rock *Union Labor Bulletin*, August 12, 1906, quoted in Kiser, "Socialist Party," 139.

23. Thomas L. Baxley, "Prison Reforms during the Donaghey Administration," *Arkansas Historical Quarterly* 22 (Spring 1963): 76–84; Calvin R. Ledbetter Jr., "The Long Struggle to End Convict Leasing in Arkansas," *Arkansas Historical Quarterly* 52 (Spring 1993): 15–27; Frances Mitchell Ross, "The New Woman as Club Woman and Social Activist in Turn-of-the-Century Arkansas," *Arkansas Historical Quarterly* 50 (Winter 1991): 341–42, 349–50 (quotation on 341); Ware, *Labor Movement*, 379.

24. De Santis, *Shaping of Modern America*, 197, 214; Randall G. Holcombe, *From Liberty to Democracy: The Transformation of American Government* (Ann Arbor: University of Michigan Press, 2002), 166–68.

25. *Fayetteville* (Ark.) *Democrat*, May 30, 1890; McMath, *Populist Vanguard*, 96–98; Hild, *Greenbackers*, 215; Brad Bauerly, *The Agrarian Seeds of Empire: The Political Economy of Agriculture in U.S. State Building* (Boston: Brill, 2016), 278 (quotation).

26. Kiser, "Socialist Party," 126, including n. 24, 129, including n. 34.

27. Hardy (Ark.) *Morgan's Buzz-Saw*, n.d., quoted in the Rolla *Missouri Sharp Shooter*, July 7, 1905.

28. Wheeler, "People's Party in Arkansas," 489.

29. Little Rock *Arkansas Gazette*, May 24, 1903. On the Populists' refusal to endorse women's suffrage at their Omaha national convention in 1892, see McMath, *American Populism*, 168. On Coxey's "good roads" plan, see Alexander, *Coxey's Army*, and Prout, *Coxey's Crusade for Jobs*.

30. Hild, *Greenbackers*, 210–11; Kiser, "Socialist Party"; Moore, Preimesberger, and Tarr, *Congressional Quarterly's Guide to U.S. Elections*, 1419; Brecher, *Strike!*, 102; Ashmore, *Arkansas*, 175; Moneyhon, *Arkansas and the New South*, 107.

31. Hild, *Greenbackers*, x (map), 210–11; Kiser, "Socialist Party" (first quotation on 142); Wheeler, "People's Party in Arkansas," 490.

32. Little Rock *Arkansas Gazette*, May 24, 1903, November 29, 1914 (first quotation); Green, *Grass-Roots Socialism*, 302, 323–28 (second quotation on 328); Garlock, *Guide to the Local Assemblies*, 12; Nigel Anthony Sellars, *Oil, Wheat & Wobblies: The Industrial Workers of the World in Oklahoma, 1905–1930* (Norman: University of Oklahoma Press, 1998), 77, 84–86; Nigel Anthony Sellars, "Working Class Union," *Encyclopedia of Oklahoma History and Culture*, accessed August 11, 2017, http://www.okhistory.org/publications/enc/entry.php?entry=WO021; Covington Hall, *Labor Struggles in the Deep South and Other Writings*, ed. David R. Roediger (Chicago: Charles H. Kerr, 1999), 186–87. A native of Mississippi, Hall was a Socialist, labor organizer, and journalist. During the 1930s he taught at Commonwealth College in Mena, Arkansas. (Roediger, "Introduction," in Hall, *Labor Struggles*, 1–23.) As discussed in chap. 2 above, the Knights of Labor made one racial exclusion in refusing to admit Chinese members, but in Arkansas this had little practical effect given the very low Chinese population.

33. Pierce, "Great Women All," 304–5, 324; J. Blake Perkins, *Hillbilly Hellraisers: Federal Power and Populist Defiance in the Ozarks* (Urbana: University of Illinois Press, 2017), 75; Brecher, *Strike!*, 102; Sellars, *Oil, Wheat & Wobblies*, 87–88, 91; Hall, *Labor Struggles*, 188–89; Nick Salvatore, *Eugene V. Debs: Citizen and Socialist* (Urbana: University of Illinois Press, 1982), 288–302, 326–28.

34. Green, *Grass-Roots Socialism*, 405–6, 414, 423, 425.

35. Biegert, "Legacy of Resistance"; Grif Stockley, *Blood in Their Eyes: The Elaine Race Massacres of 1919* (Fayetteville: University of Arkansas Press, 2001); F. Ray Marshall, *Labor in the South* (Cambridge, Mass.: Harvard University Press, 1967), 154, 158–165.

36. Marshall, *Labor in the South*, 158–65; Howard Kester, *Revolt among the Sharecroppers* (New York: Covici-Friede, 1936; repr., New York: Arno Press, 1969); Jarod Roll, *Spirit of Rebellion: Labor and Religion in the New Cotton South* (Urbana: University of Illinois Press, 2010); Jason Manthorne, "The View from the Cotton: Reconsidering the Southern Tenant Farmers' Union," *Agricultural History* 84 (Winter 2010): 20–45 (quotation on 20). Howard Kester was a Socialist and STFU activist and organizer.

37. Whayne et al., *Arkansas*, 347–50; Biegert, "Legacy of Resistance," 88–89 (quotation on 88); Johnny E. Williams, *African American Religion and the Civil Rights Movement in Arkansas* (Jackson: University Press of Mississippi, 2008), 146; Link, *Southern Crucible*, 447.

38. Samuel A. Sizer, "'This Is Union Man's Country': Sebastian County 1914," *Arkansas Historical Quarterly* 27 (Winter 1968): 306–29.

39. *United Mine Workers Journal* (Indianapolis), December 1, 1918.

40. Ben F. Johnson III, *Arkansas in Modern America, 1930–1999* (Fayetteville: University of Arkansas Press, 2000), 23, 80; Marshall, *Labor in the South*, 241–42, 299 (table 5); James C. Cobb, *The Selling of the South: The Southern Crusade for Industrial Development, 1936–1990*, 2nd ed. (Urbana: University of Illinois Press, 1993), 101.

41. Kayla Griffis, "United Mine Workers of America (UMWA)," *Encyclopedia of Arkansas History & Culture*, accessed August 13, 2017, http://www.encyclopediaofarkansas.net/encyclopedia/entry-detail.aspx?search=1&entryID=6884; Center for Union Facts, "United Mine Workers," Unionfacts.com, accessed August 13, 2017, https://www.unionfacts.com/union/United_Mine_Workers.

42. For a recent examination of the "second" or "new" Gilded Age, see Larry M. Bartels, *Unequal Democracy: The Political Economy of the New Gilded Age*, 2nd ed. (Princeton, N.J.: Princeton University Press, 2016).

BIBLIOGRAPHY

Primary Sources

Private Papers and Manuscript Collections

Butler, Marion. Papers. Microfilm. Southern Historical Collection, Wilson Library, University of North Carolina at Chapel Hill.

Clark Grange #232, Pope County, Arkansas. Records. Microfilm. Arkansas State Archives, Little Rock.

Hayes, John William. Papers. Microfilm. Glen Rock, N.J.: Microfilming Corporation of America, 1974.

Heartsill, W. B. W. Papers, 1864–1945. Center for Arkansas History and Culture, University of Arkansas at Little Rock Library.

Knights of Labor. Van Buren Assembly, No. 6307, Records, 1886–1892. Special Collections Division, University of Arkansas Libraries, Fayetteville.

Meridian Agricultural Wheel. Minutes and Proceedings Book, 1887–1889. Arkansas State Archives, Little Rock.

Powderly, Terence Vincent. Papers. Microfilm. Glen Rock, N.J.: Microfilming Corporation of America, 1974.

Watson, Thomas E. Papers. Southern Historical Collection, Wilson Library, University of North Carolina at Chapel Hill.

Proceedings

Proceedings of the Fifth Annual Session of the Arkansas State Grange, Patrons of Husbandry, Held at Little Rock, January 22, 23, 24, 25 and 26, 1877. Little Rock: Webb and Burrows, 1877.

Proceedings of the First Annual Session of District Assembly No. 78, Knights of Labor, Held at Galveston, Texas, Jan. 4–9, 1886. Fort Worth: Labor Siftings Cooperative Publishing, 1886.

Record of the Proceedings of the General Assembly of the Knights of Labor, 1878–1913. Microfilm. Madison: State Historical Society of Wisconsin, 1950.

Newspapers and Periodicals

Arkadelphia (Ark.) *Southern Standard*, 1890, 1892

Atlanta (Ga.) *People's Party Paper*, 1892

Austin (Tex.) *Weekly Statesman*, 1896
Birmingham *Alabama Sentinel*, 1887
Charlotte (N.C.) *Home-Democrat*, 1886
Chicago Daily Tribune, 1890
Cincinnati Enquirer, 1887, 1891
Dallas (Tex.) *Southern Mercury*, 1900, 1902
Fayetteville (Ark.) *Democrat*, 1882, 1888, 1890–91
Fayetteville (N.C.) *Messenger*, 1888
Fort Smith (Ark.) *Times*, 1904
Frank Leslie's Illustrated Newspaper (New York), 1886
Gentry (Ark.) *Journal-Advance*, 1906
Jasper *Arkansas Wheel*, 1886
Journal of the Knights of Labor (Philadelphia; Washington, DC) (superseded the *Journal of United Labor*), 1890–96
Journal of United Labor (Marblehead, Mass.; Pittsburgh; Philadelphia), 1880, 1884–89
Junction City (Kan.) *Union*, 1893
Little Rock *Arkansas Democrat*, 1881, 1884, 1886–91, 1898–1900, 1904, 1907
Little Rock *Arkansas Gazette/Daily Arkansas Gazette*, 1873, 1876, 1878, 1881–96, 1898, 1903–04, 1907, 1912, 1914
Magnolia (Ark.) *Columbia Banner*, 1886–88
Mansfield (Ark.) *Alliance Patriot*, 1891
Marietta (Ga.) *Journal*, 1873
Monticello (Ark.) *Monticellonian*, 1895
Nashville (Tenn.) *Weekly Toiler*, 1888
New York Times, 1874, 1878, 1882, 1886–88, 1890
Osceola (Ark.) *Times*, 1888, 1890, 1907
Pine Bluff (Ark.) *Daily Graphic*, 1904
Pittsburg (Kan.) *Daily Headlight*, 1894
Prescott (Ark.) *Times-Picayune*, 1900
Public Opinion (Washington, D.C.), 1894–95
Rolla *Missouri Sharp Shooter*, 1905
San Francisco Chronicle, 1890
Savannah (Ga.) *Tribune*, 1889, 1896
Sedalia (Mo.) *Sunday Democrat*, 1900
St. Louis Post-Dispatch, 1888, 1892
United Mine Workers Journal (Indianapolis), 1918
Washington Post, 1905
Yellville (Ark.) *Mountain Echo*, 1886, 1888

Government Documents

Annual Report of the Mine Inspector for the Indian Territory to the Secretary of the Interior for the Fiscal Year Ended June 30, 1899. Washington, DC: Government Printing Office, 1899.

Biennial Report of the Secretary of State of the State of Arkansas, 1892. Little Rock: Press Printing, 1893.

Bulletin of the Bureau of Labor. Washington, DC: Government Printing Office, 1904.

Bureau of Labor Statistics and Inspection of Missouri. *The Official History of the Great Strike of 1886 on the Southwestern Railway System.* Jefferson City, Mo.: Tribune Printing, State Printers and Binders, 1887.

Compendium of the Eleventh Census: 1890. Part 1. Washington, DC: Government Printing Office, 1892.

Compendium of the Ninth Census (June 1, 1870). Washington, DC: Government Printing Office, 1872.

Compendium of the Tenth Census (June 1, 1880). Part 1. Washington, DC: Government Printing Office, 1883.

Congressional Record. Vol. 21. Washington, DC: Government Printing Office, 1890.

Congressional Record. Vol. 22. Washington, DC: Government Printing Office, 1891.

Daniels, Charlie. *Historical Report of the Secretary of State, 2008.* Fayetteville: University of Arkansas Press, 2008.

Department of Agriculture. Miscellaneous. Special Report No. 2. Proceedings of a Convention of Agriculturalists Held at the Department of Agriculture, January 23, 24, 25, 26, 27, and 29, 1883. (Second Convention.) Washington, DC: Government Printing Office, 1883.

Report of the Committee of the Senate upon the Relations between Labor and Capital, and Testimony Taken by the Committee. Vol. 1. Washington, DC: Government Printing Office, 1885.

Report of the Industrial Commission on the Relations and Conditions of Capital and Labor Employed in the Mining Industry, Including Testimony, Review of Evidence, and Topical Digest. Vol. 12. Washington, DC: Government Printing Office, 1901.

Report on the Productions of Agriculture as Returned at the Tenth Census (June 1, 1880). Washington, DC: Government Printing Office, 1883.

Rowell, Chester H., comp. *Digest of Contested-Election Cases in the Fifty-First Congress.* Washington, DC: Government Printing Office, 1891.

Third Annual Report of the Commissioner of Labor, 1887. Strikes and Lockouts. Washington, DC: Government Printing Office, 1888.

Third Biennial Report from the Bureau of Mines, Manufactures and Agriculture of the State of Arkansas for the Years 1893 and 1894. Morrilton, Ark.: Pilot Printing, 1894.

US Congress. House of Representatives. 49th Cong., 2d sess., H.R. 4174. *Investigation of Labor Troubles in Missouri, Arkansas, Kansas, Texas, and Illinois.* Washington, DC: Government Printing Office, 1887.

———. House of Representatives. 54th Cong., 2d sess., Doc. 9. *Annual Report of the Attorney-General of the United States for the Year 1896.* Washington, DC: Government Printing Office, 1896.

Books

Appleton's Annual Cyclopaedia and Register of Important Events of the Year 1891. New York: D. Appleton, 1892.

Arkansas Democrat Co.'s Little Rock City Directory, 1899. Little Rock: Press of Arkansas Democrat, 1899.

Arkansas Democrat Co.'s Little Rock City Directory, 1900–1901. Little Rock: Press of Arkansas Democrat, 1900.

Barrett, Charles Simon. *The Mission, History and Times of the Farmers' Union: A Narrative of the Greatest Industrial-Agricultural Organization in History and Its Makers.* Nashville, Tenn.: Marshall & Bruce, 1909.

Biographical and Historical Memoirs of Eastern Arkansas. Chicago: Goodspeed Publishing, 1890.

Biographical and Historical Memoirs of Pulaski, Jefferson, Lonoke, Faulkner, Grant, Saline, Perry, Garland, and Hot Springs Counties, Arkansas. Chicago: Goodspeed Publishing, 1889.

Biographical and Historical Memoirs of Southern Arkansas. Chicago: Goodspeed Publishing, 1890.

Blood, F. G. *Hand Book and History of the National Farmers' Alliance and Industrial Union.* Washington, DC: n.p., 1893.

Castle, John T. *Supplement to Kirby's Digest of the Statutes of Arkansas Embracing the General Statutes Enacted at the Legislative Sessions of 1905, 1907, 1909, and the Regular Session of 1911.* Indianapolis: Bobbs-Merrill, 1911.

Dunning, N. A., ed. *The Farmers' Alliance History and Agricultural Digest.* Washington, DC: Alliance Publishing, 1891; reprint, New York: Arno Press, 1975.

Kelley, O. H. *Origins and Progress of the Order of the Patrons of Husbandry in the United States; A History from 1866 to 1873.* Philadelphia: A. Wagenseller, 1875.

Kester, Howard. *Revolt among the Sharecroppers.* New York: Covici-Friede, 1936; reprint, New York: Arno Press, 1969.

McPherson, Edward, ed. *Tribune Almanac and Political Register for 1893.* New York: Tribune Association, 1893.

Morgan, W. Scott. *History of the Wheel and Alliance, and the Impending Revolution.* Hardy, Ark.: s.p., 1889.

———. *History of the Wheel and Alliance, and the Impending Revolution.* 3rd ed. Hardy, Ark.: s.p., 1891; reprint, New York: Burt Franklin, 1968.

The National Economist Almanac 1890: National Farmers Alliance and Industrial Union Hand-Book. Washington, DC: National Economist Print, 1890.

Northrup, Henry Davenport. *Life and Achievements of Jay Gould, the Wizard of Wall Street: Being a Complete and Graphic Account of the Greatest Financier of Modern Times.* Philadelphia: National Publishing, 1892.

Powderly, Terence V. *The Path I Trod: The Autobiography of Terence V. Powderly.* Edited by Harry J. Carman, Henry David, and Paul N. Guthrie. New York: Columbia University Press, 1940; reprint, New York: AMS Press, 1968.

———. *Thirty Years of Labor, 1859 to 1889.* Columbus, Ohio: Excelsior Publishing House, 1889.

Simonds, John Cameron, and John T. McEnnis. *The Story of Manual Labor in All Lands and Ages: Its Past Condition, Present Progress, and Hope for the Future.* Chicago: R. S. Peale, 1887.

Swinton, John. *A Momentous Question: The Respective Attitudes of Labor and Capital.* Philadelphia: Keller Publishing, 1895.

Twain, Mark, and Charles Dudley Warner. *The Gilded Age: A Tale of To-day.* Hartford, Conn.: American Publishing, 1873.

Williams, C. Fred, S. Charles Bolton, Carl H. Moneyhon, and LeRoy T. Williams, eds. *A Documentary History of Arkansas.* Fayetteville: University of Arkansas Press, 1984.

Websites

United States Census Bureau. "Profile of General Population and Housing Characteristic: 2010. Bonanza City, Arkansas." United States Census Bureau American Fact Finder. Accessed July 28, 2017. https://factfinder.census.gov/bkmk/table/1.0/en/DEC/10_DP/DPDP1/1600000US0507540.

University of Arkansas at Little Rock. "Census State Data Center, Population by City and Town, 1840–1900." Arkansas Economic Development Institute. Accessed December 18, 2016. http://iea.ualr.edu/arkansas-census-data.html?id=168:population-by-city-1840-1900&catid=1&tmpl=component.

Secondary Sources

Books

Ackerman, Kenneth D. *The Gold Ring: Jim Fisk, Jay Gould, and Black Friday, 1869.* New York: Dodd, Mead, 1988.

Alexander, Benjamin F. *Coxey's Army: Popular Protest in the Gilded Age.* Baltimore: Johns Hopkins University Press, 2015.

Ali, Omar H. *In the Lion's Mouth: Black Populism in the New South, 1886–1900.* Jackson: University Press of Mississippi, 2010.

Allen, Ruth A. *The Great Southwest Strike.* University of Texas Publication No. 4214. Austin: University of Texas, 1942.

Arsenault, Raymond. *The Wild Ass of the Ozarks: Jeff Davis and the Social Bases of Southern Politics.* Philadelphia: Temple University Press, 1984; reprint, Knoxville: University of Tennessee Press, 1988.

Ashmore, Harry S. *Arkansas: A Bicentennial History.* New York: W. W. Norton, 1978.

Ayers, Edward L. *The Promise of the New South: Life after Reconstruction.* New York: Oxford University Press, 1992.

Barnes, Kenneth C. *Journey of Hope: The Back-to-Africa Movement in Arkansas in the Late 1800s.* Chapel Hill: University of North Carolina Press, 2004.

———. *Who Killed John Clayton? Political Violence and the Emergence of the New South, 1861–1893.* Durham, N.C.: Duke University Press, 1998.

Bartels, Larry M. *Unequal Democracy: The Political Economy of the New Gilded Age.* 2nd ed. Princeton, N.J.: Princeton University Press, 2016.

Bauerly, Brad. *The Agrarian Seeds of Empire: The Political Economy of Agriculture in U.S. State Building.* Boston: Brill, 2016.

Blevins, Brooks. *Hill Folks: A History of Arkansas Ozarkers and Their Image.* Chapel Hill: University of North Carolina Press, 2002.

Brecher, Jeremy. *Strike!* Rev. 3rd ed. Oakland, Calif.: PM Press, 2014.

Case, Theresa A. *The Great Southwest Railroad Strike and Free Labor.* College Station: Texas A&M University Press, 2010.

Cobb, James C. *The Selling of the South: The Southern Crusade for Industrial Development, 1936–1990.* 2nd ed. Urbana: University of Illinois Press, 1993.

Commons, John R., David J. Saposs, Helen L. Sumner, E. B. Mittelman, H. E. Hoagland, John B. Andrews, and Selig Perlman. *History of Labour in the United States.* Vol. 2. New York: Macmillan, 1926.

Crow, Jeffrey J., and Robert F. Durden. *Maverick Republican in the Old North State: A Political Biography of Daniel L. Russell.* Baton Rouge: Louisiana State University Press, 1977.

DeBlack, Thomas A. *With Fire and Sword: Arkansas, 1861–1874.* Fayetteville: University of Arkansas Press, 2003.

De Santis, Vincent P. *The Shaping of Modern America: 1877–1920.* 3rd ed. Wheeling, Ill.: Harlan Davidson, 2000.

Dubin, Michael J., comp. *United States Congressional Elections, 1788–1997: The Official Results of the Elections of the 1st through 105th Congresses.* Jefferson, N.C.: McFarland, 1998.

Dubofsky, Melvyn, and Foster Rhea Dulles. *Labor in America: A History.* 8th ed. Wheeling, Ill.: Harlan Davidson, 2010.

Durden, Robert F. *The Climax of Populism: The Election of 1896.* Lexington: University of Kentucky Press, 1965.

Epstein, David A. *Left, Right, Out: The History of Third Parties in America.* New York: Arts and Letters Imperium Publishing, 2012.

Fine, Nathan. *Labor and Farmer Parties in the United States, 1828–1928.* New York: Rand School of Social Science, 1928; reprint, New York: Russell and Russell, 1961.

Fink, Leon. *Workingmen's Democracy: The Knights of Labor and American Politics.* Urbana: University of Illinois Press, 1983.

Finley, Randy. *From Slavery to Uncertain Freedom: The Freedmen's Bureau in Arkansas, 1865–1869.* Fayetteville: University of Arkansas Press, 1996.

Fite, Gilbert C. *Cotton Fields No More: Southern Agriculture, 1865–1980.* Lexington: University Press of Kentucky, 1984.

Foner, Eric. *A Short History of Reconstruction, 1863–1877.* Updated ed. New York: Harper Perennial, 2015.

Gaither, Gerald H. *Blacks and the Populist Movement: Ballots and Bigotry in the New South*. Rev. ed. Tuscaloosa: University of Alabama Press, 2005.

Garlock, Jonathan, comp. *Guide to the Local Assemblies of the Knights of Labor.* Westport, Conn.: Greenwood Press, 1982.

Gleason, Mildred Diane. *Dardanelle and the Bottoms: Environment, Agriculture, and Economy in an Arkansas River Community, 1819–1970*. Fayetteville: University of Arkansas Press, 2017.

Goldstene, Claire. *The Struggle for America's Promise: Equal Opportunity at the Dawn of Corporate Capital*. Jackson: University Press of Mississippi, 2014.

Goodwyn, Lawrence. *Democratic Promise: The Populist Moment in America*. New York: Oxford University Press, 1976.

———. *The Populist Moment: A Short History of the Agrarian Revolt in America*. New York: Oxford University Press, 1978.

Grantham, Dewey W. *The Life and Death of the Solid South: A Political History*. Lexington: University Press of Kentucky, 1988.

Graves, John William. *Town and Country: Race Relations in an Urban-Rural Context, Arkansas, 1865–1905*. Fayetteville: University of Arkansas Press, 1990.

Green, James. *Death in the Haymarket: A Story of Chicago, the First Labor Movement, and the Bombing That Divided Gilded Age America*. New York: Pantheon, 2006.

———. *Grass-Roots Socialism: Radical Movements in the Southwest, 1895–1943*. Baton Rouge: Louisiana State University Press, 1978.

Hall, Covington. *Labor Struggles in the Deep South and Other Writings*. Edited by David R. Roediger. Chicago: Charles H. Kerr, 1999.

Henderson, Shannon J., comp. *Arkansas Gazette Index: An Arkansas Index, 1886*. Russellville: Arkansas Tech University Library, 1985.

———, comp. *Arkansas Gazette Index: An Arkansas Index, 1887*. Russellville: Arkansas Tech University Library, 1985.

———, comp. *Arkansas Gazette Index: An Arkansas Index, 1888*. Russellville: Arkansas Tech University Library, 1986.

———, comp. *Arkansas Gazette Index: An Arkansas Index, 1889*. Russellville: Arkansas Tech University Library, 1986.

Hicks, John D. *The Populist Revolt: A History of the Farmers' Alliance and the People's Party*. Minneapolis: University of Minnesota Press, 1931; reprint, Lincoln: University of Nebraska Press, 1961.

Hild, Matthew. *Greenbackers, Knights of Labor, and Populists: Farmer-Labor Insurgency in the Late-Nineteenth-Century South*. Athens: University of Georgia Press, 2007.

Holcombe, Randall G. *From Liberty to Democracy: The Transformation of American Government*. Ann Arbor: University of Michigan Press, 2002.

Hunter, Tera W. *To 'Joy My Freedom: Southern Black Women's Lives and Labors after the Civil War*. Cambridge, Mass.: Harvard University Press, 1997.

Johnson, Ben F., III. *Arkansas in Modern America, 1930–1999.* Fayetteville: University of Arkansas Press, 2000.

Joiner, Thekla Ellen. *Sin in the City: Chicago and Revivalism, 1880–1920.* Columbia: University of Missouri Press, 2007.

Jones, Jacqueline. *Labor of Love, Labor of Sorrow: Black Women, Work, and the Family from Slavery to the Present.* New York: Basic Books, 1985.

Kazin, Michael. *A Godly Hero: The Life of William Jennings Bryan.* New York: Knopf, 20006.

Kipnis, Ira. *The American Socialist Movement, 1897–1912.* New York: Columbia University Press, 1952; reprint, New York: Greenwood Press, 1968.

Kousser, J. Morgan. *The Shaping of Southern Politics: Suffrage Restriction and the Establishment of the One-Party South, 1880–1910.* New Haven, Conn.: Yale University Press, 1974.

Lancaster, Guy. *Racial Cleansing in Arkansas, 1883–1924: Politics, Land, Labor, and Criminality.* Lanham, Md.: Lexington Books, 2014.

Laurie, Bruce. *Artisans into Workers: Labor in Nineteenth-Century America.* New York: Hill and Wang, 1989.

Lause, Mark A. *The Civil War's Last Campaign: James B. Weaver, the Greenback-Labor Party & the Politics of Race & Section.* Lanham, Md.: University Press of America, 2001.

Ledbetter, Calvin R., Jr. *Carpenter from Conway: George Washington Donaghey as Governor of Arkansas, 1909–1913.* Fayetteville: University of Arkansas Press, 1993.

Letwin, Daniel. *The Challenge of Interracial Unionism: Alabama Coal Miners, 1878–1921.* Chapel Hill: University of North Carolina Press, 1998.

Levine, Susan. *Labor's True Woman: Carpet Weavers, Industrialization, and Labor Reform in the Gilded Age.* Philadelphia: Temple University Press, 1984.

Link, William A. *Southern Crucible: The Making of an American Region.* New York: Oxford University Press, 2015.

Loewen, James W. *Sundown Towns: A Hidden Dimension of American Racism.* New York: New Press, 2005.

Mancini, Matthew J. *One Dies, Get Another: Convict Leasing in the American South, 1866–1928.* Columbia: University of South Carolina Press, 1996.

Marion, Nancy E., and Willard M. Oliver. *Killing Congress: Assassinations, Attempted Assassinations and Other Violence against Members of Congress.* Lanham, Md.: Lexington Books, 2014.

Marshall, F. Ray. *Labor in the South.* Cambridge, Mass.: Harvard University Press, 1967.

Martis, Kenneth C. *The Historical Atlas of United States Congressional Districts, 1789–1983.* New York: Free Press, 1982.

McLaurin, Melton Alonza. *The Knights of Labor in the South.* Westport, Conn.: Greenwood Press, 1978.

McMath, Robert C., Jr. *American Populism: A Social History, 1877–1898.* New York: Hill and Wang, 1993.

———. *Populist Vanguard: A History of the Southern Farmers' Alliance.* Chapel Hill: University of North Carolina Press, 1975.

Moneyhon, Carl H. *Arkansas and the New South, 1874–1929.* Fayetteville: University of Arkansas Press, 1997.

Montgomery, David. *Workers' Control in America: Studies in the History of Work, Technology, and Labor Struggles.* Cambridge: Cambridge University Press, 1979.

Moore, John L., Jon P. Preimesberger, and David R. Tarr, eds. *Congressional Quarterly's Guide to U.S. Elections.* 4th ed. Vol. 2. Washington, DC: CQ Press, 2001.

Moreno, Paul D. *Black Americans and Organized Labor: A New History.* Baton Rouge: Louisiana State University Press, 2008.

Mountjoy, Edgar E., comp. *Official Congressional Directory.* 63rd Congress, 3rd Session. Washington, DC: Office of Congressional Directory, 1915.

Niswonger, Richard L. *Arkansas Democratic Politics, 1896–1920.* Fayetteville: University of Arkansas Press, 1990.

Nordin, D. Sven. *Rich Harvest: A History of the Grange, 1867–1900.* Jackson: University Press of Mississippi, 1974.

Otto, John Solomon. *The Final Frontiers, 1880–1930: Settling the Southern Bottomlands.* Westport, Conn.: Greenwood Press, 1999.

Painter, Nell Irvin. *Standing at Armageddon: A Grassroots History of the Progressive Era.* 2nd ed. New York: W. W. Norton, 2008.

Perkins, J. Blake. *Hillbilly Hellraisers: Federal Power and Populist Defiance in the Ozarks.* Urbana: University of Illinois Press, 2017.

Perman, Michael. *Struggle for Mastery: Disfranchisement in the South, 1888–1908.* Chapel Hill: University of North Carolina Press, 2001.

Phelan, Craig. *Grand Master Workman: Terence Powderly and the Knights of Labor.* Westport, Conn.: Greenwood Press, 2000.

Phillips, Clifton J. *Indiana in Transition: The Emergence of an Industrial Commonwealth, 1880–1920.* 1968; reprint, Indianapolis: Indiana Historical Society Press, 2016.

Porter, Glenn. *The Rise of Big Business, 1860–1920.* 3rd ed. Wheeling, Ill.: Harlan Davidson, 2006.

Postel, Charles. *The Populist Vision.* New York: Oxford University Press, 2007.

Prout, Jerry. *Coxey's Crusade for Jobs: Unemployment in the Gilded Age.* DeKalb: Northern Illinois University Press, 2016.

Reinhardt, Richard, ed. *Workin' on the Railroad: Reminiscences from the Age of Steam.* Norman: University of Oklahoma Press, 1970.

Reitano, Joanne. *The Tariff Question in the Gilded Age: The Great Debate of 1888.* University Park: Pennsylvania State University Press, 1994.

Ritter, Gretchen. *Goldbugs and Greenbacks: The Antimonopoly Tradition and the Politics of Finance in America, 1865–1896*. Cambridge: Cambridge University Press, 1997.

Rogers, William Warren. *The One-Gallused Rebellion: Agrarianism in Alabama, 1865–1896*. Baton Rouge: Louisiana State University Press, 1970.

Roll, Jarod. *Spirit of Rebellion: Labor and Religion in the New Cotton South*. Urbana: University of Illinois Press, 2010.

Saloutos, Theodore. *Farmer Movements in the South, 1865–1933*. Berkeley: University of California Press, 1960; reprint, Lincoln: University of Nebraska Press, 1964.

Salvatore, Nick. *Eugene V. Debs: Citizen and Socialist*. Urbana: University of Illinois Press, 1982.

Sanders, Elizabeth. *Roots of Reform: Farmers, Workers, and the American State, 1877–1917*. Chicago: University of Chicago Press, 1999.

Schlesinger, Arthur M., Jr., ed. *The Almanac of American History*. New York: G. P. Putnam's Sons, 1983.

Schlup, Leonard, and James G. Ryan, eds. *Historical Dictionary of the Gilded Age*. Armonk, N.Y.: M. E. Sharpe, 2003.

Sellars, Nigel Anthony. *Oil, Wheat & Wobblies: The Industrial Workers of the World in Oklahoma, 1905–1930*. Norman: University of Oklahoma Press, 1998.

Shaw, Barton C. *The Wool-Hat Boys: Georgia's Populist Party*. Baton Rouge: Louisiana State University Press, 1984.

Shi, David Emory, and George Brown Tindall. *America: A Narrative History*. Brief 10th ed. New York: W. W. Norton, 2016.

Steeples, Douglas, and David O. Whitten. *Democracy in Desperation: The Depression of 1893*. Westport, Conn.: Greenwood Press, 1998.

Stockley, Grif. *Blood in Their Eyes: The Elaine Race Massacres of 1919*. Fayetteville: University of Arkansas Press, 2001.

———. *Ruled By Race: Black/White Relations in Arkansas from Slavery to the Present*. Fayetteville: University of Arkansas Press, 2009.

Summers, Mark Wahlgren. *Party Games: Getting, Keeping, and Using Power in Gilded Age Politics*. Chapel Hill: University of North Carolina Press, 2004.

Taylor, Carl C. *The Farmers' Movement, 1620–1920*. New York: American Book, 1953; reprint, Westport, Conn.: Greenwood Press, 1971.

Troy, Gil. *The Age of Clinton: America in the 1990s*. New York: Thomas Dunne Books, 2015.

Tulloch, Hugh. *The Routledge Companion to the American Civil War Era*. London and New York: Routledge, 2006.

United States Congress. *Biographical Directory of the United States Congress, 1774–2005*. Washington, DC: Government Printing Office, 2005.

Ware, Norman J. *The Labor Movement in the United States, 1860–1895: A Study in Democracy*. New York: D. Appleton, 1929; reprint, Gloucester, Mass.: Peter Smith, 1959.

Weir, Robert E. *Beyond Labor's Veil: The Culture of the Knights of Labor.* University Park: Pennsylvania State University Press, 1996.

Whayne, Jeannie M., Thomas A. DeBlack, George Sabo III, and Morris S. Arnold. *Arkansas: A Narrative History.* 2nd ed. Fayetteville: University of Arkansas Press, 2013.

White, Richard. *Railroaded: The Transcontinentals and the Making of Modern America.* New York: W. W. Norton, 2011.

———. *The Republic for Which It Stands: The United States during Reconstruction and the Gilded Age, 1865-1896.* New York: Oxford University Press, 2017.

Williams, Johnny E. *African American Religion and the Civil Rights Movement in Arkansas.* Jackson: University Press of Mississippi, 2008.

Woodward, C. Vann. *Origins of the New South, 1877–1913.* Baton Rouge: Louisiana State University Press, 1951.

———. *The Strange Career of Jim Crow.* Rev. 3rd ed. New York: Oxford University Press, 1974.

Articles and Essays

Abramowitz, Jack. "The Negro in the Populist Movement." *Journal of Negro History* 38 (July 1953): 257–89.

Barjenbruch, Judith. "The Greenback Political Movement: An Arkansas View." *Arkansas Historical Quarterly* 36 (Summer 1977): 107–22.

Barry, Louise Spears McCants. "Answers in an Autobiography." *Ancestry* 20, no. 5 (2002): 59–63.

Baskett, Thomas S., Jr. "*Miners Stay Away!*: W.B.W. Heartsill and the Last Years of the Arkansas Knights of Labor, 1892–1896." *Arkansas Historical Quarterly* 42 (Summer 1983): 107–33.

Baxley, Thomas L. "Prison Reforms during the Donaghey Administration." *Arkansas Historical Quarterly* 22 (Spring 1963): 76–84.

Biegert, M. Langley. "Legacy of Resistance: Uncovering the History of Collective Action by Black Agricultural Workers in Central East Arkansas from the 1860s to the 1930s." *Journal of Social History* 32 (Fall 1998): 73–99.

Branam, Chris M. "Another Look at Disfranchisement in Arkansas, 1888–1894." *Arkansas Historical Quarterly* 69 (Autumn 2010): 245–62.

Brough, Charles Hillman. "The Industrial History of Arkansas." *Publications of the Arkansas Historical Association* 1 (1906): 191–229.

Brown, Kevin C. "1877 Great Railroad Strike." In *Disasters, Accidents, and Crises in American History: A Reference Guide to the Nation's Most Catastrophic Events,* edited by Ballard C. Campbell, 147–49. New York: Infobase Publishing, 2008.

Caldemeyer, Dana M. "Unfaithful Followers: Rethinking Southern Nonunionism in the Late Nineteenth Century." In *Reconsidering Southern Labor History: Race, Class, and Power,* edited by Matthew Hild and Keri Leigh Merritt, 112–25. Gainesville: University Press of Florida, 2018.

Darrow, William B. "The Killing of Congressman James Hinds." *Arkansas Historical Quarterly* 74 (Spring 2015): 18–55.

Davis, Granville D. "The Granger Movement in Arkansas." *Arkansas Historical Quarterly* 4 (Winter 1945): 340–52.

Dillard, Tom W. "Gillam, Isaac T." In *Arkansas Biography: A Collection of Notable Lives*, edited by Nancy A. Williams, 122–23. Fayetteville: University of Arkansas Press, 2000.

Elkins, F. Clark. "The Agricultural Wheel: County Politics and Consolidation, 1884–1885." *Arkansas Historical Quarterly* 29 (Summer 1970): 152–75.

———. "The Agricultural Wheel in Arkansas, 1887." *Arkansas Historical Quarterly* 40 (Autumn 1981): 249–60.

———. "Arkansas Farmers Organize for Action: 1882–1884." *Arkansas Historical Quarterly* 13 (Autumn 1954): 231–48.

———. "State Politics and the Agricultural Wheel." *Arkansas Historical Quarterly* 38 (Autumn 1979): 248–58.

Finley, Randy. "Arkansas." In *Encyclopedia of the Reconstruction Era*, vol. 1, edited by Richard Zuczek, 49-56. Westport, Conn.: Greenwood Publishing Group, 2006.

Graves, John William. "The Arkansas Separate Coach Law of 1891." *Arkansas Historical Quarterly* 32 (Summer 1973): 148–65.

Henningson, Berton E., Jr. "Northwest Arkansas and the Brothers of Freedom: The Roots of a Farmer Movement." *Arkansas Historical Quarterly* 34 (Winter 1975): 304–24.

———. "Root Hog or Die: The Brothers of Freedom and the 1884 Arkansas Election." *Arkansas Historical Quarterly* 45 (Autumn 1986): 197–216.

Hild, Matthew. "The Knights of Labor and the Third-Party Movement in Texas, 1886–1896." *Southwestern Historical Quarterly* 119 (July 2015): 24–43.

———. "Labor, Third-Party Politics, and New South Democracy in Arkansas, 1884–1896." *Arkansas Historical Quarterly* 63 (Spring 2004): 24–43.

Holmes, William F. "The Arkansas Cotton Pickers Strike of 1891 and the Demise of the Colored Farmers' Alliance." *Arkansas Historical Quarterly* 32 (Summer 1973): 107–19.

———. "The Demise of the Colored Farmers' Alliance." *Journal of Southern History* 41 (May 1975): 187–200.

James, Edward T. "T.V. Powderly, A Political Profile." *Pennsylvania Magazine of History and Biography* 99 (October 1975): 443–59.

Kiser, G. Gregory. "The Socialist Party in Arkansas, 1900–1912." *Arkansas Historical Quarterly* 40 (Summer 1981): 119–53.

Lancaster, Guy. "'Negroes Warned to Leave Town': The Bonanza Race War of 1904." *Journal of the Fort Smith Historical Society* 34 (April 2010): 24–29.

Ledbetter, Calvin R., Jr. "The Long Struggle to End Convict Leasing in Arkansas." *Arkansas Historical Quarterly* 52 (Spring 1993): 1–27.

Manthorne, Jason. "The View from the Cotton: Reconsidering the Southern Tenant Farmers' Union." *Agricultural History* 84 (Winter 2010): 20–45.

McCollom, Jason. "The Agricultural Wheel, the Union Labor Party, and the 1889 Arkansas Legislature." *Arkansas Historical Quarterly* 68 (Summer 2009): 157–75.

McMath, Robert C., Jr. "C. Vann Woodward and the Burden of Southern Populism." *Journal of Southern History* 67 (November 2001): 741–68.

Miller, Worth Robert. "Building a Progressive Coalition in Texas: The Populist-Reform Democrat Rapprochement, 1900–1907." *Journal of Southern History* 52 (May 1986): 163–82.

Niswonger, Richard L. "Arkansas and the Election of 1896." *Arkansas Historical Quarterly* 34 (Spring 1975): 41–78.

Nixon, Herman C. "The Cleavage within the Farmers' Alliance Movement." *Mississippi Valley Historical Review* 15 (June 1928): 22–33.

Oestreicher, Richard. "A Note on Knights of Labor Membership Statistics." *Labor History* 25 (Winter 1984): 102–8.

Paisley, Clifton. "The Political Wheelers and Arkansas's Election of 1888." *Arkansas Historical Quarterly* 25 (Spring 1966): 3–21.

Pierce, Michael. "Great Women All, Serving a Glorious Cause: Freda Hogan Ameringer's Reminiscences of Socialism in Arkansas." *Arkansas Historical Quarterly* 69 (Winter 2010): 293–324.

Roediger, David R. "Introduction." In Hall, *Labor Struggles*, 1–23.

Rogers, William Warren. "Negro Knights of Labor in Arkansas: A Case Study of the 'Miscellaneous' Strike." *Labor History* 10 (Summer 1969): 498–505.

Ross, Frances Mitchell. "The New Woman as Club Woman and Social Activist in Turn-of-the-Century Arkansas." *Arkansas Historical Quarterly* 50 (Winter 1991): 317–51.

Saloutos, Theodore. "The Agricultural Wheel in Arkansas." *Arkansas Historical Quarterly* 2 (March 1943): 127–40.

———. "The Grange in the South, 1870–1877." *Journal of Southern History* 19 (Nov. 1953): 473–87.

Shea, William L. "Isaac Murphy, 1864–1868." In *The Governors of Arkansas: Essays in Political Biography*, edited by Timothy P. Donovan and Willard B. Gatewood Jr., 38–42. Fayetteville: University of Arkansas Press, 1981.

Shedd, Lindley C. "Effiegene Wingo: An Early Congresswoman from Arkansas." *Arkansas Historical Quarterly* 67 (Spring 2008): 27–53.

Sizer, Samuel A. "'This Is Union Man's Country': Sebastian County 1914." *Arkansas Historical Quarterly* 27 (Winter 1968): 306–29.

Soderstrum, T. Jason. "Currency Act of 1900." In *The American Economy: A Historical Encyclopedia*. Rev. ed. Vol. 1, edited by Cynthia Clark Northrup, 117. Santa Barbara, Calif.: ABC-CLIO, 2011.

Tontz, Robert L. "Memberships of General Farmers' Organizations, United States, 1874–1960." *Agricultural History* 38 (July 1964): 143–56.

Tuohy, Martin. "Sovereign, James R. (1854–1928)." In *Encyclopedia of U.S. Labor and Working-Class History*, vol. 3, edited by Eric Arnesen, 1308–10. New York: Routledge, 2007.

Turner, Ralph V., and William Warren Rogers. "Arkansas Labor in Revolt: Little Rock and the Great Southwestern Strike." *Arkansas Historical Quarterly* 24 (Spring 1965): 29–46.

Welch, Melanie K. "Violence and the Decline of Black Politics in St. Francis County." *Arkansas Historical Quarterly* 60 (Winter 2001): 360–93.

Whites, LeeAnn. "Paternalism and Protest in Augusta's Cotton Mills: What's Gender Got to Do with It?" In *Paternalism in a Southern City: Race, Religion, and Gender in Augusta, Georgia*, edited by Edward J. Cashin and Glenn T. Eskew, 68–84. Athens: University of Georgia Press, 2001.

Wintory, Blake J. "African-American Legislators in the Arkansas General Assembly, 1868–1893." *Arkansas Historical Quarterly* 65 (Winter 2006): 385–434.

Zimmerman, Jane. "The Convict Lease System in Arkansas and the Fight for Abolition." *Arkansas Historical Quarterly* 8 (Autumn 1949): 171–88.

Dissertations and Theses

Barnhill, John H. "A History of District Twenty-One, United Mine Workers of America." MA thesis, Oklahoma State University, 1978.

Bayliss, Garland E. "Public Affairs in Arkansas, 1874–1896." PhD diss., University of Texas at Austin, 1972.

Chandler, Jerry W. "The Knights of Labor and the Southwestern Strikes." MA thesis, Florida State University, 1970.

Garlock, Jonathan E. "A Structural Analysis of the Knights of Labor: A Prolegomenon to the History of the Producing Classes." PhD diss., University of Rochester, 1974.

James, Edward T. "American Labor and Political Action, 1865–1896: The Knights of Labor and Its Predecessors." PhD diss., Harvard University, 1954.

Jones, Krista M. "'It Was Awful, but It Was Politics': Crittenden County and the Demise of African American Political Participation." MA thesis, University of Arkansas, 2012.

Jordan, Bradley S. "A Path Less Traveled: The Life and Times of Louis Porter Featherston." MA thesis, University of Arkansas at Little Rock, 2016.

Matkin-Rawn, Story L. "'We Fight for the Rights of Our Race': Black Arkansans in the Era of Jim Crow." PhD diss., University of Wisconsin—Madison, 2009.

Wheeler, John M. "The People's Party in Arkansas, 1891–1896." PhD diss., Tulane University, 1975.

Websites

Arkansas Records Catalog. "International Typographical Union, Local 92, 1884–1978." Accessed December 20, 2016. http://www.ark-cat.com/browse/fulldetail.aspx?id=1882.

Butler Center for Arkansas Studies. *Encyclopedia of Arkansas History & Culture.* http://encyclopediaofarkansas.net.

Center for Union Facts. "United Mine Workers." Unionfacts.com. Accessed August 13, 2017. https://www.unionfacts.com/union/United_Mine_Workers.

Oklahoma Historical Society. *Encyclopedia of Oklahoma History and Culture.* http://www.okhistory.org/publications/encyclopediaonline.php.

Stanford University. "Per Capita Income in the United States: 1880–1910." *Railroaded.* Accessed October 20, 2016. http://web.stanford.edu/group/spatialhistory/cgi-bin/railroaded/gallery/interactive-visualizations/capita-income-united-states-1880-1910.

Texas State Historical Association. *Handbook of Texas Online.* https://tshaonline.org/handbook.

INDEX

Page numbers in italics refer to illustrations.